MAKING FACTS MATTER

MAKING FACTS MATTER
Reading Non-Fiction 5–11

MARGARET MALLETT

P·C·P
Paul Chapman
Publishing Ltd

Copyright © 1992 Margaret Mallett
All rights reserved
First published 1992
Paul Chapman Publishing Ltd
144 Liverpool Road
London
N1 1LA

British Library Cataloguing-in-Publication Data
Mallett, Margaret
  Making facts matter: reading non-fiction 5 to 11.
  I. Title
  428.43

ISBN 1-85396-165-5

Typeset by Inforum Typesetting, Portsmouth
Printed by St Edmundsbury Press and bound by W.H. Ware

A B C D E F G H   9 8 7 6 5 4 3 2

CONTENTS

ACKNOWLEDGEMENTS

The author and publishers would like to thank the following publishers for kindly giving permission to quote from their material:

Belitha Press for material from *The Squirrel in the Trees;*

Cassell;

Dorling Kindersley for material from *The Way Things Work* by David Macaulay;

Franklin Watts for material from Michael Bright's books *Koalas, Gorillas* and *Polar Bears;*

Hodder and Stoughton for material from *Developing Reading 3–13* by Roger Beard.

Insights over the years from my conversations with children, students, teachers and colleagues find their way into this book and I am grateful to all of them.

Jill Thorn generously allowed me to have much typing done in the college office and I particularly thank Wyn Taylor for deciphering my writing so well.

Thanks are also given to the following schools, teachers and children: Jill Hawkins and Dennis Pratt of Rowdown Junior School, Croydon, for allowing me to carry out the Squirrel project; Gemma Amplett for agreeing to the use of the Space Project and to Eileen Shea, Headteacher of St Joseph's Primary School, Bromley; to Nancy Martin of the Wordsworth Trust for her help and Pat Blackwell of Home Farm School, Colchester, for sending me the fine books that her class had made which informed my example on History at Dove Cottage; Michael Thomas, Beryl Endersley and Matthew Hickling for making it possible for me to learn about fossils and about reading from Michael and Kieron at Crofton Junior School; Gillian Swallow and Nigel Shaw of Mottingham Primary School for permission to use the Bat project; Samantha, Michael, Kieron, Charlotte, Stephen and Andrew for sharing their reading enthusiasm with me; John Dixon for encouraging me to look at children as 'experts' to learn about what is involved in successful reading of non-fiction. Above all my thanks go to my family for their support, and particularly to David who often set aside his own book to read through my first drafts.

Margaret Mallett

INTRODUCTION

When we think of children's books our thoughts often turn first to stories and this perhaps is reflected in the great number of excellent works about fiction for the young. Far fewer have taken up the less immediately appealing but equally important area of non-fiction. A distinguished exception is Margery Fisher who insists in her inspiring book *Matters of Fact* (1972) that an information book, however simple, can be 'individual, strong and alive'.

On the whole, books about reading non-fiction have tended to be one of two kinds: books about older children meeting the challenge of secondary school textbooks (Lunzer and Gardner, 1979) or books mainly concerned with the organization of non-fiction in school libraries and the acquisition of study skills. There are also several useful research studies, but these, like John Chapman's books on reading, are based on research relevant to, but outside, ordinary classroom practice. Major studies, like Southgate *et al.* (1981), include the reading of non-fiction but do not place it at the centre of their work.

There are two recent studies of the demands non-fiction makes on young readers and these have informed part of this work. In *Reading all types of Writing* (1991) Alison Littlefair takes up the linguistic terms 'genre' and 'register' and applies them to all the different kinds of writing children need to respond to in the school years. Bobby Neate's book *Children's Informative Reading* (in press) describes and evaluates features of successful and less successful information books and makes recommendations for choosing and using this kind of non-fiction in the classroom.

The main contribution of the present book is to take the reader directly into classrooms where children use non-fiction and make explicit how their existing knowledge is enriched by what they read. Teachers' voices are heard too, both explaining new ideas and helping increase children's understanding of the conventions of non-fiction genres, as well as of the topic under study. At the heart of this book is the question of what children do with information once they have found it. It is argued that study skills need embedding in the context of the wider purposes and intentions children bring to their reading of non-fiction. It is not just a matter of finding out, there has to be a clear purpose for acquiring what is found. Above all, becoming a reader of informational texts involves reflecting on the ideas and concepts encountered.

This is intended to be a practical book for primary education students, practising teachers and all who are interested in the education of 5–11-year-olds. However, good practice comes from sound principles and the seven chapters in Part 1 aim to establish a theoretical framework for the classroom practice described in the later chapters in Part 2.

The first chapter aims to draw together the fruits of relevant theory and recent research studies in proposing some main principles on how children learn, and particularly the role of language in learning. The texts themselves are the substance of Chapters 2, 3, 4 and 5, which aim to describe and offer criteria for judging all the different kinds of non-fiction that children use in the primary years. Chapter 2 sets out a general classification with reference to the National Curriculum reading guidelines. The kinds of non-fiction which are organized chronologically, what we might term 'information stories' and procedural and biographical kinds of writing are considered in Chapter 3. Information books which are organized according to the logic of a topic rather than in a time sequence are examined in Chapter 4, which describes and evaluates reference material like encyclopaedias, dictionaries and thesauruses. The children's information book is considered in some detail in Chapter 5 as we need to know what demands this important and quite challenging kind of text makes. The question asked is 'what features make an information book both sound and inviting?' The next chapter, 6, focuses on what is involved in becoming a reader of non-fiction, and evaluates different approaches to nurturing reading comprehension. Chapter 7 sets out what the priorities are in establishing a school policy on non-fiction, and includes sections on making aims explicit, the features to look for in books to support some of the main curriculum areas, the role of parents and ways of assessing progress in reading non-fiction.

Part 2, Into the Classroom, presents a range of classroom examples which seem compatible with the principles set out in Part 1. These last four chapters stand on their own and some readers might like to begin with them. Chapter 8 gives a detailed account of how some of the insights of Chapters 1 and 6 might be realized in everyday project work. Chapter 9 links with Chapters 2–6: young learners are helped to understand the conventions of non-fiction: how to use retrieval devices and how to evaluate the books they are using. In line with a main principle in this book all this is firmly fixed in sustained work: a project on squirrels. Chapter 10 provides glimpses of promising practice in helping children use non-fiction across the curriculum. The National Curriculum guidelines make it clear that we need to help the children become readers of science, history and so on, but as the examples in this chapter show, a topic-centred approach is still often both an appropriate and efficient one. The classroom examples range from very short glimpses like the 6-year-olds learning how to use reference books for a purpose they can understand – identifying the birds that visit the birdtable they have set up just outside their classroom – to the longer examples considering work over several weeks like 'The Earth and Planets' science topic-enriched by the books 7-year-olds consulted, and the history work of 11-year-olds centred on Wordsworth's cottage in Grasmere, Cumbria. The voices of the children discussing and sharing their developing ideas permeate all these later chapters, but the perceptions of some young readers are heard particularly forcefully in the final chapter as Samantha, Michael, Kieron, Charlotte, Stephen and Andrew share with us their knowledge about dinosaurs, bats, space and so on.

The children in this last chapter have learnt to control their reading of non-fiction. The books are used to serve their purposes and they are impressively able to point out any shortcomings.

Two interesting things stand out about these successful young readers. First, they all have a very clear idea about how the books will serve their purposes, answer their questions and extend what they already know. Second, they very much want to both talk and write about what they have read. The two boys who made themselves experts on dinosaurs, Michael and Kieron, talked endlessly together about their common interest, and when fossils came up in a school science lesson were delighted to share with the teacher and other children the fruits of their special researches in this area. For these young readers facts matter and are worth reflecting on.

If out of all I have learned from my years as a class teacher, a supervising tutor in school and educational researcher I was asked to choose one significant observation I think it would be the great contribution talking about reading makes to learning. If we can create a classroom environment where pupils come to think of themselves as a community of young readers and writers using spoken language to share and learn, they are likely to move forward in their control over the challenging kinds of reading we include under the term non-fiction.

PART 1

LEARNING FROM NON-FICTION

1
TOWARDS A MODEL OF LEARNING

> New knowledge has to be fitted into existing knowledge, to be translated into terms of one's own experience and re-interpreted, and in this process (which can be called learning) thought and language are very close together.
>
> (Martin *et al.*, 1976, p. 17)

> Many developmental psychologists have come to criticize the picture of the lone child which they consider to be the orthodox Piagetian model. A number of researchers have demonstrated the importance of collaborative activity in enhancing problem-solving ability.
>
> (Bruner and Haste, 1987, p. 8)

A central proposition in this book is that what we know about learning in general can be usefully applied to supporting children's reading of non-fiction. Most primary schools provide children with systematic help in finding their way round the school library. Understanding how to find the appropriate book, dictionary, encyclopaedia or information book for a particular purpose is important. Children also need systematic help in learning to find their way through books by using contents pages and indexes. All this, and the ability to make summaries and notes, is often included in the term 'study skills'. The later chapters give glimpses of children acquiring these abilities in the context of interesting projects and lessons across the curriculum. The struggle to find information is worthwhile if it arises from a strong sense of purpose.

However, there is much more to learning from non-fiction than being able to find information. The challenging task is to help children make sense of and use what they have read. How is it assimilated with existing knowledge and with information from other sources, including first-hand experience? What kind of teacher and peer group support helps children truly reflect on the new concepts and ideas? Successful practice here is much less universal. Sometimes children are given little or no help in learning to control the more difficult kinds of reading across the curriculum and thus to respond in National Curriculum terms to all types of writing (Attainment Target 2, Reading English).

This chapter seeks help from theory and relevant research studies in finding a working model of how children learn so that we can come closer to understanding the kind of teacher mediation between children and secondary sources that is likely to be most helpful. Chapter 6 considers more specifically what is involved in becoming a reader of non-fiction.

From conditioning to cognition

The limitations of behaviourism

Learning theory or behaviourism has been described as the study of observable and measurable behaviour (Crystal, 1987, p. 146) and it dominated the psychology of learning from early this century right up to the 1960s. At its most general the aim of behaviourism was to produce a scientific theory of learning based on general laws. To this end there was a concentration on behaviour which could be directly observed, and mentalistic concepts like 'mind', 'interest' and 'feeling' were avoided (see useful reviews like Hilgard, 1964).

It was assumed that children's responses could be shaped, just as those of rats were conditioned in the laboratory by consistently applied rewards.

For our purposes it is important to appreciate that only the simpler forms of learning can be explained in terms of conditioned responses: for example, acquiring skills like operating a tape recorder or responding accurately to a flash card. The more advanced kinds of cognition, including of course the reflection and evaluation necessary to become a critical reader, are beyond the explanatory power of the theory. The idea that children's language might assist their learning is conspicuous by its absence. Another whole area which was ignored by behaviourists was the facilitating role of the adults' oral language. But it is the relatively passive role of the learner in the theory which is least acceptable. Why then bother to mention behaviourism at all? The new information technology reveals teaching machines as the dinosaurs they are. However, while the influence of the theory in its starker form has faded, some teaching strategies based on behaviourist ideas still persist where children's interest and intelligence are not fully engaged in their learning. Study skills, for example, can be taught as an exercise rather than embedded in a broader learning context. As long as children are put in a relatively passive role and required to carry out exercises unrelated to their broader intentions and purposes, behaviourism is still alive.

Challenges to behaviourism came from two different sources, one of them being Chomsky who argued convincingly against the dominant role of imitation in learning language. Clear accounts of Chomsky's contribution are available elsewhere (for example in Wood, 1988, Donaldson, 1978, and Crystal, 1987). For our purposes we need mainly to understand that Chomsky challenged the stimulus response theory of behaviourism and argued powerfully that children's acquisition of language is essentially creative. Evidence for this comes from the over-generalizations children make indicating they are applying a general rule which does not always work. For example, Anna at age 3 years exclaimed 'I've eaten my apple and readen my book.'[1] The main limitation of Chomsky's theory was his almost exclusive attention to language learning: other kinds of learning were neglected.

It is to Jean Piaget, the other main challenger of behaviourism, that I now turn.

Piaget's adaptive model of learning

Piaget was a developmentalist and epistemologist, not an educator or even primarily a psychologist, but his work on child development has had considerable effect on classroom practice.

Important for us are: his theory of learning by adaptation through the complementary processes of assimilation and accommodation; the idea of 'equilibrium' as a motivating force; egocentricity as a central characteristic of child logic; and finally the role of language development. A recent account of work on the stages of development can be found in Wood (1988).

Piaget's model of learning by adaptation can be applied to any type of new learning. When an individual is confronted by new objects, people, events, situations or ideas in books, two complementary and simultaneous processes are set in motion: assimilation which means the absorption into general schema of a specific piece of new learning and accommodation which is to do with the modification of internal schemes to fit a changing cognizance of reality.[2] Piaget suggests we compare this dual process to the digestive system: food is mixed with the gastric juices to become capable of assimilation, and the organs of digestion have to adjust so that accommodation is possible.

This basic mode of organizing experience through assimilation and accommodation persists throughout life. The same functional laws are obeyed whether the learning is of the earliest kind at the sensory motor stage when intelligence is rooted in action and perception, or when the individual is grappling with the most evolved forms of rational thought.

New learning involves some alteration of a child's existing schemata. However, if the gap between what is already established and what needs to be integrated is too great, learning cannot take place. This has an obvious application to learning from books. If they are too difficult through complexity of subject matter or difficulty of language the new learning cannot be assimilated. This is an extremely powerful and useful model of the learning process. Perhaps because Piaget did not think of himself as a pedagogue he does not attend to the enabling role of instruction in making assimilation of difficult material more possible. The contribution of the adult, whether parent or teacher, is an aspect which is important in this book, as the chapters in Part 2, with their emphasis on teachers and children collaborating, show.

How does Piaget suggest a balance between the processes of assimilation and accommodation is maintained? Piaget believed there is a self-regulatory mechanism, 'equilibrium'. Children lose equilibrium when curiosity is aroused. They return to a state of equilibrium when new knowledge to satisfy their need is incorporated into their understanding. The right sort of information book can help achieve this. His dynamic view of a child constructing his or her knowledge about the world challenged the behaviourists' more passive view of the child as responder to stimuli. The striving to relieve the intellectual discomfort of disequilibrium brings positive reinforcement when equilibrium is restored. Thus in Piaget's theory motivation is integrated into the learning process as a whole. It seems to follow that the child has to feel the need to move forward in taking on new learning and many teachers have acted on this by creating lively classroom environments with many objects and pieces of apparatus for the child to experience and discover. But the relatively low status accorded to language in Piaget's theory leads to an underemphasis on the potential role of verbal interaction in learning.

Piaget also tends not to present the adult as a crucial part of a child's environment, but the enabling role of the adult and the role of language as a tool of assimilation need not be incompatible with his adaptive model of learning. The teacher support for children's own questions in the course of the squirrel project (see Chapter 8) is consistent both with the intrinsic motivation germane to Piaget's assimilation-accommodation model and with the views of those who see language as a prime tool of learning.

We tend to think of adaptive learning as an essentially gradual process, but there is nothing in Piaget's theorizing to discount sudden spurts of development, a sudden reassembling of the mental structures. Something of an emotional character, a mismatch between expectation and reality, can bring this about. For example, in Chapter 11 the children learning about bats began to perceive the creatures differently when they read that the female bat shows great devotion to her baby, hiding it in a crevice in the cave for safety while she searches for food.

Central in Piaget's theory is that children in the primary years are 'egocentric' in much of their thinking, tending to see things from their own viewpoint. However, it seems that where children have a lot of curiosity and interest invested, their thinking is much more flexible than Piaget's proposition would suggest. The problems we set children should make 'human sense' and relate strongly to what they are likely to have experienced (Donaldson, 1978, Chapters 2 and 3). As later chapters make clear, writers of non-fiction need to appeal strongly to children's likely interests and imaginations. Then we find that children can become very involved indeed with questions like why red squirrels are dying out, how we can save bats from extinction and why stars look star-shaped when they are really round. The children whose work is considered in Part 2 of this book seem very different from those who feature in Piaget's rather abstract problem-solving tasks.

His emphasis on an individual child interacting with the environment rather than with other human beings is consistent with his view on the role of language. His basic position is that thought exists before language and provides the mental structures from which language develops. Piaget is not alone in believing that thought and intentions precede the acquisition of language, and indeed make the difficult task of language acquisition possible (Macnamara, 1972; Bruner, 1975; and Donaldson, 1978). However, few now accept the relatively modest role in Piaget's theory for language once a child is a verbal being.

Piaget believes that many of the classifying tasks introduced in the primary years have their roots in action and perception in the pre-school years. Before you can combine or dissociate relatively abstract classes like birds and animals you need to have classified selections of objects in the same perceptual field. Few would disagree with this. Here is the example Piaget gives:

> All birds (class A) are animals (class B), but all animals are not birds because more are non-bird animals (class A1). The problem here, then, is whether A + A1 = B and A = B − A1.
>
> (See Piaget's article in Adams, 1969, p. 175)

The children learning about squirrels in Chapter 8 faced a similar sort of task in learning that squirrels belong to both the mammal and rodent categories. All squirrels are rodents and mammals, but not all rodents and mammals are squirrels. This kind of thinking underlies the way knowledge is organized in information books and textbooks. While accepting that such thinking probably does depend on the prior establishment of other cognitive gains (see Macnamara, 1972; Donaldson, 1978; and Bruner and Haste, 1987), I believe that it can be made accessible by teachers and children talking together (Wood, 1988, p. 22).

Summary

- Behaviourists tried to produce a scientific theory of learning based on general laws, but only the simpler mechanistic kinds of learning can be adequately explained in terms of conditioned responses.

- Piaget's cognitive theory of learning presents children as active constructors of the world, overcoming problems with the kind of intelligence available at each developmental stage.

- This powerful adaptive model presents learning as a process of assimilating new material to an existing framework while simultaneously accommodating prior understandings to receive fresh input.

- The general model of learning as adaptation is capable of application to learning from books and secondary sources.

- The main limitation of Piaget's contribution is the underprivileging of language as a way of organizing new learning.

Towards language and collaboration as agents of learning
Vygotsky's linguistic model

A main emphasis in Vygotsky's work is a search for an explanation of the development of human consciousness. He therefore has a great deal to offer to educationists. While he agrees with Piaget that intelligence is rooted in activity and experience, unlike Piaget he gives great weight to the roles of instruction and social interaction in human development. Piaget recognizes language as an important means of crystallizing and communicating thinking, but Vygotsky maintains that once a child gains control over language his or her whole intelligence is transformed. He views language as an instrument of organizing thinking and indeed he would argue that certain kinds of thinking only come into being through language.

Children learn to talk because they want to communicate with other human beings. Vygotsky recognizes two kinds of speech: egocentric or speech for oneself, often in the form of talking out loud, and social speech for others. He claims that speech is essentially social in its origins and egocentric speech soon 'goes underground' as inner speech or thought. The planning and organizing function of egocentric speech is carried on internally by thinking. So the pattern is: first social speech, then the addition of egocentric speech which branches off to become inner speech and a tool of thinking; meanwhile social speech continues its development, becoming a more mature instrument of communication.

Vygotsky maintains that behind verbal thought lies the 'plane of thought itself'. He insists that there is no rigid correspondence between the units of thought and speech. Indeed the 'post-language symbols' with which we think began as speech, but have been freed from the constraints of the spoken language and the limiting force of conventional public word meanings. James Britton (1987, p. 24) draws our attention to this freedom that characterizes the fluidity of thought we need to 'impose organization' upon our thoughts when we want to communicate them.

Because the child, motivated by social needs, handles freer forms of speech, he or she becomes able to carry out 'mental operations more subtle than anything he or she can put into words'.

The claim that human consciousness is achieved by the internalization of shared social behaviour is an even more central theme in Vygotsky's *Mind in Society* (1978) than in *Thought and Language*. If indeed education is 'an effect of community'[3] there are strong implications for how teachers, who are powerful agents of a culture, organize the learning environment and their own role within it. Before explaining some of the implications for instruction I would like to turn next to Vygotsky's contribution to our understanding of the development of concepts, for this too has enormous potential for guiding classroom practice.

Vygotsky stresses that concepts are not taken on ready made. The acquisition of the word may be the beginning rather than the end point in understanding the mature meaning. In short, word meanings evolve during childhood. Vygotsky notes, for example, that there are several stages in coming to understand a concept like a triangle. First, in a task involving assembling triangles the child is guided by the concrete, visible likeness and only forms an associative complex limited to a certain kind of perceptual bond. Although the reuslts are identical, the process by which they are reached is not at all the same as in conceptual thinking.

The true concept only emerges when the abstracted traits are synthesized and this synthesis becomes the agent of thought. Vygotsky maintains that his experimental results reveal that it is language which is significant in directing 'all the processes of advanced concept formation'. It is only when a true concept is acquired that a child can generalize what has been learnt to other situations (Vygotsky, 1962, p. 66).

This gives language a far more significant role in the development of conceptual thinking than we find in Piaget's theory. In the case of younger children it is the spoken form of language which organizes mental activity. Vygotsky goes on to note the profound effect becoming a reader and a writer has on the young learner's critical awareness of his or her own thought processes. The constancy of the written word makes possible reflection upon meanings. As I intend to show later, this has had a great impact on other educational thinkers and researchers, not least Jerome Bruner. However, only slowly are these understandings about the role of language in its spoken and written form being fully applied to everyday primary school practice.

Vygotsky does make explicit some of the pedagogical implications of his theory and I turn now to some of his ideas which have direct relevance to instruction: his analysis of the relationship between 'spontaneous' and 'non-spontaneous' concepts, the notion of the 'zone of proximal development' and the related idea of the role of the adult in promoting intellectual growth.

Piaget described the ideas which we arrive at by inference from our everyday experience, notions like 'dog', 'angry' and 'plate', as 'spontaneous' concepts. Vygotsky adds to this the idea of 'non-spontaneous' or 'scientific' concepts taken over from others, often in a relatively formal context like a school. These latter concepts are essentially verbally mediated and are 'empty categories' until infused with the life-blood of our own experience. In human learning there is a two-way process constantly taking place as the experience-saturated spontaneous concepts move upward, while the verbally mediated non-spontaneous concepts descend in a mutually supportive and enriching manner. This seems to me entirely compatible with Piaget's complementary processes of assimilation and accommodation.

In any classroom programme it is the teacher's role to help the bridging of the gap between the two kinds of concept. Thus, to take as an example the 'Squirrel' project in Chapter 8 of this study, the children come to the project with spontaneous notions about squirrels: they are small furry animals with large tails; they live in woods but in Kent the grey squirrel is also found foraging in dustbins; they are killed by foxes but are also seen dead on the roads. These spontaneous notions were refined by contact with non-spontaneous concepts in the video film, in books and the teacher's comments: squirrels become part of a category of creatures, 'rodents'; their woodland environment becomes a 'habitat' and they are seen as both 'prey' and 'predators' in the food chain. In Chapter 8 it is suggested that by helping children to organize their prior knowledge verbally and in a group context the teacher can prepare the way for the integration of these spontaneous ideas with the new ideas school learning provides.

Vygotsky has much to say about instruction and the teacher's role: learning can accelerate when a more mature person explains something by thinking through strategies out loud to a less mature person. This assistance helps a child manage a particular task with help, but more importantly, he or she internalizes strategies for planning and organizing their own thinking. For Vygotsky this self-regulation of mental activity is the key to intellectual progress. It begins with social interaction which makes possible the inner dialogues which regulate thought and leads to mature, culturally developed ways of learning.

However, bringing about what David Wood (1988, p. 212) helpfully terms 'shared constructions' of knowledge and expertise is not a straightforward matter. As Wood points out, some children retain and generalize what they are taught, others are less successful. The way the adult structures the task, verbally and through demonstration, draws attention to the most important features for the child to remember. The verbal support and advice of the adult is highly significant and this whole area will be taken up again in different ways throughout this book. It is therefore helpful to look at Vygotsky's notion of the 'zone of proximal development'; at its simplest this refers to the tasks, activities and kinds of problem-solving a child can manage with help at a particular time. Thus it has to do with the gap between what a child manages competently with help and what he or she would manage unassisted. This is an exciting and useful way of looking at the potential role of instruction, and not surprisingly, since Vygotsky's *Mind in Society* was published in English in 1978, the idea has given rise to much interest and research (see, for example, Wood *et al.*, 1978).

The next section considers the views of current developmentalists of the cognitive school and at how they draw on both Piaget and Vygotsky in refining their own theory of pedagogy.

The later cognitive theorists: Bruner, Macnamara and Donaldson and the importance of context and collaboration in learning

Jerome Bruner shares some assumptions with Piaget but there are important differences of emphasis, and in recent years Bruner's research and thinking has drawn closer to Vygotsky's. Bruner is a psychologist and developmentalist who has worked with adults, whose reasoning powers he studied, children of all school ages and more recently very young infants. Bruner's interest centres on processes: on individual differences in creative problem-solving. Like Vygotsky, he places great emphasis on the role of language in the development of knowledge and understanding. This section considers the importance of context and of collaboration in learning in Bruner's theory, and in related thinking and research by some of those who would feel reasonably comfortable under the broad umbrella of cognitive psychology.

In his early work, Bruner described developmental stages superficially similar in some ways to those of Piaget. The 'enactive' stage from birth to about eighteen months is, like Piaget's sensory motor stage, a period of action-based thinking. This is followed by the 'iconic' stage when a child can create internalized images of experiences and things. The 'symbolic' stage arrives later; it includes language and transforms the child's capacity for thinking. The capacity to symbolize enriches the child's existing experiencing and thinking. Perhaps it is misleading to call these ways of processing experience 'stages' as this suggests they are immature modes to be replaced. In fact, some of our thinking throughout life remains both 'enactive', skills learning being an example, and 'iconic', which would include some kinds of problem-solving.

Bruner's views have changed over a long working life. He has made these changes of perspective explicit in recent works, for example in *Actual Minds, Possible Worlds* (1986) and in *Making Sense* (1987). The child is essentially a social being, 'one who plays and talks with others, learns through interactions with parents and teachers'. Further, through such social life, the child acquires a framework for interpreting experience, and 'learns how to negotiate meaning in a manner congruent with the requirements of the culture' (Bruner and Haste, 1987, p. 1).

Bruner has always seen 'making sense' in the context of what a particular culture offers to an individual growing up in it. However, like Piaget, he began by perceiving a problem-solving child as interacting with objects in a relatively isolated way. Now Bruner's focus is on the child as a *social being* whose competences are interwoven with the competence of others.

While Piaget sees formal logic as a description of the ultimate destination of intellectual development, Bruner sees logic as only one of several ways of thinking.

The resources of a particular culture affect how a young learner develops. The children's pattern of development is affected by the ways in which older members of society relate to the new members and what they consider needs to be learned. Something as commonplace as interpreting a picture or photograph in western culture would be difficult for children who have not been helped to infer solidity and depth by cues, like the relative size of the things portrayed. Even within our culture we sometimes assume pupils can make sense of diagrams and illustrations in books when in fact they have not the experience, skill and knowledge to do so without help. This is an issue taken up in a practical way in Chapter 8. Bruner pointed out that perceptions of such things are not natural but learnt. He recognizes that the processes that underlie intelligent and adaptive thinking are communicated, often in subtle ways, from the mature to the less mature.

Bruner stresses that it is the role of the adult as interpreter while interacting with the child that is so significant. It is not a matter of imitation, which dominates the behaviourist model of language learning considered earlier, but of extending, with help, the rules in action to the semiotic sphere.

The later cognitive developmentalists emphasize processes of self-regulation rather than the emergence of underlying logical structure. Powers of concentration are developed over time and, as Wood (1988, p. 70) points out, perceptual/attentional activities demand 'guided selection, memory and interpretation'. These abilities are developed within a cultural context and, as Bruner has written consistently over several decades, the interpretative skills of the more mature in a society are needed to help the less mature use all the resources, human and technological, which that culture offers.

In literate societies like ours much of the learning children have to do takes place in institutions called schools and tends to be less context bound. Bruner argues that effective teaching engages pupils with the specific ways of thinking peculiar to the different academic disciplines. What Bruner calls the 'syntax' of a subject, its typical procedures, facts, formulae and methods of validation, have to be explained. However, it is equally important that children understand the 'structure of the tasks' they are asked to grapple with in school. What is the purpose of what they are doing, what are the overall aims and the shorter-term goals? As the enthusiasm of the young readers in Chapters 7, 8 and 9 suggests, children need to practise the role of being historians or scientists to control their reading and learning, otherwise only 'empty tricks or procedures' will be learnt and children will not inherit the discipline itself (Wood, 1988, p. 84).

The classroom examples in Part 2 show that knowledge gained from books has to be integrated into these broader contexts. Piaget's work challenges the belief that motives outside the satisfaction of the activity are needed, and Bruner's work reinforces this. The work itself has to be intrinsically interesting enough to motivate the young learners. This suggests that we need to structure the overall programme carefully and to present the tasks within it, including the reading tasks, in an interesting way for particular young learners. The learning environment needs to encourage the pupils to formulate their own questions: particularly in the case of the younger children, practical outings awaken and sustain interest and enjoyment. However, much that a child in a culture like ours needs to learn cannot be encountered first hand. Film, photographs, maps, diagrams, charts and books play a part in bringing alive what Donaldson terms 'disembedded' learning.

As the classroom work in Chapter 8 aims to exemplify, the secondary sources need to be introduced and organized to encourage collaboration and discussion. Bruner and others believe a major step forward in current views on pedagogy is the new status of collaboration in learning, of perceiving learning as a social act. I believe that this applies also to reading reference and information books. In the past it has tended to be rather a solitary activity.

This leads to a widely recognized acknowledgement of the role of language in classroom learning and collaborating. A major new emphasis is now placed on the idea that language is embedded in a communicative context that includes non-linguistic cues (Macnamara, 1972). We gain a sense of what people mean because we have access to a wide range of cues that tell us what the context is and the problem people are referring to. Bruner points out that non-linguistic clues like gestures and movements reveal subtleties like the degree of importance of what is being said. In many of our interactions speech is embedded in a more general communicative context.

Pre-school children do their learning in context; for them speech and thought are nearly always embedded. This accounts for the young child's ability to engage in apparently logical exercises like negation which would be beyond them if presented in disembedded language.

In school setttings, however, we are sometimes obliged to consider what words mean since there cannot always be a perfect embedding in a context. Even here we do not derive meaning from the words alone. Bruner observes that we make them 'mean' by locating them in our known world (Bruner and Haste, 1987, p. 15).

This recognition of the central role of speech in learning, alongside its embeddedness in a wider learning context, has considerable implications for classroom practice as I intend to explore further in Chapter 8.

Summary

- Vygotsky, like Piaget, views intelligence as rooted in action but, unlike Piaget, gives great weight to the roles of instruction and social interaction in human development.

- Piaget recognizes language as an important means of crystallizing and communicating thinking, but Vygotsky believes certain kinds of thinking only come about through language.

- Vygotsky considers the role of the adult to be significant in moving children's thinking forward: thinking through strategies with a maturer person brings a child nearer to independent competence.

- Bruner and the later cognitive psychologists have drawn close to Vygotsky both in their emphasis on the role of language in the development of knowledge and understanding and their belief that 'making sense' often results from collaborative learning.

- Learning takes place in contexts which are both linguistic and non-linguistic.

Moving towards a new synthesis

It was observed in the introduction to this chapter that no one theory explains the full complexity of human development and learning. No single existing approach answers every question. However, it is suggested in this study that certain insights or themes about how children learn in general might helpfully be applied to their reading of non-fiction to support classroom work. What then are some of these understandings?

Firstly, the three main developmentalists, Piaget, Vygotsky and Bruner, agree that the child actively constructs his or her intelligence through interaction with the environment. Chomsky too presents a picture of the child actively applying the rules of syntax in becoming a language user, although he pays minimal attention to environmental factors. It is clear that an active child needs to be helped to formulate his or her own questions and to be fully and intelligently engaged in every aspect of the learning situation. The dynamic nature of learning is evident in Piaget's adaptive model of learning as assimilating new to existing knowledge and accommodating the established framework to take in the new learning. If the new learning, whether it is from first-hand experience or activity or from a secondary source like a book, is of too alien a nature, and the gap between existing knowledge and the new information is too great, learning cannot take place. This has important implications for choosing and using information books. However, Piaget's notion of 'readiness for learning' has been challenged, at least in its more extreme form, and in the examples in Part 2 of this book we find children reading beyond their usual level when their interest is strong.

This leads to the second insight which informs this book. Although the child is active in his or her learning, the sensitive adult whether parent, caregiver or teacher can make a difference. The right sort of intervention can allow a child to reach for an idea which might not be accessible without help. Judging children's 'zones of proximal development' requires experience and skill; one child, apparently at the same stage as another, may have a more elastic capacity for further learning. Clearly this idea is important where the teacher is giving help on an individual basis. Can a teacher engage in what Bruner terms 'scaffolding discourse' with a group or even a whole class? Sometimes new learning begins with a class discussion. This provides the opportunity for the teacher to help the children organize their prior experience and knowledge, in Vygotsky's terms their 'spontaneous' concepts, to prepare the way for new learning or 'non-spontaneous' concepts. In Chapter 8 an attempt is made to help nine-year-olds organize their common-sense ideas about squirrels before formulating their own questions and then seeking information from books. Throughout work of a sustained nature like this the teacher can help take the children's thinking further in class or group discussion than might have been the case if learning was more solitary. This is why many have reservations about work which is too much structured by worksheets, cards or computer programmes, thus cutting the children off from the verbal interaction with teacher and peers which would give their learning point and vitality.

It is of course interaction with the other children in the class that leads to the shared purposes and intentions which make extrinsic kinds of motivation unnecessary. My third theme is indeed that learning is essentially social. Vygotsky confronts us with a paradox: what is first engaged with through social interaction is then internalized as a tool of thought and self-regulation. This is how the ways of thinking characteristic of the particular culture in which we have our being make their impact on us. Bruner and others have accepted and developed the idea that children learn best collaboratively. In the case of primary schoolchildren this means making talk about activities and about their reading and writing central to the learning. Spoken language can help bring alive for children the new ideas and information they find in books.

A fourth theme has to do with the recognition that learning takes place in a context in which both linguistic and non-linguistic cues combine to make meanings available to young pupils. Donaldson and Macnamara have shown how language is embedded in other kinds of learning from the earliest stages. How we help children to integrate verbal and non-verbal kinds of learning and first-hand experience with what they find out in secondary sources continues to be a pedagogical challenge to which we have only partial answers.

These four themes, that children are essentially active in their learning, that the adult's discourse can move a child forward in a special way, that learning is essentially social and collaborative and that it takes place in context involving both linguistic and non-linguistic elements, provide an organizing framework for considering how we might best support children's reflections on the information they find in non-fiction.

Notes

1. For a delightful selection of further examples see Whitehead (1990), p. 48 and p. 59.

2. See Piaget (1953) *The Origins of Intelligence in The Child*, Routledge and Kegan Paul, p. 36, for interesting examples of the process of assimilation in infants.

3. In this part of my analysis I draw on James Britton's interesting article on Vygotsky in *English in Education*, Vol. 21, no. 3, 1987.

Further reading

Britton, J. N. (1987) Vygotsky's contribution to pedagogical theory, *English in Education*, Vol. 21, no. 3, Autumn.

Bruner, J. S. and Haste, H. (eds.) (1987) *Making Sense: The Child's Construction of the World*, Methuen, London.

Crystal, D. (1987) *The Cambridge Encyclopaedia of Language*, Cambridge University Press.

Donaldson, Margaret (1978) *Children's Minds*, Fontana, Glasgow.

Piaget, J. (1953) *The Origins of Intelligence in the Child*, Routledge & Kegan Paul, London.

Vygotsky, L. S. (1962) *Thought and Language*, MIT Press, Cambridge, Mass.

Wadsworth, B. (1981 edition) *Piaget's Theory of Cognitive and Affective Development*, Longman, London.

Whitehead, M. R. (1990) *Language and Literacy in the Early Years*, Paul Chapman Publishing Ltd., London.

Wood, D. (1988) *How Children Think and Learn*, Blackwell, Oxford.

2
KINDS OF CHILDREN'S NON-FICTION

> Teachers are required to make possible 'The development of the ability to
> respond to all types of writing'.
>
>> (Attainment Target 2 Reading. English 5–16, Statutory guidelines)
>
> In order to make a good job of selecting books, teachers need to know books
> as well as know their children.
>
>> (McKenzie and Warlow, 1977, p. 62)

Non-fiction is a broad term used to cover kinds of writing which have to do
with information about the phenomena human beings experience in the
world. It contrasts with fiction – stories, poems and plays – which draw also
on the inner world of the imagination and explore human experience in a
different way.

This chapter aims to identify the different kinds of non-fiction with which
children need to become familiar in the primary school years. If, as required by Attainment Target 2 Reading (*English in the National Curriculum (No. 2)*, DES, March 1990), we are able to help children to develop
'the ability to read, understand and respond to all types of writing' it is
helpful to become clear about what types of non-fiction there are and the
demands each of them makes on young readers.

This short chapter offers a simple categorization of the kinds of non-
fiction writing typically used in the primary years. It then relates this categorization to the requirements of the National Curriculum – English Key
Stages 1 and 2. It suggests that material used in Key Stages 3 and 4, in their
simpler forms, often have a place among the texts offered to younger
children. Chapters 3, 4 and 5 draw on this scheme and introduce the principal characteristics and desirable features of the different kinds of text.

Genre and register

Different styles or 'genres' of writing are characterized by their distinctive
language and subject matter (Crystal, 1987, p. 73). Each style of writing is
also the outcome of a particular kind of thinking. Children need help in

becoming familiar with these different kinds of thinking and writing. The linguist M. A. K. Halliday refers to the way in which spoken and written language is expressed as its 'register'. (Halliday, 1978, p. 32). The 'register' depends on what is being spoken or written about (the field), how the language is used (the mode) and to whom we are speaking and our attitude to the subject (the tenor).

Each school subject has its own register as do the reading materials associated with it. Children need to become familiar with the registers of the different genres. They can then begin to take control of and be active in their reading: they can read to learn. However, since the different kinds of reading material cross subject boundaries they can be considered under some broad headings.

Categories of writing for children

The traditional way of categorizing writing is as follows: narrative, description, exposition and argument (J. N. Britton *et al.*, 1975, p. 4). These categories are helpful as a way of describing the work of mature writers but less useful in considering writing for, and indeed by, children. The basic division between fiction and non-fiction remains, but in categorizing the non-fiction written for children one major division exists. This is between non-fiction with a narrative, chronological or sequential form and non-fiction organized by topic or subject. The broad non-fiction categories in this book are narrative, non-narrative (reference) and non-narrative (exposition). These broad categories and their suggested subcategories are set out in the next three chapters.

Chapter 3 examines non-fiction with a narrative form including:

- writing organized chronologically where the information is given in a story form – 'information stories', biographies, autobiographies and diaries;
- writing organized procedurally in, for example, instruction booklets and manuals.

Chapter 4 examines one category of non-fiction with a non-narrative form:

- reference books: dictionaries, thesauruses, encyclopaedias and atlases.

Chapter 5 considers another main category of non-fiction non-narrative:

- non-narrative picture books;
- expositionary texts, writing which describes, explains or sets out an argument ('information books').

Children's information books can often be categorized as expositionary texts. They are an important part of reading undertaken across the whole of the curriculum. For this reason they are given particular attention throughout this book with some criteria for evaluating them being suggested (see Chapters 5 and 7).

Non-fiction in the National Curriculum

How far do these genres appear in the National Curriculum and at what stage are they introduced? Those genres introduced at Key Stages 1 and 2 in *Programmes of Study, English Ages 5–16* are set out below, with the suggestion that some of the genres, introduced at later stages, can also be used in the primary classroom.

Narrative non-fiction

Key Stage 1 (ages 5–7)

- Interest books and information books – organized within a time sequence (paragraphs 16.22 and 16.23).

Key Stage 2 (ages 7–11)

- Non-fiction information stories would be one category (paragraph 16.29).

Note: Diaries and biographies are mentioned for Key Stages 3 and 4 (ages 11/12–14 and 14–16; (paragraph 16.30) but since they are widely used in the primary years they are discussed in Chapter 3.

Writing organized procedurally

Key Stage 1 (ages 5–7)

- Notices and books of instructions (paragraph 16.22).

Note: Programmes of study for Key stages 3 and 4 suggest the following: guide books, sets of instructions, manuals, stage directions and forms (paragraph 16.34). Many of these, in their simpler forms, are used in the primary years and it seems odd that none are mentioned in the programme of studies for Key Stage 2. They are included in Chapter 3.

Non-fiction – non-narrative

Reference books:
Key Stage 1 (ages 5–7)

- Plans, maps, diagrams and computer printouts (paragraph 16.22).
- Dictionaries, word-books, computer data, road signs and logos (paragraph 16.23).

Key Stage 2 (ages 7–11)

- List of contents, indexes, library classification and library catalogues (paragraph 16.28).

Note: The programmes of study for Key Stages 3 and 4 include thesauruses, atlases, encyclopaedias, subject reference books and databases (paragraph 16.42). Many children are ready for and are provided with these earlier and therefore they are considered in Chapter 4.

Expositionary texts

Key Stage 1 (ages 5–7)

- Interest books – non-chronological (paragraph 16.22).
- Information books – non-chronological (paragraph 16.22).

Key Stage 2 (ages 7–11)

- Non-fiction (newspapers and magazines as well as non-chronological information books) and advertisements (paragraph 16.29).

Note: The programmes of study for Key Stages 3 and 4 include travel books, consumer reports, textbooks, contracts, information leaflets, publicity material, newspapers and magazines (paragraph 16.34), leader columns and pressure group literature (paragraph 16.40). Some of these are often part of the primary school reading programme and are included in Chapter 4.

Chapters 3, 4 and 5 describe the kinds of reading material categorized above likely to be found in the non-fiction section of good school and class libraries, and identify some general pointers to what features make such books good examples of their kind.

Children deserve the liveliest, most useful and attractive books we can provide. A main limitation of non-fiction compared to the best stories is that knowledge, and attitudes to existing knowledge, are constantly changing. Conscientious renewing of books and other material is therefore necessary. Fiction has a special power to engage and enchant, but non-fiction can be just as exciting in its own way.

Summary

- Non-fiction is an umbrella term sheltering many different kinds of writing.

- Each category and subcategory is characterized by distinctive subject matter and language and can be described as a 'genre'.

- Each school curriculum area has its own 'register', i.e. the way the spoken or written language is expressed: what is spoken or written about is the 'field'; how the language is used is the 'mode' and to whom we are speaking and your attitude to the subject decides the 'tenor'.

- Categories of non-fiction are considered under the following headings in the next three chapters (see also the summary in Appendix I):

Chapter 3 Kinds of Non-Fiction: Narrative
Information stories
Biographies
Procedural writing

Chapter 4 Kinds of Non-fiction: Non-Narrative 1 – Reference Books
Dictionaries and thesauruses
Encyclopaedias
Atlases and map books

Chapter 5 Kinds of Non-Fiction: Non Narrative 2 – Information Books
Non-story picture books
Expositionary – information books

Notes

In this chapter I have drawn on some of Alison Littlefair's analysis of categories of children's books in her book *Reading All Types of Writing* (1991).

Further reading

Littlefair, Alison (1991) *Reading All Types of Writing*, Open University Press, Milton Keynes.
DES (1989) *Programmes of Study, English Ages 5–16*, National Curriculum, HMSO, London.

3
KINDS OF NON-FICTION: NARRATIVE

> The narrative habit is not confined to fiction but is embedded in every kind of discourse.
>
> (Meek, 1991, p. 183)

> There is a wealth of evidence that young children find that writing organized chronologically provides a sympathetic framework for making sense of the world. Our daily lives consist of streams of events in a time sequence and it is hardly surprising narrative is an important way of making sense of the world for both adults and children.
>
> (Barbara Hardy in Meek *et al.* (eds.), 1977, p. 12)

The stories read to young children are usually their first introduction to book language. While sheer enjoyment is the most important reason for sharing a story, children also learn a great deal about the world from them. The special contribution of stories is their ability to explore both the outer world and the inner world of the imagination and to involve both thinking and feeling. These stories come under the umbrella of 'fiction'. But as well as being drawn into a stream of events, the young reader has an opportunity to evaluate and ponder on what is happening. James Britton takes over two terms from D. W. Harding, distinguishing between a 'participant' role towards experience and a 'spectator' role; the former has to do with acting in the real world and non-fiction belongs here while the latter has to do with improvising and ruminating on experience and fiction is one outcome of this (Britton, 1970, p. 97). However, there is no crude distinction between books that entertain and books that inform. We can learn to reflect through stories. Clive King's *Stig of the Dump* tells children much about the lives of cave people as well as involving them in a story. We can be enchanted by narrative texts that have a much more obvious informational focus. David Macauley's *Cathedral: The Story of Its Construction* intrigues as well as explains. There is therefore a broad category of non-fiction texts which can be described as non-fiction narrative. Within this category are firstly what we might term 'information stories', secondly biography, diaries and letters and thirdly procedural material like instruction booklets and manuals.

Information stories

The main way in which narrative non-fiction differs from what we usually think of as stories is its narrower focus. An information story is largely concerned to tell us about the actual phenomena. Let me give an example of a story which is not an information story. In *Squirrel Nutkin* Beatrix Potter delights readers with the exploits of an imaginary squirrel. Some squirrel-like behaviour is evident, for example the need to gather nuts and a playful resourcefulness. The illustrations convey perfectly the form and movement of the creature. However, we are not limited to the literal truth. Squirrels do not go out in boats and they do not take presents to persuade owls to land on islands! Children learn at an early age that in stories animals sometimes talk (e.g. Russell Hoban's Frances books about bears), people can visit imaginary places with fabulous creatures (Max in Brian Wildsmith's *Where the Wild Things Are*) and that our belief in the ordinary laws of science has sometimes to be set aside (e.g. Dahl's *The Magic Finger*). Familiarity with such fictional devices helps them develop some expectations about the genre. There are, however, narratives which have a story form, but whose primary purpose is to inform. For example in *Sciurus: the Story of a Grey Squirrel*, Jan Taylor never deviates from behaviour he has observed as a naturalist studying the creatures in woodlands near Windsor Park. In the foreword his invitation to young readers makes this clear; indeed it makes explicit how he conceives the genre. He mentions how he carefully observed and recorded what squirrels did and what happened to them, and drew on this in writing his account. All squirrels 'like Sciurus will have to escape from predators, learn how to open nuts, and how to establish social relationships with other squirrels' (Taylor, 1978, p. 11). Even so Chapter 1 starts like a story: 'Sciurus woke with a start; something strange had given him a fright. He knew very little about the world because he was only thirty-two days old, but he was using his senses and learning fast'.

This story about Sciurus is good of its kind: the illustrations by Harold George are clear, detailed and accurate. The book is organized in chapters, which stand on their own. For example, when the 9-year-olds whose work is described in Chapter 5 of this book were learning about 'winter dreys' it was helpful for the teacher to end the session with a reading of Chapter 4 of *Sciurus,* 'Winter Home'. Unlike conventional fiction, the book ends with a 'further reading' section – another feature which signals the nature of the genre to young readers.

Early information stories

Sciurus is an example of the mature form of the genre for older juniors, but 'information stories' take their place alongside other kinds of book from the earliest years. One major type is the books Peggy Heeks refers to as 'induction aids' (Heeks, 1981). These books centre on the experience of the very young child: narratives about dressing, shopping, visiting the park and playing with friends (for example, Sarah Garland's *Going Shopping*). The everyday events in a familiar environment reflected in these books helps make children feel secure – 'the known is less frightening than the un-known' (Cass, 1967). However, other books in this category aim to intro-duce the unknown in an unthreatening way and prepare young children for the broader experience they will soon be facing. Books serving this aim have titles like 'First Day at Nursery School' and 'Visiting the Dentist' (or Doctor or Optician). *Staying Overnight* by Kate Perry and Lisa Kopper follows through a little boy's experience, showing how anxieties about a night away from home are overcome.

Information stories at Key Stage 1

The themes covered broaden further as children reach school age: books describing festivals like Christmas, Chinese New Year and Diwali, often following through the activities of one child or one family, and books about the lives of children who have handicaps like deafness fit here.

Within this type, first there are those accounts which have a realistic background often with colour photographs and those which are more per-sonal and which come close to being stories but which still relate to places and activities children know about, like Errol Lloyd's *Nina at Carnival*, and Khurshia Hasan's *Manzur goes to the Airport* (English and Bengali text).

All of these operate on the principle that young children like to find their own world and experience reflected in books, and that of others they are likely to meet.

A second type of book brings to children's attention information and experience from the wider world: what it is like to go on a journey by boat, aeroplane, bus or train. In this category we also find books about different occupations like nurse, doctor or fire officer, often following through one person's working day. *Doctor* by Tim Wood, following through a working mother's day, and *Postwoman*, also by Tim Wood, are good examples which have clear texts and good photographs and which challenge sexual stereotypes.

A third category is the early books to help children find out about science, geography and history and to relate the new ideas to their own everyday experience. By following through a day, a week or longer in a child's life in another country geographical and cultural ideas can be ab-sorbed through the familiar narrative form. As with all books there are good and less good examples. The better books are accurate with written text that draws the young readers into someone else's experience, sometimes indicating what is different and what is similar between our own and other cultures. Stereotyping needs to be avoided in both text and illustration. A good example of this kind of book for Key Stage 1 is Nadia Kabeer's *Ann in Bangladesh*. It is about a relatively comfortably off family showing not everyone is poor in the Third World.

Early narrative information books about the life-cycle of animals like squirrels, foxes and hedgehogs are frequently found in infant classrooms. Barrie Watts' *House Mouse* is a good example; beautiful photographs tell the story of how a mouse is born and grows to adulthood. As with all the books in this series (suited to Key Stage 1 and the early part of Key Stage 2), the young readers or listeners are invited to re-tell the story using small versions of the photographs throughout the text. Following through the life of one creature, plant or object is easier and more interesting for younger children than a more general approach.

Where drawings rather than photographs are used we need to guard against too 'Disney-like' a portrayal of animals. It is also best to avoid rather twee names like Buffie the Barn Owl and Dizzy the Donkey! (We can just about cope with Sciurus as a name for a squirrel.) This seems likely to cause some genre confusion in the young reader.

Many natural phenomena have a clear life-cycle and the narrative form is a sympathetic and appropriate way of providing information. We need to apply the same standards of accuracy to narrative information books as we do to other factual books. The story form should not be an invitation to wild and unhelpful minglings of fact and fantasy. The wonder of nature can be communicated without such confusion.

The familiar story form suits younger children, and some older readers still seek out this kind of narrative framework as we shall see in the Squirrel case study in Chapter 8.

This is not an immature genre discarded as children move through the primary years. We have already seen how challenging *Sciurus* is and there are many other books with a narrative organization which also provide advanced information. Sarah Bisel's *The Secrets of Vesuvius* traces the author's research at Herculaneum, and shows what seems to have happened to one family when Vesuvius erupted in AD 49. Ruth Thompson's *How A Book is Made* follows through all stages of production from initial idea (for A. Browne's Piggybook) through to end product.

David Macauley's architectural picture books are good examples of this genre for Key Stage 2 and above. *Cathedral, Pyramid, City* and *Castle* all tell the story of how each was typically built or made. An overall narrative framework often opens with a general introduction, and there is evaluation of what is done and of thoughts and attitudes throughout.

Biography

Biographies written for primary age children can draw young readers into a story and encourage enjoyment of history. The basic overall organization is a narrative one, but some careful choices are made about what to leave in and what to miss out so that evaluation of a person's life is constantly made. What are the good points about the most successful books in this genre?

It is helpful to place the person under study in his or her historical context. This is achieved in Olivia Bennett's biography of *Annie Besant*, partly by including many contemporary photographs, for example the photographs of the pinched faces of the match girls whose cause Annie championed, and partly by sometimes breaking away from the narrative to comment and provide information. We learn, for example, that 'most opportunities for training or further study were open only to men' (Bennett, 1988, p. 8). Thus Annie's achievements are seen to be all the more remarkable given the difficulties for ambitious women in Victorian times. A time chart and list of key dates in social reform makes this 'In her own time' series useful as a contribution to historical understanding. Another way of providing strong historical background is by providing fact files alongside the narrative pages. Richard Tames does this very effectively in the Life Times series. Thus in *Mother Teresa* there are important facts about leprosy and the partitions of Bengal so that young readers can come closer to understanding the social conditions in which her work is carried out. Sheer admiration for what has been achieved against all the odds is inspired by some biographies, for example *Rosa Luxemburg* by Wendy Forrest: Rosa became an international socialist leader at a time when women could not even vote. The better biographies, even for young readers, manage to indicate the complexity of human beings, even those who have made great contribution to the welfare of humankind. In *Guglielmo Marconi* (Richard Tames) the inventor's flirtation with fascism is not hidden, but included alongside his achievements.

There is no point in hiding the unbearably sad or unpleasant things that are part of people's lives. The appalling details of the Frank family's capture and death which contrasts so sharply with the friendly and hopeful tone of Anne's diaries (extracts are used) are included in Tames' *Anne Frank*.

A main problem in more conventional information books is how to invite young readers in. Good biography by the very nature of its form can achieve this and be an important source of historical information.

Autobiography, in the form of diaries or letters, provides primary evidence for historical work. Anne Frank's diary is perhaps the best way for children to learn about the horror and unacceptability of Nazi anti-semitism.

Older juniors can, with help, sometimes draw on adult work: for example, the children on a historical project at Dove Cottage had used part of

Dorothy Wordsworth's letters and journals (see Chapter 10). The provision of this kind of source material enables young readers to judge people's actions and beliefs for themselves.

Procedural writing: manuals, instruction books

The earliest examples of this genre ('procedural writing' is the term used in Littlefair, 1991) are notices and simple books of instructions. Teachers often write their own instructions, for example for using the tape recorder, paper trimmers and other everyday classroom equipment, and place them on the wall for easy reference.

I agree with Littlefair when she expresses surprise that there are no suggestions in Key Stage 2 (7–11) for the texts appropriate at this stage (Littlefair, 1991, p. 35). Many science books for this age range set out instructions for simple experiments. The tone, use of headings and lists typical of this genre becomes more familiar with use.

As well as reading this type of writing children often produce their own instructions. Sarah, aged 7, produced a simple version of the book about using the classroom computer for the teacher and the other children. Richard, aged 8, wrote a book about how to play chess. A student teacher encouraged 6-year-olds to write down their recipes for Caribbean dishes. The kind of thinking involved here, to do with ordering practical action, is very typical of children at Key Stage 2.

Summary

- A large number of the books for young children in the non-fiction part of libraries have an organization which follows a time sequence in the way that a story does. However, the permissible themes, scope and incidents are much more narrowly conceived than those in a storybook classified as fiction.

- The 'information story' can be a sympathetic way of inviting young readers into new learning as it uses a familiar form.

- Biographies for young children have a special power to draw the young readers into the life and times of the person under study. While the main organization is narrative, analysis and evaluation is also present.

- Procedural reading material from simple notices and instructions on the classroom walls to instruction in information leaflets and manuals has important uses throughout the primary school years.

Further reading

Barrs, M. (1987) Mapping the world, in *English in Education*, vol. 21, no. 1.
Beard, Roger (1987) *Developing Reading 3–13*, Hodder and Stoughton, London.
Perera, Katherine (1984) *Children's Reading and Writing*, Basil Blackwell, Oxford.

4
KINDS OF NON-FICTION: NON-NARRATIVE 1 REFERENCE BOOKS

Study skills include the ability to find information for specific purposes by using card indexes, dictionaries, encyclopaedia and other reference books.

(Southgate *et al.*, 1981, p. 6)

A dictionary should be fun.

(*Richard Scarry's Picture Dictionary,* introduction)

The 'skills' of looking up words in a dictionary, or information in an encyclopaedia, are learned only when the context for use of these skills is significant for the learner.

(Meek, 1991, p. 919)

The main types of reference books used by 5–11-year-olds are dictionaries, encyclopaedias and atlases. The reference genres are identified by certain conventions which we need to help children acquire partly by demonstration in context. As well as describing each kind some criteria for selecting good examples at different stages are set out. Dictionaries are invariably alphabetically arranged word lists with meanings; in encyclopaedias topics are sometimes arranged alphabetically and sometimes thematically. A thesaurus (from a Greek word meaning 'treasure house') catalogues the English language according to meaning. Children need systematic help in using all of these. This help is best provided within the context of real tasks to serve a purpose they can understand. Providing help 'as the need arises', however, is in my experience too vague as a policy. This kind of learning is best built into the programme, when the lessons are planned. For example, in the Squirrel case study I planned to use encyclopaedias both general and on animals so that the children would be encouraged to look up relevant words such as 'rodent', 'mammal' and 'arboreal'.

Dictionaries and thesauruses

Children need to acquire more than the ability to understand the aphabetical organization of dictionaries. Other features of the genre are the tendency of compilers to write in phrases as well as in sentences, the fact that several different meanings of a word are often provided and the abbreviations which appear.

Decisions by compilers about the content of dictionaries, the choice of words included and those left out, are difficult to make whether the dictionary is aimed at adults or children. Before choosing a dictionary it is worth checking that the words most likely to be looked up are there and that there are also some new interesting and challenging ones. One strange omission in the main dictionaries available for the primary years is the lack of any sexual terminology (Fox, 1989, p. 62).

The concept that words are fascinating and open up ideas is reinforced in the better dictionaries. In the invitation at the beginning of his *Picture Dictionary* for very young children, Richard Scarry writes 'a dictionary should be fun'. This is certainly a dictionary children would enjoy browsing through. As we would expect from this author the pictures and text are amusing and integrate perfectly.

Contextualizing of words is a feature of most dictionaries for the younger end of the primary years (Octopus, Hamlyn, Chambers and Scarry). In Scarry's dictionary under 'address' we have: 'Betty has written Grandma's address. This is where Grandma lives. Do you know your address?' Alongside is a picture of an addressed envelope. This helps make the meaning secure. Such contextualizing of terms also gives an opportunity to include the spelling of inflectional variations like past tenses.

Definitions are not always free of controversy and we need to be sure that on the whole these are illuminating rather than confusing or drearier than they need be. The entries in John Grisewood's *Kingfisher Illustrated Dictionary* for the 8–12-year-old age range often have a nice speculative flavour. It is suggested, for example, that the idea of the existence of the mythical creature, the unicorn, may have been the result of people mistaking the oryx, a desert antelope, for a white one-horned horse.

The specialist dictionaries for older juniors support the keen interests children of this age often acquire for some favourite subject or topic. I am grateful to two of the young experts whose enthusiasms are celebrated in Chapter 11 for drawing my attention to the merits of Michael Benton's *Prehistoric Animals: An A–Z Guide*. As Kieron remarked, 'it shows that there were lots of prehistoric creatures not just dinosaurs'. This is a book adults and children can enjoy together. It offers up-to-date information on both the history and science of fossils, and comparisons between species. For younger children, R. Matthew's *A Dictionary of Dinosaurs* would be more accessible. The latter could be used alongside Aliki's delightful account of a child's research into fossils, *Dinosaur Bones*.

Perhaps a true concept of what a dictionary is and how we use it is best acquired by children making their own personal dictionaries, and this is well established in good practice.

Thesauruses of antonyms and synonyms are available for the primary years. I have often used them, for example, in the context of poetry writing. Although the National Curriculum does not require them to be introduced until the secondary school stage, help with using a thesaurus seems to be appropriate for the older juniors. It reinforces the idea of language as essentially creative and varied, and offering us an exciting range of options to express our meaning. In his preface to the *Oxford Children's Thesaurus* Alan Spooner hopes that 'it includes a wide enough vocabulary to make it interesting and thought provoking'.

Encyclopaedias (and major resource books)

A set of encyclopaedias can cost a hundred pounds, or much more, and teachers will wish to study several sets before making a choice. To prepare a short list it is helpful to consult a guide. To my knowledge, the most comprehensive and fair minded is Tucker and Timms *The Buyer's Guide to Encyclopaedias*.[1] This appeared in revised form in May 1991. The National Curriculum's subject-centred emphasis has led to renewed interest in a set of volumes summarizing all kinds of human knowledge.

Multi-volume encyclopaedias are prepared for three main age ranges, broadly: elementary sets for children under 12, intermediate sets for those aged 10 years and over and advanced sets for older children and adults. It is the first of these which mainly concerns us in the primary years, although middle schools and families buying for home use might choose an intermediate set.

Awareness on the part of the compilers of the kinds of project 5–11-year-olds are likely to be undertaking should be evident: this would certainly involve a good knowledge of National Curriculum requirements at Key Stages 1 and 2. This might also mean that encyclopaedias following too closely the school curriculum of other countries might now be less appropriate. On the other hand, an internationalist approach is attractive particularly when, as in the *Children's Britannica*, it is combined with some special coverage of Britain.

Here I can only briefly set out features which seem important in choosing encyclopaedias for the primary years. A fully comprehensive encyclopaedia would result in a weighty set of books and at the primary stage, since some topics are likely to be more relevant than others, compilers can, to some extent, be selective. The editor of the new *Oxford Children's Encyclopaedia* commissioned a survey of what children look up: volcanoes, Vikings, Normans, Romans, dinosaurs and so on. So we are looking for good clear treatment of the most important topics at the primary stage.

As is the case with most kinds of non-fiction, we seek books which provide sound factual information but also ideas and speculation to awaken curiosity and interest. A good motivating feature of *Children's Britannica* (revised reprint published 1991) are the stories about historical characters which run alongside factual accounts. *Childcraft*, for children in the early years of schooling, includes stories, games and projects appropriate to each volume's subject (for example, Mathemagic, Art Around Us and Celebrations).

Naturally we expect good retrieval devices in reference material and, in learning about what this genre offers, children need to find out how to get to the items they seek quickly. The survey carried out by the *Oxford Children's Encyclopaedia* editors found that an alphabetic format was much preferred to a thematic organization.

Most modern compilers take great trouble over indexing. The *Children's Britannica*, in 20 volumes, devotes the final one to a 630-page index which, as well as directing young readers to appropriate parts of the volumes, also provides short, useful definitions. The *New Book of Knowledge* (updated edition 1991) provides a large well-organized main index and each of the 21 volumes has its own index. *Childcraft* (1989 edition) also provides a general index to its reference books as well as for each of the 15 books.

Illustrations, photographs and drawings are important in making reference books inviting or otherwise. Colour illustrations are generally more numerous in updated encyclopaedias (Tucker and Timms, 1991, p. 4). In Chapter 9 of this book we find a strong preference for colour pictures and photographs amongst the children. However, often black and white diagrams are more appropriate and *Children's Britannica* provides a great variety. Sometimes the illustrations vary in quality from volume to volume. The *Childcraft* Resources Set presents high quality art work in the 'Art around us' volume, but pictures in other volumes are on the insipid side (Timms and Tucker, 1991, p. 36).

Encyclopaedias specially designed for the primary years usually avoid dry reference-book language. Stories, bits of biography, ideas for projects all help to interest and motivate. The long, dreary sentences typical of the genre are off-putting (Littlefair, 1991, p. 38). We also need to look at the whole format and how the text integrates with illustrations. We should not forget that the actual print size matters to the younger children.

The most recently prepared or updated encyclopaedias are avoiding a narrow ethnocentric view of the world. *The Oxford Children's Encyclopaedia* (in 7 richly illustrated volumes) mentions the implications of colonialism, for example, under 'aborigines': it is made clear they 'resented the settlers taking over their land, especially the sacred sites'.

So far the encyclopaedias discussed have been sets rather than less detailed single volumes. For younger children a single volume like the *Kingfisher Children's Encyclopaedia* and the *Dorling Kindersley Children's Illustrated Encyclopaedia* can be less daunting. Both of these are alphabetical, give instructions about use (symbols, etc.) and are clear and easy to handle. I looked up 'octopus' in each volume and found that, as well as basic facts, each included boxes of extra information about particular kinds of octopus. Each also included the kind of detail that interests and motivates the very young. The *Kingfisher* explains that some of the 50 kinds of octopus are as big as 9 metres but that most are 'no longer than a person's fist'. The *Dorling Kindersley* mentions that one member of this family of sea creatures – the male cuttlefish – 'turns black with rage when it is angry'.

Children usually need quite a lot of help in using encyclopaedias whether they are sets or single volumes. Talking about the signs, symbols and cross-reference systems is best done with individuals or small groups in the context of everyday classroom work. Encyclopaedias often give the first summary of a topic a child needs. It sometimes provides a framework for researching a topic in other books. All this needs to be made explicit and demonstrated. Work with encyclopaedias can be more enjoyable if it is collaborative.

Before moving on some mention should be made of the new computer-based encyclopaedias, for example the *Information Finder*, on CD-ROM, which uses the text of the *World Book Encyclopaedia*. At £390 this would be a big investment for a primary school, and would probably only benefit the older and abler children. The latter would have access to computer encyclopaedias at the local public library. Rather than replacing the book form the new advances have encouraged the use of computer technology in updating, indexing and generally speeding up the production of books.

Atlases and map books

Maps communicate information visually. Very young children often acquire the principle of mapping by being helped to make simple maps of their own. In a typical activity five-year-olds were comparing the sizes of pieces of toy furniture as part of topic work on 'Homes'. With the teacher's help they drew round the furniture on squared paper and looked down at the view. After cutting out the shapes they coloured them and arranged them on a sheet of paper representing a room (*Junior Education*, September 1991, p. 26).

The next stage is often to 'read' maps of the area near their homes and school. Once the way information is represented on a map is understood, children can begin to use maps and map-type books. The map books for the youngest children often present one country. They tend to begin with a clear colourful map, and then to provide on subsequent pages information through simple text and illustrations about history; famous people is a favourite focus (for example, *This is China* by Chris Masters). Gradually these texts introduce us to a country's present circumstances with facts about customs, products and communication systems (Margery Fisher in *Growing Point*, 1985, p. 3942). Map books of this kind are a good support for topic work.

Compilers of map books and simple atlases which include the continents of the whole world use carefully considered strategies to try to link the information to children's existing ideas and experience. In *Philips Children's Atlas* information boxes explain about occupations, flags, stamps and so on. The *Kingfisher Children's World Atlas* uses bright clear photographs and pictures indicating the way of life in the countries on the maps.

In fact the format and layout of the best atlases for the very young is much improved. Contents pages are clear and inviting and the countries of each continent are often colour coded (for example, *Philips Children's Atlas*).

The new *Dorling Kindersley Picture Atlas of the World* has a large format and gives a three-dimensional impression. As well as the mountains, rivers and seas, places of interest, well-known people, products, animals and customs of each area are shown. The same large format is used for the Dorling Kindersley specialist atlases which include *The Great Dinosaur Atlas, The Space Atlas, The Animal Atlas* and *The Great Atlas of Discovery*. They all have well-designed information boxes and clear 'How To Use This Atlas' sections. They are aesthetically pleasing, easy to use and above all – great fun.

World atlases aimed at older primary and secondary school children often include political and religious information (*Hamlyn's Children's World Atlas*). This can date rather swiftly. Events in the Soviet Union in the summer of 1991 made political maps in atlases published only a few months earlier seem prematurely out of date.

Similarly tables of statistics on health, population and so on, quite sensibly included in new editions of atlases (see, for example, *Philips Modern School Atlas*), are in need of constant updating.

Quite a number of atlases for the 10 and over age range begin with a useful section about the world and its formation (*Collins Children's Atlas*, revised edition). There is more about what to bear in mind when choosing atlases for different ages and stages in Chapter 7 under geography books.

Summary

- Dictionaries often provide more than one word meaning for each item, tend to use phrases rather than sentences and include abbreviations which are explained at the front or back. All these features need to be understood by young readers and help by demonstration and direct teaching is necessary.

- Early dictionaries try to contextualize the items by embedding them in sentences and including helpful illustrations. This is also a way of bringing in the spelling of inflections like past tenses and plurals.

- The liveliest dictionaries not only anticipate the words children are likely to want to look up, but also include unusual and intriguing words which would encourage browsing and reinforce the idea that language is creative, interesting and exciting.

- A children's thesaurus is a useful classroom reference book; since it is organized around word meanings, the synonyms and antonyms provided help children refine their vocabulary and indicate the enormous range of options a writer has.

- Children's encyclopaedias include single volumes and sets of up to 20 books. New computer technology has greatly enhanced general layout and organization of retrieval devices. The best encyclopaedias challenge and interest as well as inform.

- The best early atlases and map books have clear, colourful and accurate illustrations and an inviting large format; they use strategies like information boxes to help children make links between what they know and the new information.

- The best atlases for older primary age children are also clear, aesthetically pleasing, up to date and accurate, but have more detailed information, for example, political and religious background to countries and statistics on health and population.

Notes

1. I acknowledge the contribution of Tucker and Timms (1991) in informing my analysis of encyclopaedias.

Further reading

Littlefair, Alison (1991) *Reading All Types of Writing*, Open University Press, Milton Keynes.
Meek, Margaret (1991) *On Being Literate*, The Bodley Head, London.
Southgate, V. *et al.* (1981) *Extending Beginning Reading*, Heinemann Educational Books, London, for the Schools Council.
Tucker, N. and Timms, S. H. (1991) *The Buyer's Guide to Encyclopaedias*, from Simply Creative, 246 London Road, Charlton Kings, Cheltenham, Glos. GL52 6HS.

5
KINDS OF NON-FICTION:
NON-NARRATIVE 2
CHILDREN'S NON-STORY PICTURE
AND INFORMATION BOOKS
(EXPOSITION)

> An information book must communicate facts and ideas to its readers, of whatever age or capacity, in such a way that they develop the will and the mental equipment to assess these facts and ideas.
>
> (Fisher, 1972, p. 474)

> It is time we started recognizing one of our traditions: the primary school information book – carefully written, beautifully produced, uncensored and sometimes unloved.
>
> (Graham Hart, *Times Educational Supplement,* 13 October, 1989, p. 65)

The earliest non-narrative texts, apart from labels and notices, which children experience are usually the non-story picture books for the pre-school and early school years. These are the forerunners of the genre known as children's information books so I examine them first.

The rest of the chapter considers in some detail the nature of the information book genre with sections on the global or overall structure, the language, the illustrations and the retrieval devices. Attention is paid to how information books can be inviting and accessible and suggests that there may be some transitional genres to provide a bridge to mature non-narrative prose. The important question of unwelcome bias in books ends this chapter.

Non-story picture books

Books organized around the theme of numbers or letters, for very young children, can be introduced as early as their first year. The educational advantages are obvious – reading and counting are anticipated and the baby becomes familiar with the shapes of numbers and letters. Looking at the pictures together, parent and child talking about them, is highly enjoyable. Interpreting pictures and even photographs is learnt (see the discussion of Bruner Chapter 1 p. 12). The realization that print 'means' is also learnt. The baby learns to connect the black marks on the page with the adult's voice and then the knowledge that the meaning arises from the writing will have 'lodged in her bones' (Butler, 1988, p. 16).

Favourites at this stage include Brian Wildsmith's *ABC*, John Burningham's *ABC* and Rodney Peppe's *The Alphabet Book*. In the last of these the illustrations are simple and clear and there are sentences like 'this is the anchor . . . that holds the boat'.

Dick Bruna has an appropriate style and children like the very bold print and primary colours: his *b is for bear* is a favourite. Other non-story picture books are organized according to a concept like shape, size, opposites, odd one out and up and down. Often the written text is minimal and the pictures are meant as a starting point for conversation. Sometimes continuity between pictures is achieved by having the same child shown in different contexts. In John Burningham's *Opposites Book* the same little boy in a yellow hat and blue trousers is seen: on a double page he observes a tortoise and then a hare with the captions 'slow' and 'fast'; in another he holds a baby's hand, then an old lady's hand to extend the written word 'young' and 'old'.

Fiona Pragoff's picture book on the same theme, opposites, uses photographs rather than drawings and we follow through the same little boy in the same environment with his toy bear.

Both books reflect the mingling of fact and fantasy in a young child's mind. While Burningham's pictures, for example, of the child lifting an elephant to indicate the concept 'heavy', have a delightful sense of the ridiculous, Pragoff enters into the idea of treating the toy bear as if he is joining in the activities.

This kind of picture book is not an immature form which recedes as children grow older. Some publishers like Macdonald Educational (for example, *Starters Long Ago* books) and Usborne (*Understanding . . . Farm Animals,* etc.) have specialized in pictorial information books for the early and middle primary school stages. These are a transitional genre leading towards books with a greater proportion of writing to illustrations.

Some picture books reinforce the idea that acquiring information can be fun at any age. Anno's superb history and geography books create an exhilarating mixture of legend, custom, literature and all the things that make up a place's character. *Anno's Britain*, for example, includes Chaucer, Churchill and Land's End. *Anno's Italy* and *Anno's Medieval World* provide similarly rich experiences for any reader from the older primary school stage upwards. Of course, these do not replace the more conventional information books described later in this chapter, but I would certainly include them in displays and talk about them with groups and even the whole class to enrich a geography or history theme.

Older children often enjoy books intended for a younger audience. Some over-10s love to agonize over the disturbing choices in John Burningham's *Would You Rather . . .*, for example 'Would you rather your dad did a dance in school or your mum had a row in a café?' I would use this playful sort of book to develop English work, their own writing and drama.

Charles Keeping's imaginative picture books, bringing alive the life of the inner city community, can also be the starting point of children's own art, language and dramatic activities. Perhaps books like *Railway Passage* are not easily placed in a firm category. The old age pensioners, couples, individuals and children that people the black and white drawings are in one sense fictional, but also educate us about city life.

Summary

- Picture books, with a topic-based rather than a chronological structure, are often amongst the first non-narrative reading material young children experience.

- Text and illustration integrate in communicating meanings in the picture book genre but pictures are not necessarily just simple visual expression of the text; they may extend or even challenge what is written. Above all they often entertain and provide a playful focus for adult-child conversation.

- The picture book genre is not an immature or transitional form but rather a type of book which can be enjoyed at any age.

Information books[1]

The more subject-centred approach of the National Curriculum makes information books a key genre in the primary years. These are illustrated books, usually on one topic, identified by the title, for example 'Squirrels', 'The Victorians' or 'Stars and Planets'. Information books make up a large part of the non-fiction section of class and school libraries. While it is probably true that story genres are most familiar to children when they start school, it is unlikely that the information books at school will be their first experience of non-chronological writing. As well as the non-story picture books described in the previous section children see signs, labels, notices and captions. Nevertheless, some features of the information book genre can present a challenge to young readers. These include factors to do with the global structure, the language, the illustrations and the retrieval devices. Each of these is looked at in some detail to help teachers to understand the nature of the genre and the demands it places on young readers, and to provide a framework within which to choose appropriate texts.

The global structure

It is the global or generic structure of a text that identifies it with a particular type or genre of writing (M. A. K. Halliday, 1978, p. 138). This means the organization of the book into sections which are ordered in a certain way. In a very interesting paper Christine Pappas[2] (1986) suggests that children's expectations of the global structure of texts is an important factor in their developing ability to understand and control this kind of reading material. She examined 100 children's information books and concluded that there are three obligatory elements, without which a text could not be considered to belong to this genre.

The first is 'Topic Presentation' and this, as we might expect, introduces the topic of the book. For example, *The Squirrel in the Trees* (Coldrey, 1986), one of the texts the 9-year-olds in the case study in Chapter 8 used, begins on page 2 with a heading 'Tree living squirrels around the world' and the first sentence is: 'Squirrels that live and shelter in the trees are common in many countries.' The account under this introductory heading explains how all the tree squirrels are helped by their tail to move and function in the trees. The variety of trees different squirrel species prefer is mentioned.

The second obligatory feature is termed 'Description of Attributes'. The 'attributes' are the essential features of the subject of the book. These features can either be blocked together or interspersed throughout the text. In *The Squirrel in the Trees* the 'attributes description' applies to the different kinds of tree squirrel which are the subject of the book. On page 2, still within the topic presentation, we are told that 'Tree living squirrels can be no bigger than mice', Indian giant squirrels are 'as big as cats' and flying squirrels 'have two flaps of furry skin stretching between their front and back legs' which 'open out like a parachute when the squirrel jumps allowing it to glide through the air'. Later on page 6 we return to a further 'attributes' description complicated by the fact that the book is about all the different kinds of tree living squirrels, and we get a generalized statement: 'There are many different colour varieties throughout the world, but greyish-brown and brownish-red are some of the commonest'. Thus in this book the Description of Attributes is interspersed and not a discrete element in the book.

The third and final obligatory feature, 'Characteristic Events,' is, as Pappas discovered, nearly always the largest element in an information book. They include typical processes like feeding and events like giving birth. This element is certainly the largest and most detailed in *The Squirrel in the Trees* and is mainly contained under headings like 'Movement', 'Food and feeding', 'Activities', 'Behaviour', 'Starting a family', 'Growing up', 'Natural enemies', 'Ways of escape' and 'Squirrels as pests'.

As well as these three obligatory elements, Pappas describes three elements which are optional. The first of these, 'Category Comparison', is important in *The Squirrel in the Trees* because in each section it is necessary to modify generalizations about squirrels with reference to particular varieties. Unlike most squirrel books for the primary years, which only compare grey and red squirrels, species common in Britain, this one takes on a large number of species, all of which, as the title suggests, are tree-living. The description of the tiny pygmy squirrels and the large Indian squirrels which was quoted as an example of 'Attribute Description' also exemplifies the 'Category Comparison' element. In this book the feature appears in the text in different ways at different times.

The second optional element identified by Pappas, 'Final Summary', sums up the main information in the book. This seems to be lacking in *The Squirrel in the Trees*. The last sentence of the book might be viewed as a sort of conclusion – not summarizing the information in it but in a sense deriving from it: 'So it is very important that we keep plenty of large areas of wild, unspoilt woodland and forest, in which squirrels and other woodland creatures can survive'.

The third optional element, 'Afterword', adding extra information at the end of a book, is present in the example under discussion.

For some reason Pappas does not include retrieval devices as an optional feature of information books. This is perhaps unfortunate since in my work in school both teachers and pupils often mentioned the quality of contents pages, indexes and glossaries as important in how well a book supports research for a topic. I would not expect all non-fiction texts to offer this feature, it is often not necessary in books for very young children. We would exclude from class libraries many individual and lively books if we insisted on a blueprint for information books. However, it seems to me that a contents page, with headings and subheadings to organize it, is very often useful when children are using books for research.

How useful then are the identifying elements Pappas proposes in relation to children's information books?

In Hasan's terms (1984a, 1985b) by recognizing three obligatory elements we gain an idea of what would or would not count as an information book. Teachers, of course, identify them on intuitive, common-sense grounds. Nevertheless, Pappas' attepmpt to make explicit these intuitive judgements is useful. While these elements, both obligatory and optional, once pointed out are fairly obvious, the variable order and interspersion of elements is not.

Is it the case, as Pappas believes, that the way in which information books are structured affects how easy or difficult it is for children to understand them? Pappas suspects that books which do not treat the Description of Attributes and Characteristic Events as discrete categories, but rather intersperse them through the text, are likely to be more challenging. This might be particularly the case for the youngest children who are just becoming familiar with the structure of the new genre. Pappas suggests that the order in which the elements are presented may also be an important factor in how easy or difficult a young child finds a particular text. The existence of the optional Category Comparison element, for example the comparing of different kinds of tree squirrels in *The Squirrel in the Trees*, seems likely to be a complicating factor for some young readers. This suggests that a book like *Tomato* by Barrie Watts (1991) would be relatively accessible for the young reader just tuning in to the register of information book: it concentrates on one category – 'tomatoes'; the order of the elements moves in an uncomplicated way from Topic Presentation, Description of Attributes – colour, seeds, etc. – to Characteristic Events which follow the life-cycle of the growing seeds through stages to the mature tomato. The Characteristic Events element is perhaps inevitably in narrative form, because it is about the life-cycle of the tomato plant. However, the early part of the book and other cues like the pictures and diagrams reveal it as an information book rather than a story. The final Summary is presented in the form of the key illustrations, reduced in size, and in the same sequence as in the main body of the book. It is suggested that the young reader describes the stages in his or her own words, using the pictures as a guide.

Tomato clearly qualifies as an information book if we accept Pappas' criteria. Thus a text can tell about events through time and still belong to this genre. This kind of text, discussed in Chapter 3, which is organized partly or mainly on a chronological basis seems a good way of introducing the information book genre to children sympathetically.

As well as the Stopwatch series to which *Tomato* belongs (with many other delightful books with titles like *Bumblebee, Conker, Newt, Spider's Web* and *Strawberry*) we have series like Life-Story published by Eagle Books and Animal Babies, published by Walker Books for Sainsbury's, all structured to appeal to children of Key Stage 1. Quite a lot of Key Stage 2 children are still most comfortable when dealing with a specific example of a phenomenon and with a partial time-sequencing approach. Not all topics can be presented like this, and as they move through the primary years children need help in learning how to read text organized round a topic and not through time, in other words books more like *The Squirrel in the Trees* than *Tomato*.

The language of information books

Non-narrative information books are organized on the basis of the demands of the subject or topic. The language used reflects this. A certain lexis is associated with particular topics. We can identify a core of concepts we would expect to be covered in, for example, a topic book on squirrels for children. The squirrel books used in the case study described in Chapter

8 included sections headed drey, gestation, hibernation, rodent, arboreal, habitat, and species. Part of coming to understand a subject is to do with making sense of the technical terms that help describe it. In books for primary age children we look for the embedding of new vocabulary in a strong contextual support: both writing and pictures can help here. In *Under the Sea* (Claire Llewellyn, 1991), one of a new science series for Key Stage 1 children, a headline 'Pollution of the Sea' is accompanied by a striking and moving picture of an oil-saturated sea-bird emerging from an oily sea. The supporting text communicates effectively and simply the chain of events a polluted sea sets in motion:

> What does the sea look like when it is polluted? How does this happen? What happens to the tiny creatures of the sea when there is pollution? What happens to the fish, and the animals and birds which feed on them?

The syntax of an information book is distinctive; sentences are often quite densely packed. Information is arranged hierarchically and a difficulty for primary age children is coping intellectually with the generalizations realized in language. Headlining can help indicate what are main and sub-topics and careful use of headings and colour coding of pages to do with different aspects of a topic, for example, basic information or projects to try out, can help show children how an information book works. Because of the general nature of the content of many information texts the tone tends to be rather impersonal. Thus we read near the beginning of Ralph Whitlock's *Squirrels* the following sentence: 'Squirrels scientifically belong to the great order of rodents, or gnawing animals, of which the best known examples are rats and mice'.

Here the reader is encouraged to think of squirrels as one species within a larger category. This kind of thinking is more characteristic of the later primary and early secondary school years. However, the sentence quoted above is the second sentence in the book. The first is: 'Have you ever seen a squirrel with an acorn scurrying up a tree trunk?' This question, appealing directly to the young reader's likely first-hand experience, is close to the rhythm of speech and therefore provides a sympathetic invitation to the rest of the book.

The use of personal pronouns indicates an author has some insight into the needs of the young readers the book is intended for. In Propper's *The Squirrel* there is a first page that draws the reader into the context of the book:

> Squirrels live deep in the woods where it is cool and dark. If you can see half-eaten pine cones lying on the ground beneath fir trees, you can be sure that there are some squirrels not far away. Listen and watch for them.

Two concepts from linguistics are helpful in analysing texts: register and cohesion. Put simply, 'register' refers to the fact that spoken and written language varies according to the situation[3]. The theory of register attempts to uncover the general principles which control this variation thus helping us to understand *what* situational factors determine *what* linguistic features (M. A. K. Halliday, 1978, p. 138). Halliday, more than any other modern linguist, has drawn our attention to the importance of context when language is used. He insists that any piece of text arises in a particular setting in which particular purposes are embedded. A successful reader of a text is sensitive to the context and the author's purposes in writing the text. The classroom studies in this book (see Part 2) seek to demonstrate that the total learning situation in which information books are read and discussed and the way teacher and pupils relate greatly affect success.

The Open University Reading Research Project Team found that another factor, children's sensitivity to the cohesion of texts, was important in their reading development. 'Cohesion' is to do with the internal unity of a text. Studies of cohesion examine the ways in which the text is knitted together and 'the different kinds of stitches in use' (Barrs, 1987, p. 12). Barrs differentiates between global cohesion (citing a list as an example) and local cohesion which is the 'knitting' together of ideas found in a sentence. A list lacks local cohesion. At the same time it is possible to produce a text which has local cohesion but is not globally cohesive (see Perera, 1984, for an example). However, a satisfactory text has both local and global coherence (see Chapter 6 for a further account of global and local cohesion).

Making lists can be a preliminary stage in producing a piece of writing. The children making their own information books (see Chapter 6) began by listing the sort of things they wanted to include. Adults too make lists to serve as plans for their writing. Making a list of items and later on putting them into a hierarchy according to their greater or lesser importance can be an important stage in producing a non-narrative text. Producing this kind of writing which follows an abstract principle is more difficult for both adults and children than a narrative or chronological organization. Barrs suggests that early writing which seems to be a loose collection of facts round a topic may in fact represent a first attempt to search for a different organizing principle than narrative. Those like Gunther Kress (1982) and Katherine Perera (1984) who have examined children's first attempts at non-narrative writing have tended in Barrs' view not to recognize that 'listing' is a way of widening experience.

I believe that we can conclude from this analysis that understanding mature non-narrative text requires a certain level of cognitive development since different kinds of reading and writing demand different kinds of thinking. As we shall see in Chapter 7, non-fiction texts which support each curriculum area can be written to appeal to different ages and stages.

Illustrations

The photographs, drawings, maps and diagrams used in children's information books communicate facts and ideas as well as the written text. These
are discussed as an aspect of every kind of text referred to in this book. In
part 2 children's response to illustrations in the books they are working
with is described.

In general we seek books in which the illustrations are clear, accurate
and useful and which complement the text. The language, for example the
labelling of the illustration, needs to be clear and unambiguous. We cannot
assume children understand how to 'read' diagrams as we see in Part 2,
Chapter 8 where children struggle with a 'food chain' diagram.

Publishers work to a budget, of course, and sometimes too much is
crammed into one page. A jumble of sketches, maps and photographs is
best avoided. A book needs to be aesthetically inviting. Ian Redmond's
beautiful photographs in *Elephant* (Walker Books) serve an excellent text
very well. Drawings too can be aesthetically pleasing as in David Macauley's fine architectural illustrations in *Cathedral, Pyramid* and *Castle*
(Collins).

The main questions we need to ask about the illustrations in a text are:
are they clear and accurate; do they complement, explain and extend the
written text; are they attractive and pleasing to the age group for whom
they are intended; do they include pictures of girls and children of ethnic
minorities where appropriate; are the illustrations free of stereotyping?

Retrieval devices

Contents pages, indexes and glossaries are often a feature of non-narrative
texts and are particularly important when children are using books for
research rather than for browsing. The *Times Educational Supplement* received 180 entries for the 1990 Junior Information Book competition. The
comment was made that 'It is unusual, now, to have a book submitted
without index, glossary or other apparatus where these are necessary'. The
last four words are pertinent. Non-fiction for the very young tends not to
have any of these, for example Aliki's *My Five Senses* or Franklin Watts'
Ways to . . . Change It series. A text has to have reasonable substance to
justify retrieval devices. The books in the Stopwatch (A & C Black) series
for young children have an index but there seems no real need for a
contents page.

While we need a core of information books in the main curriculum areas
with well organized retrieval devices, there is not a blueprint which must be
adhered to. Indeed the 1990 winning entry in the *TES* competiton, Judy
Hindley's *The Tree*, lacks even page numbers, but is a delightfully original,
quirky and almost poetic work. As Vivien Griffiths comments: 'You

couldn't base a school library on books like *The Tree*, we still need our "bread and butter" information books, but its excellence lies in its difference from the rest and that is what makes it a winner.'

Nevertheless, where retrieval devices are appropriate and present they need to be of good quality. Information retrieval is part of the requirement of National Curriculum, Attainment Target 2 English: Reading, and includes the ability to trace information through an automated electronic system as well as from printed materials like books. Teachers consulted in the course of my research for this book expected information books for junior children to have at least good contents pages and indexes.

A good contents page sets out the structure of a book and indicates its scope. Publishers are becoming more skilful in using contents pages to reveal how the material in an information book is organized. In the Squirrel project, the case study described in some detail in Chapter 8, the 9-year-old pupils appreciated the headings and subheadings in the contents pages of Davies' *Discovering Squirrels*. For example, the main heading in Chapter 2 is 'Different kinds of squirrel' and the subheadings, identifying the three main categories of squirrel, are Tree, Flying and Ground squirrels. Some of the newer science series, for example Science Starters 1990 (Watts), include this kind of detail. *Weight and Balance* by Barbara Taylor has a contents page which communicates the scope of the book clearly: each main heading is in heavy type and includes subheadings:

Weighing machine
Spring balance; weighbridges; steelyards; sensitive balance.

Each section of the book is represented by a triangle of an identifying colour, red triangles indicating when a step-by-step investigation starts. The type of book, its subject matter and complexity are important factors in how detailed the contents page needs to be. David Macauley's book *The Way Things Work* is an ambitious overview of technology and key inventions for all ages with an appropriately detailed contents page, and a separate more detailed page introducing each of the four main sections.

The contents pages of children's books to support science, nature study, mathematics, history and geography are usually best set out in a clear, unambiguous manner indicating the structured outline of the subject. The more catchy alternative lists require a certain level of verbal sophistication or prior knowledge of the subject for their interpretation (Von Schweinitz, 1989).

Von Schweinitz chooses not to name the author or publisher of her supporting example on *The Media*, but the contents list includes 'What are the media?', 'What makes a good story?', 'All the news that's fit to print', 'Subversive Agents', 'Beautiful People' and so on. These headings could be mystifying rather than illuminating to the young people and Von Schweinitz's point is a valid one. However, I think there is a case for playful contents pages for some readers in some contexts. Many of the 9-year-olds whose work is described in Chapter 8 claimed to enjoy the humour of Jessica Holm's contents page in her book *Squirrels* which has sections on 'Some other members of the squirrel clan', 'Nest sharing', 'Do reds and greys mix?' and 'Gadding about'. Used together with the index the maturer readers managed to find the information they wanted in this book.

The index is intended to work with the contents page to make retrieval of information possible. More specific information is sought in the index and items discussed in sections across the book are listed.

The very earliest non-fiction may not cover enough to justify an index or it may simply be inappropriate or unnecessary, as, for example, in the Franklin Watts lively 'Ways to . . .' Series (titles include *Ways to . . . Change it, Ways to . . . Build it*). Barrie Watts' *Tomato* (Stopwatch series) has a simple index suitable for the 6–8-year-old age range. The index includes all the key concepts covered; for example 'Seed', 'Seed-coat' and 'Sunlight'.

There is a problem for indexers when information books cover a large range of topics rather superficially. It is frustrating for a young reader to look up a word and find only a slight mention. Apart from the indexing problems posed we need to question the value of such general books for a younger primary age range.

Another obvious weakness is failing to include ideas, terms and phenomena covered in the book in the index. Each topic for a particular age range usually has some core concepts we would expect to be covered. Their omission in the index might reflect a serious weakness in the book. Also to be avoided are lists of pages where a topic appears, when helpful differentiation could have been given. Differentiation of a long index topic becomes increasingly important as children move through the primary years. Under 'Magnetism' in David Macauley's *The Way Things Work*, a book for any age, we have a detailed entry as follows:

Magnetism 294–309, 322–3, 340, 370
    Magnetic compass 371
    Magnetic field coil 181
    Magnetic induction 50
    Sound recording 243, 245, 247

This helps direct the readers quickly to the aspect of the topic they need.

On the other hand, good indexes avoid relegating to a sub-topic under a main entry items which deserve a full alphabetical slot of their own. Eleanor Von Schweinitz (1989) gives the extreme example of a book on the environment which lists 'Whale' under 'Hunting' and 'Greenhouse effect' under 'Weather'.

There are ways of making an index easier to use by spacing it helpfully: for example, in one of the books used in Chapter 8, Jessica Holm's

Squirrels, there is a space between each group of items under one alphabet letter, and the first word of each new letter is in strong print. Slightly different help for the same purpose, making retrieval as swift and efficient as possible, is given in the layout of the index in the Franklin Watts' Wildlife series. For example, the index in Michael Bright's *Koalas* is set out as follows:

A	Aborigines	5, 6, 8
	Alaska	10
	Albino koalas	23
	Antibiotics	16, 17
	Australian Koala	
	Foundation	11, 16, 24
	Australian Koala	
	Society	17

This kind of spacing makes an index considerably more inviting.

Newer information books, aimed at the older junior age range, are increasingly featuring glossaries. Full definitions of some of the key concepts in the book are provided. The entries here should of course relate to parts of the text and not be a home for new ideas not incorporated in the body of the writing. Neil Ardley's *Sound Waves to Music* (Hands-on-Science Series) gives a definition of fourteen key concepts. Under 'compact disc' in the index we are referred both to the part of the book where it is covered and to the glossary entry which gives a more succinct definition. John Elkington and Julia Hail's book *The Young Greens' Consumer Guide* has the glossary at the beginning of the book so that a young reader's attention is drawn to the key concepts, thus preparing themselves for what is likely to be covered in the text.

In addition to contents pages, indexes and glossaries, some information books provide lists of books under 'Further Reading'. *The Young Greens' Consumer Guide* mentioned above has quite a substantial and nicely organized list under 'Other Books to Read'. There are sections on non-fiction, fiction and some books for the very young. Even slight annotation would have added further to the worth of the list. However, the long and useful Lists of Organizations and Useful Addresses are excellently annotated. As well as the more obvious ones like The National Trust, Friends of The Earth and World Wildlife Fund for Nature (WWF) there are less known organizations like Woodcraft Folk (including children's crafts and games), the Woodland Trust (encourages participation – helping plant trees) and the Field Studies Council (provides courses for schools and families on environmental issues). Here is the annotation for another lesser known society, the Henry Doubleday Research Association (HDRA):

Encourages and researches into organic gardening and farming, and works to save many threatened British seed varieties from extinction.

Lists of further reading and useful organizations put a particular book in a helpful broader context, and suggest the book itself may be a starting point for further research.

Summary

- Information books vary in style and complexity but research evidence suggests that to qualify as an example of the genre three elements have to be present: topic presentation, description of attributes (essential features of subject of the book) and characteristic events.

- Early books in which 'characteristic events' can be presented, at least partially in time stages, seem to help a transition from story forms to the information book genre.

- It seems also to be helpful for younger readers if descriptions of attributes of the subject are blocked together rather than dispersed throughout the text.

- The language register of information texts can be difficult for young readers. Strategies which help are the careful contextualizing of new terms, use of personal pronouns and a conversational tone where appropriate.

- Illustrations need to be accurate and to complement, explain and extend the text as appropriate.

- Illustrations should not reveal a sexual or ethnic bias and stereotyping of particular groups needs to be avoided.

- Where children are using information books for research the quality of the retrieval devices is extremely important. We seek contents pages, glossaries and indexes which are well designed and easy to use.

Resources other than books

Chapter 7 refers to resources other than books needed for particular curriculum areas. Chapters 8–11 in which we move close to children in the classroom refer to the newspapers, charts, posters, magazines, archive material, video films, slides, TV programmes and computer databases which are also sources of information and ideas.

Some general criteria

These last four chapters have described the main types of reading material under the very broad classification of 'non-fiction' and given some good examples of each kind. The next two chapters focus on young learners as readers of non-fiction. In Chapter 7 I will be looking at the criteria teachers use in choosing books to support learning in particular curriculum areas.

In the last two sections of this chapter I want to look at some more general issues that usefully inform our selection of non-fiction.

Making facts matter

Even if we make sure books have the sort of desirable qualities already discussed like clear format and layout, attractive and useful illustrations, good retrieval devices and so on, we cannot be sure they are exciting or involving enough to sustain interest.

A great mistake some writers of children's information books make is to imagine we should protect children from unsavoury facts by sticking to the bland and the predictable. However, seeing something disturbing like a grotesque magnified head of a predatory insect (Whitlock's *Spiders*) or reading the cruel details about the slaughter of elephants (for example, in Ian Redmond's *Elephant*, Walker Books) intrigues and motivates. In Chapter 1 it was noted that in Piaget's model, learning takes place where there is disequilibrium, an uncomfortable feeling that is only relieved when we try to find out more in an effort to understand. In Chapter 10 one of the classroom examples shows 8-year-olds talking about the ideas in Miles Barton's book *Why do People Harm Animals?* This helped the teacher deal with some of the questions the children were asking.

Other books deal with controversial and sensitive issues like bullying (*Let's Talk About Bullying* by Angela Brunsell), illness (Living With . . . Series on *Diabetes, Blindness, Heart Disease* and *Aids*, Saunders and Farquhar) and sex (Mathias and Thompson, *My Body A–Z* and *Our New Baby* by Fogerstom and Hansson). All these can be used by parents and teachers at appropriate times. The problem is not with books such as these where authors have given a lot of thought to how to explain potentially distressing things, but with books on other topics which have a controversial element which is never made explicit so that children never become moved or excited by it. Let me give an example of what I mean. A class of 9-year-olds had been enjoying *The Sheep Pig* by Dick King-Smith; some of them searched for information books as their interest in how we rear and treat pigs had been aroused by the story. The books in the library which included Jane Miller's *The Birth of Piglets* and Ruth Thompson's *Understanding Farm Animals* were all right as far as they went. The problem was that they described what typically happened to the animals without ever making it explicit that certain practices like putting sows in farrowing pens and ringing young pigs were controversial.[4] Yet it was just this kind of controversial issue that fully involved the children's interest.

Almost every subject you can think of has value-laden features. All kinds of moral decisions have to be made in science. For example, once space technology exists how much of a developed nation's income should be spent on this rather than on other things? Should new drugs be tested on animals? It is not the case that children need 'the facts' before they can cope with the controversies – the ethical element is part of the whole truth about a topic. The different viewpoints can usually be explained from the earliest stages in a way that children can begin to understand. Of course, a salacious and unnecessarily gory approach is not recommended – but rather an honest presentation of the different aspects of a subject. The increasing number of books on 'green' and environmental issues often do a good job in introducing controversial matters and some of these like Geistdoerfer's *Whales, Seals and Dolphins* and Taylor's *Waste and Recycling* get on to the Earthworm Award shortlists.

While we need a core of 'bread and butter' information and reference books we also need some which are ingenious and unusual and which show that not only stories are memorable.

Non-fiction explores the outside world and some books celebrate the sheer beauty of the natural world. *The Tree* by Judy Hindley with an almost poetic text describes trees' pollination methods but also provides the place of each species in history and folklore. *Where The Forest Meets The Sea* by Jeannie Baker tells of the thoughts and activities of a young boy exploring a prehistoric rain forest, exquisitely illustrated with photographs of collages made from natural materials. Naomi Russell's *The Stream From a Raindrop to the Sea* is a book so individual it is almost impossible to assign it to a category.

Other books celebrate the aesthetic beauty of the parts of the world made by human beings, for example David Macauley's *The Ways Things Work* with its outstanding drawings of computers, levers, typewriters and all manner of other machines. Ian Graham's *Space Shuttles* brings alive through clear text and excellent diagrams this amazing engineering feat. Peter Lafferty's *Wind to Flight* combines impeccable layout, indexing, and so on, with a sense of the sheer excitement of science partly through suggestions for simple projects and experiments – making a simple spray gun with a drinking straw and empty bin – and shows imaginatively how a principle like using an air stream can be used to spray paint, sort out rubbish and float a Hovercraft.

All these authors seem to have addressed themselves to the questions: what is a young reader likely to know already? What do they need to know in addition? How can this information be conveyed in a clear and interesting, even imaginative way? Many have a speculative tone. Aliki's *Dinosaur Bones* makes it clear that scientific enquiry continues. Often the active participation of the reader in the form of simple tasks and experiments is sought. Sometimes a Further Reading section or list of useful addresses gives ideas about how to go on to further study.

Bias in learning materials

It has already been argued that what is objective fact or truth is more problematic than publishers and selectors of children's non-fiction sometimes assume. The same information can lead to different viewpoints and opinions.

There has also been more consciousness of the problem of books which offer a partial or ethnocentric view of the world and books which present the sexes and people of different class and racial origins in a stereotyped way. These issues will inform the 'choosing books across the curriculum' section in Chapter 7, but at this point we need some general guidelines on choosing non-fiction which avoid misleading and offensive kinds of bias.

Of course, all books are biased in that each one is the product of one person's unique experience and viewpoint. This cannot be avoided, and knowing the perspective from which an author writes helps us form our own judgement (Klein, 1985, p. 1).

What are the kinds of unwelcome bias which can occur in children's non-fiction and how can we avoid them? First of all there is bias by omission. Our total provision should include books concerned with women's experience of the world and the perspective of people living in different parts of the world. For example, Hamish Hamilton's 'In her own time' series mentioned earlier helps put women's contributions at the centre rather than on the margins or in mere footnotes in books about men's lives and achievements. But as well as books about women who managed, against all odds, to make public contributions of distinction we need to draw children's attention to the lives of ordinary women and men throughout history. A good example of a book bringing our attention to more ordinary lives is *Washday* by Ruth Thompson; through photographs, adverts and contemporary accounts this aspect of women's work is explored from 1900 to the present day. We need to make a point of including such books if they are good of their kind.

Otherwise good geography books often show many more males than females in the illustrations, in spite of the observation of the United Nations' 1980 report that women constitute half the world population and perform two-thirds of the work hours. Such books should be avoided or at least the omission made a focus for discussion. Similarly teachers are increasingly seeking history and geography books which show fairly the achievements and viewpoints of all peoples in the world.

A second main kind of bias is the misrepresentation of females and black people in written text and in illustrations. Teachers and publishers are now much more aware of these matters. Often a book which fails on these grounds is also unacceptable because of more general weaknesses: by definition an information book which is sexist and racist is not a sound and reliable book. For an excellent analysis of the whole issue of bias in books and other reading materials see Gillian Klein, *Reading Into Racism* (1985). Letterbox Library specializes in non-sexist multi-cultural books for children which are also good on general criteria.

Rather than draw attention to examples of unwelcome bias in books, since this has already been done in detail (Klein, 1985; Dixon, 1976), this book aims to give examples of books which are acceptable on these criteria and good of their kind generally.

The National Curriculum has greatly affected the content and style of publishers' output. One danger that must be avoided is the provision of large quantities of books, inevitably in the series format always liked by publishers, narrowly tied to attainment targets and programmes of work. A frenzy of such recipe writing could lead to functional and charmless books. As the main purchasers, schools and libraries have the ultimate power to discourage this. Since programmes of work are constantly, and quite rightly, being modified and changed such narrowly conceived texts could be rapidly out of date. We therefore need to establish the qualities we should look for in choosing information books to enrich children's work across the curriculum. I suggest the following:

- Controversial matters, often present only implicitly, are explained in a way children can understand in the better information books.

- Books which intrigue, fascinate and occasionally, where appropriate, even shock are likely to motivate young readers, even relatively reluctant ones.

- All books are biased in the sense that they present an author's point of view and particular experience, but some books, by omission or by stereotyping or misrepresenting certain groups are biased in an unacceptable way.

- The arrival of the National Curriculum has predictably brought about a great number of series of children's information books. Some of these are better than others and teachers need to apply criteria carefully in making their selection. (See Chapter 7, p. 77 for a detailed summary of criteria.)

Notes

1. The sections on information books are based on an unpublished Ph.D. thesis: M. Mallett, Non Fiction in the Primary School Years: A Study of some Factors Associated with Success in Helping Children Reflect on Ideas and Information in their Reading.

2. Pappas developed her criteria for deciding whether a text was or was not in the

information book genre by asking the five identifying questions set out by R. Hasan (1984):

- What elements must occur in every text belonging to the genre?
- What are the optional elements, those that may or may not occur?
- Which elements can repeat?
- Is there a fixed order of occurrence?
- Is there an optional or variable sequence for some elements?

3. A clear account of registers is set out in Doughty *et al.* (1972) *Exploring Language*, p. 185–6. See also Alison Littlefair (1991) for an interesting account of how 'genre' and 'register' can be applied to children's reading development.

4. This classroom example is described in Mallett (1992a). See also R. Jones' book *Fantasy and Feeling in Education* for a fascinating account of children becoming motivated to find out about the social structures of the Netsilik tribe after reading about practices like female infanticide.

Further reading

Fisher, Margery (1972) *Matters of Fact*, Brockhampton Press.

Halliday, M. A. K. (1978) *Language as Social Semiotic*, Edward Arnold, London.

Klein, Gillian (1985) *Reading Into Racism*, Routledge and Kegan Paul, London and Boston.

Meek, Margaret (1991) *On Being Literate*, The Bodley Head, London.

Neate, Bobbie (in press) *Finding Out about Finding Out*, Hodder & Stoughton, London and Sevenoaks.

Von Schweinitz, Eleanor (1989) Facing the facts, in *Books For Keeps*, March.

Wilson, Jennifer (1989) Information books, in Nancy Chambers (ed.) *The Signal Collection of Children's Books*, pp. 68–88.

6
BECOMING A READER OF NON-FICTION

> Reading to learn what is known must include the habit of freshly wondering; knowledge must be reconstructed by the learner.
>
> (Margaret Meek, 1991, p. 170)

This chapter considers what is involved in learning from the written word and how information from first- and second-hand sources can be integrated. Reading involves much more than the transfer of meaning from one mind to another. When we read we apply our knowledge of sentence structure and word meaning as well as our existing knowledge to carry us through the text and often we are able to build a sense of what is likely to be coming next as we read. The words themselves are not read as if they were a list which is then, as a separate process, assigned a cumulative meaning. Rather, as we read the words are grouped into units that are both meaningful and grammatically structured.

Taking this model of reading as an essentially active process of creating meaning out of a text, how helpful are aids to reading comprehension like DARTS and reading laboratories, and how can we build the teaching of study skills into a meaningful context?

Constant collaboration between teachers and children over books and using the spoken language to make ideas and information in written form come alive are key elements in promising practice. Anything we can do to encourage the 'freshly wondering' in the quotation from Margaret Meek which begins this chapter is worth while.

Learning from written material

First-hand experience

Children's earliest learning is embedded in meaningful everyday contexts. Much of it is physical: learning to crawl, walk, climb stairs, use a spoon and get dressed. It is also social, achieved in the presence of others – parents, caregivers and older siblings. The activities and tasks parents and teachers of young children share and talk about – unloading shopping, digging in the garden, cooking and playing games – are accompanied by talk: talk to focus attention, to direct activity and to evaluate and share experience.

The principle that young children continue to learn from first-hand experience is evident in the practical mathematics and 'hands on' science, craft, design and technology and cross-curricular project work (still possible since the implementation of the National Curriculum) found in primary school classrooms. The emphasis on learning by manipulating objects in a stimulating environment is compatible with Piaget's theory that the roots of intelligence lie in action.

However, it is widely thought that classroom practice was influenced for many years by the relative underprivileging of the role of language in learning in Piaget's model of development (see Chapter 1). The work of educationists over the past twenty-five years has shown that language is much more central to the learning process. Language is more than the crystallizer of what of what has already been learnt, as proposed by Piaget. The assimilation of new material is greatly assisted by children and teachers talking together, as the work of Britton (1970), Rosen and Rosen (1973), Barnes (1976, 1988) and many others shows.

In some cultures nearly everything children need to learn is learnt in context, carrying out actions and tasks. However, societies like ours demand kinds of learning that are not embedded in a particular context. Such knowledge and information has to be mediated verbally by teachers and parents or else acquired from books. A major educational concern is how to help children integrate information from first- and second-hand sources. How do we help them bridge the gap between what they know from experience (Piaget and Vygotsky's spontaneous concepts) and what they hear from the teacher or read in books (Piaget and Vygotsky's scientific concepts). The more subject-centred organization of the National Curriculum makes us search anew for helpful strategies to make book learning come alive for children of different ages and abilities.

Learning from print

The great advantage of written language is its permanence. Readers can proceed at their own pace and go back and re-read when they wish. The listener, unless speech is recorded, has less flexibility and must catch things first time. But there are features of written language that make it challenging. Texts have to stand on their own without the kind of physical context spoken language has. Katherine Perera gives a good example of how situational clues help in oral communication. A primary school teacher comments, 'The noise of that pneumatic drill is quite intolerable'. Even if the children have not come across the word 'pneumatic' before, the noise outside gives a strong clue, and to interpret 'intolerable' they only have to look at the teacher's facial expression! (Perera, 1984, p. 273.)

A second factor which makes written text more difficult for all of us, but particularly young readers, is that it lacks the speaker's tone, speed of speech and pause. To a limited extent punctuation can help and writers and publishers of children's books sometimes try to use layout and line divisions to show how phrases relate to each other. But, as Perera points out, listeners know immediately by the speaker's pitch, stress and even loudness which is the new and important information. Readers, on the other hand, have to hold the developing text rather carefully in their memory so that they can identify the information focus even when it does not occur in its most usual position at the end of a clause (Perera, 1984, p. 273). There are often visual clues to help compensate: punctuation; top and side headlining; the use of different kinds of type to indicate the status of different kinds of information; and the organization of the book into chapters (see section on global cohesion in this chapter and in Chapter 5).

Thirdly, written language contains grammatical constructions which are not normally found in everyday speech. There is often much embedding of sentences and sometimes use of passive rather than active voice. Writers of children's non-fiction do try to avoid this and often use questions and other forms more typical of spoken language. Non-fiction can also be made more accessible by making links with young learners' experience, by avoiding using too many words likely to be new and by mostly preferring syntactic structures that resemble the patterns of speech.

Global cohesion

The overall organization of non-fiction work, what linguists like Perera (1987) and Pappas (1986) call the 'global structure', is important in determining how easy or difficult a text is for a young reader. Good, clear top and side headlines, division into chapters, the use of different kinds of type to give hints of relative emphasis and the place of a particular piece of information in the hierarchy all help. It should also be clear, and not left implicit, how the different sections of a book relate to one another and contribute to the whole. It is very obvious when aspects of the global structure are unsatisfactory. No amount of beautiful illustration or general attractiveness of a book can compensate for lack of clear organization (see Chapter 5 for an account of the work of Christine Pappas).

Local cohesion

This concept was discussed in relation to non-narrative writing in Chapter

5. We need to return to it now to understand what is involved in becoming a reader of this kind of text.

As well as overall unity and integrity (global cohesion), texts need to work at a more local level. Each sentence needs to be knitted carefully into the one before it and after it (Barrs, 1987, p. 10). Halliday and Hasan have done pioneering work in the area of text cohesion at sentence level. One outcome of this was their book *Cohesion in English* (1976). In his research for the Open University Reading Unit, John Chapman applied some of their ideas to how a knowledge of cohesive ties helps reading comprehension in the primary years. Lists and copious examples of the different kinds of cohesive tie found in written English are available in Halliday and Hasan (1976) and Chapman (1983). I also recommend Roger Beard's clear analysis with examples taken from *The Hobbit* (Beard, 1987, p. 33). As we might expect, all these researchers found that syntactical patterns which evolve later in childhood, and those which occur in written texts rather than in spoken language, present most difficulties for young learners. Of course, we want young learners to grow as readers, and this is partly achieved by their having opportunity to meet new and more complex sentence constructions, appropriate to different kinds of writing. Only offering them texts with short abrupt sentences denies them the opportunity and indeed sometimes produces writing which is difficult to read. Beard (1987, p. 38) following Harrison's analysis (1980) identifies five syntactic patterns which often occur in non-fiction and which tend to be difficult for young readers.

- Passive verb forms: 'Hazelnuts and acorns are liked by squirrels'.
- Nominalization: making a noun phrase from a verb.
- Modal verbs: 'could', 'should', 'might' and 'may'.
- Including of many clauses in a sentence. When we read, each segment of text is held in short-term memory while we process it and relate it to other segments. Once this processing is completed we do not need to remember the precise words, only the gist of the meaning. The inclusion of too many clauses in sentences hinders the comprehension of young readers by putting a strain on their short-term memory.
- Compression: writing with too many ideas condensed into a few, possibly rather short sentences. In fact some repetition of ideas and key vocabulary is helpful.

Sometimes complex meanings and carefully constructed arguments have to be expressed in more complicated language. We want children to learn to cope with this, but it seems sensible to introduce the new forms in stages. Some syntactic forms are not essential and are best avoided in writing for younger learners. These include concealed negatives, two or more negatives in the same sentence, difficult connections (consequently, hence, moreover) and the kind of breaks in children's books which cut across phrases. (These and many more are carefully discussed in Katherine Perera, *Children's Reading and Writing*, 1984, p. 327.)

Children's perceptions of the readability of texts

What is often termed the 'readability of a text' simply refers to the sum total of all the elements in a piece of written material which affect the reader's success. 'The success is the extent to which they understand it, read it at optimum speed and find it interesting' (Gilliland, 1972, pp. 12–13). The concept of readability has tended to be boiled down to what can easily be measured, for example sentence length and vocabulary. There are formulae which can be used for such measurement and the different kinds are described and evaluated by Harrison in Lunzer and Gardner (1979). On the whole, teachers' judgements are likely to be as reliable, particularly if several teachers work together to decide which books seem most suitable for particular ages and stages.

In my own work in school I have often discussed the issue of the readability of different texts with individual children and groups of children. Michael and Kieron, the two young fossil experts whose reading enthusiasms are shared in the final chapter, were able to suggest which books were best for 'younger children just beginning to learn about fossils and dinosaurs' and which were 'more for older children already interested'. In the Squirrel project (Chapter 8) children mentioned size of print, whether the book was in story form, the number of pictures, simply labelled diagrams and amount of writing in relation to the number of illustrations as factors in assessing the difficulty of a book. They mentioned 'hard writing' as a factor, and when pressed to explain further suggested this meant 'long sentences and difficult words'. When the children made their own books on Squirrels (see Chapter 8) and compiled word lists or glossaries, it seemed to help them read the information books they were using.

Oral and written language and cognitive development

What are the implications of becoming literate for children's intellectual development? All human societies develop an oral language but some, for various reasons, do not have a written form. Interestingly in some oral cultures some of the purposes served by written language in other cultures are taken over by their spoken language (see Gordon Wells, 1985, Chapter 7 for an interesting account of the evidence). We therefore have to be careful not to claim that literacy affects the basic repertoire of cognitive processes. We are on safer ground in arguing that literacy has an important effect on which cognitive processes are selected at a particular time and the speed and efficiency with which they are employed (Lock and Fisher, 1984, p. 219).

In cultures like our own the acquisition of literacy, unlike the acquisiton of speech, takes place for the most part in the relatively formal context of the school. The more complex kinds of written language allow us to build an abstract and coherent theory of reality. David Olson (1984) believes this explicit formal system both shapes the cognitive processes of educated adults and underpins western culture. The difficulty for our children is that there is a mismatch between the kind of thinking implicit in the general theories of science, philosophy and so on and the thinking which encompasses their daily activities in the practical world. However, another element in Olson's argument needs to be questioned. It is worth quoting it in full: 'Ordinary language, with its depths of resources, while an instrument of limited power for exploring abstract ideas, is a universal means for sharing our understanding of concrete situations and guiding practical actions. And it is the language which the child brings to school.' (Lock and Fisher (1984) p. 240.)

I cannot do justice here to a very interesting but complicated analysis, but I feel that while there are important differences between oral and written language it is possible to create too great a separation between them. A major theme of this book is that it is ordinary spoken language, the children's and the teacher's, which helps make accessible the objective knowledge which is at the centre of the curriculum. Spoken langauge allows young learners to express their thoughts and wonderings about the world and to begin the active process of reformulating new knowledge so that it can be assimilated into what they know already. This is not to deny that competence in philosophy and mathematics is often hard won. However, spoken language can be an instrument for gradually acquiring new ways of thinking and new ways of relating to experience.

Indeed, spoken language can be a bridge to the kinds of thinking which Margaret Donaldson has termed 'disembedded', that is thinking which is not centred in an immediate context. Much non-fiction deals with phenomena we cannot directly experience. Bruner has termed the ability to learn through written material 'analytic competence' (Bruner *et al.*, 1966, p. 284 and p. 310).

Writing is more abstract than talking and a purely linguistic context, independent of immediate reference, introduces children to the special power of language to extend our own physical context. We use a meta-language to talk about language. As soon as children have conversations about what something 'means' or how a 'word' or 'phrase' is chosen they have become able to be aware of taking their own decisions about what they write and, for that matter, say.

Thus talk can be about ideas and abstractions and things away from the classroom. Perhaps the important issue is not so much the mode, whether or not children are talking or writing, but the way in which language is used. I feel certain that talking about the ideas and information in books and about what is good and less good about particular books develops reading ability and the range and complexity of reading material a young learner can attempt.

Transitional forms

Reading and writing tasks which organize information into hierarchies of concepts and which require some understanding of the process of classifying and evaluating material naturally make more demands on a young reader than narrative or descriptive texts. The former are a product of mature cognitive development.

Chapter 5 seeks to show that there are transitional forms of writing for children which create a bridge from narrative forms to mature, non-narrative text. Such transitional texts include books which are completely or partly organized chronologically and those which echo conversation in syntax and tone.

The Stopwatch nature series (A & C Black) has both features. Baker and Freebody, in their interesting study described in *Children's First School Books* (1989), found many examples of these traditional forms in school classrooms.

In Chapter 8 we find some children aged 9 still coping best with books which have a time sequence but which also include the appropriate introduction of more general information. There is, therefore, a case for regarding narrative and non-narrative forms more flexibly, as forms which can both appear in a single book. Some of the books with this characteristic are excellent and to treat them as a 'transitional genre' does them less than justice. For example, Beverley Halstead has produced a fascinating story about Ajax, a brontosaurus, taking us from his hatching to his death, one hundred and twenty years later. At appropriate points in the story there are boxes giving the evidence for what is unfolding in the story. For example, one box justifies the view that 'Ajax' is a vegetarian: 'We can be certain the brontosaurus was a plant-eater from its teeth, and sometimes plant remains are preserved in the stomach' (Beverley Halstead, *A Brontosaurus: The Life Story Unearthed*).

Implications for practice

Pre-reading activities

What does what we know about learning from the written word tell us about good practice and about ways of preparing children to use secondary sources? Not all the following strategies must be put into action before a child can take up an information book. They are suggestions for focused class work in any subject area across the curriculum. The same headings are used to structure part of Chapter 8 which follows a project carried out by the author with a class of 9-year-olds.

Organizing prior experience

If children are to assimilate the information in books with their existing knowledge it is first helpful to talk through the topic with them. This sharing of 'what we know already' about, say, electricity, Saxon churches or volcanoes alerts us to 'what we might like to find out from books'.

Offering new experience

Sometimes this preliminary discussion can be helpfully followed by some sort of first-hand experience. Children learn very easily from what they do and see, and motivation is often awakened and sustained by an outing to a museum or farm or, in science, some kind of 'hands on' experience.

Alternatively a talk by a visitor to the school can be a starting point. In the case study in Chapter 8 the experience offered was a wildlife video, not first-hand experience, but an opportunity to acquire new information in a sympathetic form.

Formulating questions

The initial discussion combined with the new experience usually gives rise to a great number of questions. These can be jotted down and can direct the first bout of book research. Having your own clear purpose makes it less likely you will be dominated by someone else's structure and organization of a study of a subject.

Discussion

Class or group discussion after the early book research creates a context for reading out loud from relevant parts of books or summarizing orally what is written. The discussion provides an audience for the children's propositions and gives their work a collaborative centre.

Teacher and children can then agree a flexible plan for future activity and the ways of representing their findings. These might include: making books, shared writing tasks, setting up labelled displays, art and craft work, oral presentation of findings to another class, making a video film of the progress of the work and further outings or input from visitors.

Study skills

This term usually refers to the ability to find the most appropriate books in the library and, once the books are found, to use retrieval devices quickly and efficiently. I would also include the ability to use the conventions of spelling and punctuation in written accounts and to know how to check them. Because I believe producing oral or written summaries or notes is to do with reading comprehension I refer to them in the next section.

We will be looking in more detail at how children can be helped to use the library and to find books and resources to support their work in the next chapter.

Retrieval devices

Once the books are found children need to be able to use contents pages, indexes and glossaries to find their way to the parts most relevant to the task. This may sound obvious but the team taking part in the major Schools Council project, Extending Beginning Reading, comment that it was rare during their visits to many schools to see any teaching of bibliographical, dictionary or study skills (Southgate *et al.*, 1981, p. 159). The use of retrieval devices is firmly embedded in Attainment Target 2: Reading, but teachers are left to find the best ways of teaching these skills. The features of retrieval devices which make them easy to use are set out in Chapter 5. However, children still need help in using even the most clearly written. This help needs to be given by demonstration and direct teaching in the context of everyday work. In the case study in Chapter 8 the nine-year-olds learnt about retrieval devices by discussing as a class the relative merits of the different books they were using. Then they applied what they had learnt in making contents pages, indexes and glossaries in their own information books for a younger class.

Dictionary skills develop over the primary years if they are systematically built into classroom practice. Exercises unrelated to any sensible purpose are deadly and unlikely to encourage a love of language. There are many opportunities to give dictionary work a value. Sometimes individuals need a lot of help in going beyond using dictionaries as spelling aids. The status of different meanings and interpreting abbreviations all need to be taught. During the Squirrel project (Chapter 8) different children took responsibility for looking up the meaning and spelling of different vocabulary like 'predator', 'habitat' and 'arboreal'. They read out what they had found and we talked as a class group about the abbreviations used. The spelling of the words was a subject of discussion and so was the way dictionaries use punctuation to separate meanings. All this was systematic and related to clear purposes (see Chapter 9 for an account of the developing ability of children to use and evaluate retrieval devices). The words which formed part of the vocabulary of our topic were the basis of the word lists which they learnt to call 'glossaries' and which were included in the books they made. Identifying appropriate glossary words helped the children with their reading of information books.

Perhaps in Britain we have suffered the effects of an unfortunate dichotomy: on the one hand traditionalists demanding systematic teaching and on the other hand progressives allowing children 'to make choices' and teaching 'when the need arises'. Few teachers fit into these extremes. By definition good primary school work has to be 'child centred' in the sense that instruction and materials must be capable of being understood and interesting to children at the various ages and stages. Not everything can be absolutely fascinating all the time, of course, but if some of the chores of learning are centred in broader programmes like interesting topic work children will see the point. For example, I have often heard teachers say something like 'You do need to check your spelling and write this again neatly so that we can double mount it for our classroom display which the parents will be looking at'. Hard work is worth the effort if we can see a purpose to it.

Helping reading comprehension

Can reading comprehension be broken down into a set of subskills? The most ambitious project using schoolchildren as subjects was carried out by the Schools Council's Project team on 'The Effective Use of Reading' in the 1970s. Tests were designed to identify possible subskills like interpreting metaphors, finding main ideas and drawing inference from one part of a text. These were given to 257 10–11-year-olds in Nottinghamshire and Derbyshire. No evidence emerged that such subskills existed. Understanding seemed to be a unitary ability to do with a young learner's willingness and ability to reflect on whatever he or she is reading. One obvious way of encouraging this is to help children summarize what they read.

Scanning and skimming

Scanning is the kind of reading we do when looking at train timetables or through dictionaries. In children's everyday work they sometimes need to scan a text for a date or the name of a city or to look for answers to their own or other people's questions. It becomes more complicated when the answer is worded in a different way from the question.

Skimming is more to do with discovering the gist of what a passage or chapter of a book is basically saying. 'In reading the initial paragraphs of a book, the list of contents and the final paragraph, the reader is skimming' (Pumfrey, 1991, p. 215).

We need to demonstrate these reading techniques in context as children move through the junior years.

Notes and summaries

Learning to take notes is another valuable ability which can be acquired in the context of real tasks. Some teachers help a group or even a whole class to summarize new ideas taken from books during a lesson. Together they compose notes on the blackboard or on the computer and children make copies in their own books. This worked well in the Space project with 7-year-olds (see Chapter 10). The notes made collaboratively on the board gave all the children a framework for their writing by showing the way information in books is organized. The abler writers were then able to expand these basic notes.

We need to show how main ideas can be written boldly or in a particular colour, while subordinate ideas can be in smaller print or a different colour. Points under one heading can be numbered and written as phrases, so that when the notes are used to write an account sentences can be assembled. In this way copying and very close paraphrasing is avoided. I find older juniors are able to use notes to give short talks in groups or to the whole class, expanding phrases into whole sentences quite competently.

Becoming able to summmarize the main points from a text is a demanding activity and related to children's intellectual level. Research studies carried out at the Centre for the Study of Reading in Illinois (see Osborn *et al.*, 1985) suggest that this ability can be supported by the teacher inviting children to summarize texts as they read them, going back over the text to clarify questions. The acquisition of this kind of ability is not only helped by teacher demonstration, but also by direct teaching (Bereiter in Osborn *et al.*, 1985, p. 317). Children need help in summarizing modest amounts of text in spoken words before they can be expected to do it in writing (Southgate *et al.*, 1981, p. 323). In writing their own information books the children in Chapter 8 constantly tried to adopt syntax and vocabulary that the younger children would understand. The motivation to do this kind of rewriting, which is very challenging for all of us, was the need to satisfy an audience. This suggested how large the writing should be, how many illustrations were needed, the nature of the retrieval devices and complexity of vocabulary and syntax. I agree with Roger Beard (1987, p. 129) that rewriting is a strategy which might help in a variety of curriculum areas. Teacher and child could then review the drafts in the kind of conference approach pioneered by Donald Graves (1983).

Before leaving note-taking and summarizing I would like to mention some very interesting work carried out by Sheldon (1986) in the area of using diagrams to foster reading comprehension. I recently visited an infant school where the children had been helped to make their own diagrams of how a chick emerges from an egg, after hearing about this from a book read by the teacher. This diagrammatic kind of referent is sometimes called 'modelling'. There are many different applications of this approach: structured formats showing hierarchies of people in roles; growth patterns in graphs; intersecting circles showing how some things fit into two categories with some overlap; simple time-lines of chronological events, maps and plans. Not all texts can be summarized in this way and not everyone finds this approach helpful; some prefer ordinary written notes (Beard, 1987, p. 161).

Directed Activities Related to Texts (DARTs)

This book has emphasized the importance of embedding the reading of non-fiction in meaningful work. I believe this encourages the kind of commitment and the quality of reflection on ideas we seek. However, I see no reason why there should not sometimes be the kind of group discussion we think of when we hear the acronym 'DARTs'. This includes collaborative 'guesses' at how to fill gaps in a text in a semantically and linguistically appropriate way (cloze procedure)[3] and reordering paragraphs in a logical sequence. However, I believe that the activities are more justifiable if they have curricular relevance. Here is an example showing how Roger Beard suggests a programme of mixed activities of 'superDARTs' in which the activities are planned to fit in with evolving work. A topic on water could include 'a text analysis activity on some introductory information on the local river, a text completion activity on the key concept words of the water cycle; a sequencing activity from a text on the stages of a river; and a prediction activity on a novel or short story' (Beard, 1987, p. 155).

Thus carefully planned activities on these lines, perhaps particularly for the older end of the primary school, can help children develop reading strategies to approach both fiction and non-fiction.

Reading laboratories (Science Research Associates – SRA)

SRA have published what are known as reading laboratory materials. These consist of cards, in containers, grouped according to different reading age demands. It is claimed that by working through a series of comprehension exercises improvements will be brought about in the speed and accuracy of children's reading. Fawcett studied the progress of 11–15-year-olds, about of half of whom had and half of whom had not used reading laboratories intensively. The result is reported in Lunzer and Gardner (1979). He concludes that the intensive use of reading laboratories developed pupils' reading abilities. There has been some criticism of the design of Fawcett's study (see Beard, 1987, p. 145). Of course, it is the decontextualized nature of the material used in reading laboratories that causes concern. We would not want to rule out anything that might help less successful readers who have reached secondary school stage, but on the whole I am in sympathy with the view that if the time, effort and expense that have gone into preparing and using reading laboratories had been put into other teaching approaches the gains might have been even better.

Schema theory

An alternative approach to the search for subskills is to look for the structures of meaning the reader brings to a particular genre. The schema theory, bringing expectations and knowledge to a text, contrasts with the thinking behind traditional comprehension tasks. This line of research stems from F. C. Bartlett, *Remembering* (1932) and emphasizes the importance of the prior knowledge the reader brings to reading. Thus it fits well with Piaget's adaptive model of learning in which the new is integrated into existing knowledge which accommodates in turn to the new input.

On reading some of the interesting research being carried out into schema theory in the USA (for example Spiro *et al.*, 1980), and after carrying out the Squirrel project (Chapter 8), it seems to me that the teaching strategies of organizing prior knowledge and asking children to formulate their own questions to take to the text are entirely compatible.

The contribution of microcomputers[1]

Microcomputers offer programs involving young learners in text generation and analysis, for example 'Wordplay' from the MEP Primary Project pack. Young learners type in lists of nouns, verbs, adjectives and adverbs and the computer produces groupings based on a pre-programmed selected order.

'Tray' invites the reader, or better still a group of readers, to play with a hidden text using knowledge of syntactic cues and tuning in to an author's meaning and writing style. In one version the punctuation marks are the only clue! It is claimed this gives children insight into how they read. The reservation is that the emphasis should not be on what the machine can do but on what children think they can do with it (Beard, 1987, p. 263; Meek, 1991, p. 225). Certainly word processing functions enabling children to compose, read and then redraft their own writing and to produce and modify diagrams can be extremely helpful in the classroom. Reading drafts from a computer screen encourages children to 'read as writers'[2] and this has a pay-off when they read other people's writing.

Word processing is particularly helpful to children with special educational needs since they can produce legible script, redraft quickly rather than laboriously by hand and use the spelling checks (Pumfrey, 1991, p. 289).

Summary

- The teaching of study skills needs to be systematic and part of an agreed school policy. Rather than create mechanical exercises for children to perform we need to harness the teaching of the skills to the needs of the work in hand.

- Children need help in making oral summaries before they can manage written notes.

- DARTs activities, including cloze[3] procedures, can, if properly used, teach children about important features of book language. For the primary age range they are best tied to relevant curricular activities.

- Reading laboratories provide decontextualized material. There is some evidence that some groups benefit but again tasks are best set in broader contexts.

- Children bring expectations and existing knowledge to a text. Teaching strategies which organize this knowledge and help children formulate their own questions harness these.

- Microcomputers provide the opportunities of learning about language in general and reading in particular through games and activities. This has a place but must not be allowed to dominate the programme.

- The word processing function transforms redrafting, taking away the laborious effort needed, particularly for children with special educational needs.

Enjoying non-fiction

If we want to encourage voluntary reading of non-fiction we have to present the books and resources not only as helpful in serving a function but also as a source of enjoyment. One major conclusion in Chapter 1 was that children are active in their learning and therefore in their reading. Bringing their own questions to the text helps them to use the books creatively and not passively. A look at helpful theory in the first chapter also reinforced the idea that children are social beings and love to collaborate. This means quite simply that we need to provide opportunities for talking about the ideas and information in the books and resources being used in each curriculum area.

Reading non-fiction out loud

Children become familiar with the syntax of spoken language because they hear and use it constantly. They also usually hear stories or see them acted out on video or television so that the typical syntax of story-telling is likely to become familiar. Other kinds of writing, particularly those organized on a non-story or non-chronological principle, are much less likely to be read out loud. The language of information books tends to be more formal and organized in its sentence structure. Thus it is a good idea to build into everyday practice reading out loud from the books children are using. Some parents share this kind of reading with children. Richard Feynman, the Nobel Prize-winning atomic physicist, tells how when he was only about three his father would regularly take him on his knee and read *Encyclopaedia Brittanica*, reading a bit of the text then translating it into ideas and images the young child could understand. On one occasion, the topic was a type of dinosaur which was 20 feet by 10. Father Feynman paused and explained that if the creature was in the room where they were sitting his head and neck would need to poke out of the door and his arms would spread through the windows (Feynman and Leighton, 1986). This was of course a most effective way of helping a child achieve the imaginative leap in making the abstract accessible, but Richard Feynman remembers most the excitement and pleasure. If this quality of reflection on what a text communicates can be associated with enjoyment the chances of becoming a reader who interacts with text to make it mean anew are likely to be increased.

Non-fiction helps satisfy the young child's great curiosity about the world of people, plants, animals, inanimate objects and events and feelings about all these things. But knowledge is not just a matter of acquiring facts, it includes coming to understand the significance of the facts. This is what Feynman's father helped his young son to do.

I believe teachers have an important role as models of readers of non-fiction. Very young children enjoy the teacher reading out of simple information books like Lynne Patchett's *My Shell* from A & C Black's Simple Science series and *Night Time Animals* by Joanna Cole. After the age of 7 children need to be introduced to the wider range of non-fiction discussed in Chapters 3 and 4. The dilemma is that their reading ability may not yet enable them to tackle the harder texts themselves. They need the adult's mediation. In the Squirrel case study in Chapter 8 I read out loud from the different information books at the end of each session. Non-fiction is sometimes quite difficult to read because of the way the sentences are organized. Children were encouraged to prepare sections from the books they had been reading. This meant that the children were introduced in some cases to written forms they would not otherwise have encountered. Where appropriate some of the differences between talk and writing were discussed.

They were also able to delight in fascinating information about flying squirrels and to enter into the mystery of the disappearing red squirrel species. Reading good non-fiction out loud is pleasurable and encourages voluntary reading.

Making books

In the early years of childhood young children draw and produce attempts at writing to represent and make sense of their world (Bissex, 1980; Kress, 1982). It is now fairly well established good practice to build on this in school by encouraging children to enjoy a real sense of authorship by making both story and information books. Sometimes a group of children collaborate in this. This kind of co-operative effort is sometimes accompanied by appropriate use of metalanguage; for example, 'words', 'writing', 'mean', 'contents page', 'glossary' and 'index'.

The teacher often acts as scribe for the younger children. Children draw on the book language they have read or had read to them in making information books; their efforts to write in turn help them understand more about how information books are organized.

The teacher's contribution is to talk about the book at the planning stage and to share in the decisions which help to make it like a 'real book'. Whether the book is bound and hard-backed or sewn or stapled and soft-covered, written in long hand or word-processed, the important thing is that it should be as attractive and satisfying as possible to the young author. There is extra incentive if the audience is to be a younger class, but sometimes the book simply joins the classroom collection.

Collaborating and sharing

My own classroom practice has changed as a consequence of my developing understanding of learning (see the final section of Chapter 1). I am still concerned that individuals achieve the highest standard of work of which they are capable and I aim to provide quite a lot of one-to-one interaction. However, I now appreciate that the challenging process of becoming a reader of non-fiction is not best achieved alone. My aim is to try to create a community of young readers and writers who provide the first audience for each other's developing ideas. I see myself as a mediator or facilitator between children and books by reading out loud, paraphrasing, explaining text and diagrams: in short as a model of a reader of non-fiction.

The sharing of children's wonderings about the topic in hand sometimes draws forth a response from others. For example, when Michael and Ben expressed curiosity about the near disappearance of the red squirrel from Britain, Tara persuaded her parents to video a programme by Jessica Holm, an expert on squirrels. The video was shown in class. This led to Michael bringing in Jessica Holm's book on squirrels from the public library. It is a simple point, of course, but somehow it is more satisfying to hear the teacher read out of a book you have brought into school than from one he or she has selected. Commitment and motivation need to be high to make the struggle with difficult written material worthwhile.

Summary

- Children need to feel motivated to tackle challenging non-fiction texts.

- Reading out loud exposes young learners to the organization and vocabulary of book language in a community atmosphere which encourages enjoyment of the new ideas.

- Making books involves using and reformulating new information with a particular audience in mind. This gives the writing a purpose children can understand.

- It is oral discussion and sharing which can enliven information in books and help make a class a community of young readers, writers and users of the spoken language.

Notes

1. As well as full length texts, for example Blanchard, Mason and David (1987), there are useful critiques pointing out the strengths and limitations of computers as aids to reading comprehension: in Beard (1987), p. 267; Meek (1991), p. 222; and Pumphrey (1991), p. 228. The last book gives the most favourable view of information technology in general ('the third industrial revolution') and microcomputers in particular.

2. This is Frank Smiths' term in *Reading like a Writer* (1984).

3. A cloze procedure involves presenting readers with a passage of text from which a number of words have been deleted. Particular categories of words may be missed out, or words in particular positions in a sentence. The procedure is diagnostic since a young reader's ability to predict what is likely to come next using linguistic and semantic clues can be assessed. However, it can also be an opportunity to learn about language as a system, particularly where several young learners collaborate over supplying appropriate words to fill the gaps. The discussion and re-reading likely to be encouraged promotes learning. For further information see Southgate, V., Arnold, H. and Johns, S. (1981) *Extending Beginning Reading*, Heinemann Educational Books for the Schools Council, London, Chapter 17.

Further reading

Baker, C. D. and Freebody, P. (1989) *Children's First School Books*, Basil Blackwell, Oxford.

Barrs, Myra (1987) Mapping the world, in *English in Education*, Vol. 21, no. 1.

Beard, Roger (1987) *Developing Reading 3–13*, Hodder and Stoughton, London.

Chambers, Aidan (1991) *The Reading Environment*, The Thimble Press, Glos.

Chapman, L. J. (1987) *Reading 5–11*, Open University Press, Milton Keynes.

Lavender, Ralph (1983) Children using information books, in *Education 3–13*, Vol. 11, no. 1, pp. 8–12.

Meek, Margaret (1991) *On Being Literate*, The Bodley Head, London.

Perera, Katherine (1984) *Children's Reading and Writing: Analysing Classroom Language:* Basil Blackwell in association with André Deutsch, Oxford.

Pumfrey, Peter (1991) *Improving Children's Reading in the Junior School: Challenges and Responses*, Cassell Educational, London.
Southgate, Vera *et al.* (1981) *Extending Beginning Reading*, Heinemann Educational Books, London, for the Schools Council.
Wade, B. (ed.) (1991) *Reading for Real*, Open University Press, Milton Keynes and Philadelphia.

7
A SCHOOL POLICY ON NON-FICTION

A school which wants to sort out its own approach to reading must make its principles explicit.

(Somerfield, Torbe and Ward, 1983, p. 1)

At their best, school libraries offer pupils the resources that study requires: access to reference books, information in different forms, a place to read socially.

(Meek, 1991, p. 175)

You need somebody, preferably full-time, at least with sufficient time, who is well-informed and who orders, buys, catalogues, updates what is in the classroom.

(Griselda Barton in McKenzie and Warlow, 1977, p. 67)

The education system in England and Wales has been transformed by the requirements of the Education Reform Act 1988 from a localized to a centralized system. As well as changes in how schools are financed and governed a new school literacy has arrived. Margaret Meek comments that never before in our educational history has there been such a detailed plan for 'schooling literacy and learning'. This makes it more essential than ever that schools have each their own clear development plan. This chapter looks at organization of non-fiction at a central level: how can the school language policy assist good provision and successful use of books and other resources?

Making principles explicit

The first of the quotations which head this chapter expresses the belief of Somerfield *et al.* that a school policy on reading begins with teachers making their principles explicit. Teachers plan and implement a comprehensive programme of language and reading. However, non-fiction is the special focus here. The following principles aim to provide a framework for this kind of reading, but of course each school formulates its policy in its own way.

- Reading non-fiction should be as enjoyable in its way as reading stories and poems.

- The organization of non-fiction is part of the role of the language co-ordinator, often, but not necessarily, the teacher whose curriculum strength is in English.

- A range of different non-fiction genres, each good of its kind, should be selected for school and class libraries: encyclopaedias and dictionaries; biographies and autobiographies; non-book resources like letters, maps and archive materials; information books organized both chronologically and on a subject basis.

- Well-organized, clearly written and interesting books to support each curriculum area are sought, bearing in mind the desirable features distinctive to each subject.

- The collection should include books across the curriculum for different ages and stages and for pupils with special learning needs, who may need material suitable for their chronological ages expressed simply.

- At each level we want more than the bare facts: help towards understanding and evaluating 'the facts' is needed. The best texts provoke further questions.

- Strategies for helping children to become involved with the books are best worked out collaboratively at language meetings. Such strategies include: the imaginative use of display, teaching of study skills and note-taking, discussion of non-fiction in school assemblies and in the classroom, reading out loud where appropriate and the involvement of parents jointly with teachers and children.

- Assessment of children's progress in reading the different kinds of non-fiction is best integrated with work in progress. The National Curriculum English guidelines, Reading: Attainment Target 2 provide a scheme for what might be achieved at different points along Key Stages 1 and 2 (see Chapter 2).

The rest of this chapter aims to expand on these principles under the following headings: the role of the language co-ordinator; school and class libraries; display; choosing books across the curriculum; involving parents; and assessment and the National Curriculum.

The role of the language co-ordinator: implications for teacher training and INSET

Primary school teachers are generalists whose main expertise is in children's learning between ages 5 and 11. However, the National Curriculum guidelines are arranged in subject areas. In line with this, teachers following a B.Ed. or BA Ed. honours course for primary teachers read, in addition to their education studies, a school subject such as English, history, geography, science, religious studies, art and design, mathematics, physical education, drama and music. This enables them to have a curriculum strength which means they offer subject expertise to the school and to their colleagues. Naturally teachers with special responsibility want to order books and materials and help shape policy in teaching strategies in these curriculum areas. However, as the third quotation above from comments made by Griselda Barton makes clear, we need one person to co-ordinate the whole language programme including the reading of non-fiction. There are clear implications for INSET here and for initial teacher education. As tutor in charge of a new course entitled 'The English Curriculum Course' I am at present meeting the challenge of preparing students who are reading educational studies with English for their new role. The following sections deal with the different elements of a language and reading co-ordinator's job.

School and class libraries

The school library

The books and resources here are available for the use of every class. They are catalogued by author's name, title and subject in a card index or computer system. The important thing is that the catalogue system and the borrowing system are both clearly understood.

Most school libraries have an abridged Dewey system with a subject index and fiction catalogue. Some flexibility is desirable. Information books on specific topics (for example, Macdonald's Starters and Franklin Watts When I was Young history series) could be grouped together as a collection. Children would need to have some means of knowing that information on, for example, the weather or the Victorians was to be found therein (Howe, 1985, p. 5).[1]

The National Curriculum has brought into the primary school sphere some topics in geography, history and science which formerly were more likely to be part of the secondary school programme. Primary libraries need to reflect this in both provision and arrangement. Clear labelling, illustrated sign-posting for younger children, a library notice-board and display area and large, clear, alphabetically arranged charts clearly indicating where resources on every topic can be found are all helpful.

A member of staff, often nowadays the language/English co-ordinator, often has special responsibility for the book stock, but every teacher will attend planning meetings and ask for particular new resources to be considered for purchase.

Although a pleasant, spacious room seems a good location for the central collection of books, sometimes a less attractive but more accessible space is to be preferred. We want children to see the books and notice displays and stands containing new books as often as possible. A school I know has the book stock in the entrance and children can often be seen browsing and looking things up.

Advice on the best way of siting and cataloguing books is available from the local schools service librarians. They will visit to advise also on the balance of stock and will lend from their own collections, for example information books to support a special topic the school or a class are involved in.

The language co-ordinator and indeed all the staff need to know what the library contains in order to direct children's work. The borrowing system needs to be clear and easy to use and capable of indicating which classes use non-fiction most and least and which books seem most well liked and used. The latter information helps staff evaluate the provision and the modes of communicating to children what is available.[1]

Non-book library resources

The new programmes of study for history and geography make it essential that school libraries integrate all kinds of printed materials in addition to books. 'Jackdaw' type folders can usefully be made up of a mixture of materials on one topic (Howe, 1985, p. 2). Non-book library resources[2] could include some of the following:

- Computer programs
- Jackdaw folders
- Publishers' catalogues
- Games
- Timetables (travel) and directories (*Yellow Pages*)
- Wallcharts, pictures, postcards, photographs, posters
- OHP transparencies
- Instruction manuals
- Children's own books
- School archive material (e.g. log-book)
- Atlases, maps, charts, gazettes, guides
- Newspapers, magazines, colour supplements (e.g. projects from *Child Education* and *Junior Education*)
- Teletext: Oracle and Ceefax
- Filmstrips, slides

- Tapes, cassettes and records
- Leaflets and pamphlets

Vocabulary to do with books and resources

If children are to become critical readers they need to hear and then use some of the following vocabulary in context so that they can talk about their library research and reading: table of contents; glossary; index; preface; foreword; content; chapter; section; heading; anonymous; appendix; bibliography; biography; card catalogue; editor; author; footnote; illustration; summary; pen-name.

Class library

Although the books in the small class libraries in most classrooms are usually catalogued with the central stock, these collections sometimes remain permanently in the classroom. From time to time they may be augmented to display books from the central stock to support a particular theme or topic. Children and teachers may also 'lend' their own books from time to time to enrich the classroom stock. Some classroom non-fiction such as encyclopaedias, atlases and dictionaries is available in multiple copies to meet the likely demand.

Displays

Non-fiction displays to complement work across the curriculum are useful both in the classroom and more centrally in the hall, library or entrance hall to share one class's work and interests. I find an attractive display encourages the kind of browsing and chatting which reinforces the idea that non-fiction is enjoyable and to be shared. Sometimes children's writing and drawing can complement the books, and labels and cards can suggest questions and activities. I like to involve children in the setting up of displays, perhaps giving different groups the responsibility in turn. A piece of cloth cleverly arranged over a shoebox can make a little platform against which to prop an open book. Little flower arrangements and other attractive, interesting and relevant objects help the display work well aesthetically.

In his book *The Reading Environment* Aidan Chambers suggests some variations on themes for displays. Suggestions particularly appropriate for non-fiction display include: new books; one particular author (Aliki perhaps or David Macauley); a selection of books about a celebration, topical occasion or something in the news (earthquakes, hurricanes); award-winning books (perhaps books which have recently made the Earthworm short list); and information books reviewed by children in the class (Chambers, 1991, p. 26).

Making displays of non-fiction part of the school and classroom environment gives this kind of reading a value and invites children's voluntary engagement with the books.

Choosing books across the curriculum
General criteria

In Chapter 5 some general criteria for choosing information books were suggested. It is helpful briefly to list these here:

- Attractive format, print and layout.
- Illustrations that integrate well with the text.
- Clear, lively writing.
- Not too many new words all at once.
- Words likely to be unfamiliar to be well embedded in the context.
- Efficient, easy to use retrieval devices: glossary, contents page and index.
- For younger readers, plenty of books which have a natural chronological sequence, for example life-cycles of creatures or life stories of people.
- Clear topic presentation at the beginning of the book.
- Good overall organization (global structure).
- Good linkage at sentence level (local cohesion), that is, not lists of very loosely related facts.
- For young children conversational writing, that is, language which, to some extent, echoes speech as a helpful transition towards mature book language (some books for the older end should be resembling the latter).
- Freedom from stereotyping, misrepresenting or omitting of female people and ethnic minorities.
- Factually reliable in our present state of knowledge about a topic.
- Not presenting as neutral information and issues which can be seen from different viewpoints.
- Books which present facts plus an evaluation or questioning of information.
- Including alongside 'bread and butter' books a good selection of lively and thought-provoking books which encourage voluntary reading and browsing.

Some of these criteria are more important than others when it comes to particular subject areas. Suggestions follow below about choosing books in the main content areas: geography, history, science and mathematics.

Geography

Key Stage 1

Much of children's learning of geographical skills and physical, human and environmental geography is through first-hand and practical experience: making simple maps, exploring the local area, investigating soils and visiting places of interest.

The first secondary sources are pictures, photographs, simple maps and globes. People travel more and see other countries in television programmes. There is still a need for books about geographical topics, however, as these give time for reflection and resavouring of information through pictures and maps as well as writing. Geography books need to be up to date and as accurate as our present state of knowledge allows. The kinds of book enjoyed by the 5–7-year-old age range include simple map books, picture books about the inhabitants of other countries, either in their country of origin or in a new country, books about places and transport, and accounts of people's occupations.

Maps and map books (AT1)

These are considered in Chapter 4 where it is suggested that the best early map books are in simple bold colour, often concentrating on one country and providing information about the local customs, climate, produce and so on.

Books about people from other countries (AT4)

Books about other children and about doing things together are inviting to the very young. In Ming Tsow's *A Day with Ling* (1982, Hamish Hamilton, photos by C. Cormack) Anne spends time with Ling and enjoys shopping at the Chinese supermarket. The narrative continues with Anne trying to use chopsticks and to write Chinese characters. This is the kind of book which can inspire children's own writing about visiting their friends whose cultural roots are in other lands. The story form makes it accessible to young children who are soon drawn into the sequence of events. Dual-language picture books like *Rumana's New Clothes* and *Munzer Goes to the Airport* (English and Bengali) are also often in story form and provide information about cultural backgrounds in a sympathetic way.

Michael Rosen's *Everybody Here* (Bodley Head, 1982) is not organized as a narrative but draws the young reader in through a magazine-like array of exciting recipes, maps, letters and photographs. This also encourages children's own sharing and book-making.

Two other books deserve a mention: *Delhi Visit* and *Uzma's Photo Album* published by A & C Black. English-born children visit their parents' homelands, India and Pakistan, and compare the two cultures admirably.

Places and transport (AT2)

Many young children are interested in the size and speed of things and there are many books on cars, ships and trains. The best go beyond bland facts and figures and inspire an imaginative response. Donald Crew's books on *Trains, Freight Trains* and *Harbour* contain double-spread pictures likely to encourage lively conversation and questions. They are picture books but the small amount of writing avoids banality and introduces relevant vocabulary, for example in *Harbour* we find terms like 'warehouses', 'piers', 'wharves' and 'docks'. Movement is also suggested as the different boats crowd the harbour, some slow moving like liners, others 'fast police boats'.

Another book that entertains as well as informing is Rowland Berry's *Mechanical Giants*. This invites the young reader in through large coloured pictures and lively language that helps children make the required imaginative response. 'Big George', for example, uses a bucket 'big enough to hold two large cars and still have room for someone to walk around in it . . . so enormous that if it was put on a football field, it would stretch the field length of the pitch'. Then we have the Puller-pusher with 254 wheels, and the Canadian Pacific coal train, 2.4 kilometres long and with 108 cars. This author is making the most of comparisons in writing that Richard Feynman's father did orally (see p. 68).

Books about particular journeys, by boat, car and train, sometimes written in the first person, suit this younger age group as well.

Jobs and occupations (AT4 and AT5)

There are a great number of series of books in this category and we need to avoid the dull and banal. Watts have brought out a new 'My Job' series with excellent photographs, for example *Postwoman, Truck Driver* and *Doctor*.

Key Stage 2

Books for the 7–11 age range reflect children's increasing capacity to take on the complexity of the world. Below we examine each of the book categories which structured our look at Key Stage 1.

Maps and atlases (AT1 and 3)

These are discussed in Chapter 4. I like the large atlases such as the *Dorling Kindersley Picture Atlas of The World*. My daughter doing Advanced Level Geography was impressed by the quality of information and layout. It is clear, up-to-date, interesting and aesthetically pleasing. There is an excellent section on how maps are drawn and the problems of showing something which is really round on a flat surface (see Space project, Chapter 10). However, most of the atlases and map books coming out now benefit from the new information technology and quality of information and presentation is high.

Books about people from other countries (AT2, 4 and 5)

Seven- to eleven-year-olds still need to be invited into books, and narratives focusing on one person's or a family's experience in another country remain well liked. The use of the first person can bring a special vitality to the writing as we find in Tony Tigwell's *Sakina in India*. The sights, scents and texture of life in a North Indian village is well communicated by writing and illustrations: we almost smell the mutton cooking and the smoke from the wood and cow dung fire and hear the noise of the bus outside and the running noise of the family room inside.

The third person account can distance the experience somewhat as in Mary Regan's *French Family*. Barry Milton uses dialogue in *Oil Rig Worker* to bring the experience of working a fortnight on and a fortnight off. 'Sometimes you don't know what day it is.'

In discussing both *Sakina in India* and *Oil Rig Worker*, Jennifer Wilson comments that books about human geography can be an excellent context for laying bare sensitive issues in a natural unforced way. Sakina resents her family's valuing of her brother's education more than her own, and the consequences of the oil rig worker's unusual work pattern for family life is gently explored (Wilson, 1982).

Physical geography (AT3)

There are a lot of series for the 7–11 age range and we need to choose accurate, attractive books which encourage children's own questions and which go beyond the setting out of facts to attempts at explanation. Watts' Picture Library series offers good support for topic work: titles include *Rivers and Lakes; Hurricanes and Tornadoes; Volcanoes; Deserts and Mountains*. The need of older juniors for more structured and advanced information and explanation is provided by series like Watts' Story of Earth (*Island, Lake, Cave, Desert*), and Oxford's Young Geographer Investigates (*Our Universe; The Earth*). Books like these are a bridge between early geography picture books and the textbooks of the secondary school.

Human geography (AT4) and environmental geography (AT5)

There are also many series on aspects of human geography for older primary school children. We need some texts which take on current issues like religious groupings and birth control. We find all this in Wayland's Countries of the World Series by David Cumming including *India, Pakistan, The Caribbean, Japan and Greece*. The photographs of bathing in the Ganges and significant buildings like Taj Mahal are enormously helpful in communicating the character of the places. This series, for the 9 plus age range, has exemplary contents pages, glossaries, indexes, maps and information boxes.

Other good series of this type of geography book include the Franklin Watts' 'Inside . . .' series, (e.g. *Inside Japan*) Hamish Hamilton's 'The Way We Live' series (e.g. *Dance of Shiva*) which is well liked by younger juniors and Franklin Watts' 'Let's go to . . .' series which has over 70 titles including *Iran, Libya* and *Lebanon*. Those that I looked at have clear format and good retrieval devices and manage to give a realistic picture of the more troubled nations.

Older geography books and encyclopaedias with geography items may be unwittingly ethno-centric and those over 10 years old will certainly be out of date. If you want to replace this kind of resource you might consider Anne Smith's books *Aborigines, Plains Indians* and *Inuit* in Wayland's 'People of the World' series. The good things in each culture are brought out while problems for certain people and societies in the modern world are also made explicit. These books would stretch the older, abler juniors. They are particularly good at showing how the past affects the present and they encourage the kind of reflection that makes a committed reader.

History

Resources for history work are used for three main purposes. First to encourage knowledge and understanding and the ability to describe and explain historical change; second to come to appreciate how history is interpreted; third, where the sources are primary documents, to acquire evidence from historical sources and form judgements about their reliability and value. The National Curriculum history attainment targets reflect these three purposes and therefore teachers are encouraged to provide a rich array of books and other materials like maps, photographs, letters, artefacts, slides, videofilm, cassette recordings and archive materials. All of these can aid our primary purpose which is to help children make links between the present and the past. (The Historical Association, has many leaflets and booklets on resources for primary school history.)

Key Stage 1 (5–7 years)

'Pupils should be given opportunities to develop an awareness of the past and of the ways in which it was different from the present. They should be introduced to historical sources of different types.' (*History in the National Curriculum*, March 1991.)

This approach to history with its emphasis on enquiry, questioning and communication fits well with Bruner's idea of the child operating like a young historian from the earliest stages. It is also in keeping with the view taken in this book of the child as active learner.

As well as written sources it is required that children look at objects in museums and old houses, pictures and photographs about the past (family photographs can be brought in from home) and computer-based material. Thus schools will in most cases have to reorganize the resources to meet the specific National Curriculum requirements. But in any case teachers have always been faced with the job of finding attractive, well-written history books for the different stages in the primary years. The response of some publishers to the requirements of the National Curriculum has been to produce huge programmes of materials including series of topic books, posters, cassettes and study packs. Some of these are exciting: Longman, for example, have some inviting titles for their 12 Key Stage 1 topic books including *Our Gran, Teddy Bear, Birthday*, and *Children in History*. It is suggested that purchasing about four books on each topic will make poss- ible small group discussion and collaboration. They would also be starting points for children's own attempts at making books. Small, well-illustrated topic books like these with clear print for the very youngest children have been rather lacking until now (Blyth, 1988, p. 81). However, rather than rely solely on one publisher's programme I think teachers might do better to examine a range of materials and select what they like best, supplement- ing their collection with good history books, not necessarily part of a pub- lisher's integrated scheme. Joan Blyth recommends Dinosaur history books (for example, *Castle Life*), A & C Black (for example, *People Around Us*), Usborne (for example, *Usborne First History*), Longman (for example, *Into The Past*) and the Cambridge University Press Activity Books (Blyth, 1988, p. 81). Just because books do not have 'National Curriculum' stamped on them does not mean they should not be con- sidered. In any case the programmes of study will inevitably be modified when progress schools are making is evaluated.

Key Stage 2

Pupils should be taught about important episodes and developments in Britain's past, from Roman to modern times. They should have opportunities to investigate local history. They should be taught about ancient civilizations and the history of other parts of the world. They should be helped to develop a sense of chronology and to learn about changes in everyday life over long periods of time.

(DES, 1991, *History in the National Curriculum*)

At the time of writing pupils are required to be taught 9 study units of which the core study units are: Invaders and Settlers; Tudors and Stuarts; Victorian Britain; Britain since 1930; Ancient Greece; Exploration and encounters 1450–1550. Three or four supplementary study units on themes like writing and printing over long periods, local history units and studies of a non-European civilization can be selected from pages 31 and 32 of *History in the National Curriculum* (DES, 1991).

This then is the framework in which we are required to work, but as I suggested earlier, I think it is best thought of as just that – a framework – rather than a strait-jacket. We are still left with the task of choosing lively materials which will motivate the young learners.

In searching for good history materials much of what was covered in Chapters 3, 4 and 5 on choosing information books applies. The young learner needs to be invited into the book by beautiful illustrations, including photography, drawings, maps, family trees, time-lines and so on and a clear attractive format. Younger juniors can be put off by pages too densely packed with writing. We seek text which is accurate and unpatronizing but which does not over-condense information, which contextualizes new vocabulary and which to some extent echoes the friendlier syntax of conversation. Rosemary Stones of Collins Publishers told me that their 'best seller' in children's history books is Sainsbury's *The Kings and Queens of Britain*. It certainly looks attractive with the small square portraits of the monarchs on the front and it would probably appeal to parents as well as the over-8s for whom it is intended. In Chapter 5 a plea was made for including the amusing and the controversial in children's books. Blandness is the enemy of motivated reading. I was glad the author of this book tries to include intriguing details; for example, on page 8 we learn that James I was 'a messy eater and had a bad stammer'.

There are some good well-established series for children in the junior years including the Macdonald Starter series (with a new volume entitled *My First Library*), Wayland's How They Lived series, Wayland's History in Evidence series and from Hodder and Stoughton's Investigating series, the two for history by Pamela Mays on *Towns and Villages* and *Roads, Canals and Railways*. I also like the activity-based books in Franklin Watts' Jump! History Books – *Ancient Egypt, The Vikings*, and so on.

Junior age children often enjoy historical biographies and these are covered in Chapter 3 on narrative non-fiction. The important thing here is to seek books which are not just a stream of fact, but which include evaluation and controversy and which encourage the young reader's speculations by indicating the same facts can give rise to different interpretations.

Some living writers choose to write about their life and times and include contemporary photographs, newspaper cuttings and contemporary documents. These are not quite biographies, but rather special information books which can often intrigue adults and children. The Watts' Early Twentieth Century series has begun with two fascinating books for readers of 7 and upwards: *World War II* by Neil Thompson and Charlie Jones and *When I was Young* by Ruth Thompson and Nancy Emery. The latter describes in great detail the routines of Nancy Emery's life in the early

1900s. Excellent photography and illustrations make this a sound book of its kind. The fact that the author is still living helps create the link between present and past that the National Curriculum guidelines rightly encourage us to make clear to children.

Summary

- A good selection of primary sources – museum artefacts, family photographs, video film, etc. – help develop an enquiring, problem-solving approach.

- The best books are clear, well-illustrated and written in a way that encourages discussion and reflection on the links between past and present.

- Collections should contain, in addition to some 'bread and butter' books, truly imaginative and unusual texts including biographies and autobiographies.

Science

Teachers have to select from a burgeoning harvest of books, most at a glance attractive and beautifully illustrated. However, glossy pictures cannot compensate for tedious text. What then do we look for? We certainly want children to recognize what they know from first-hand experience and to be helped to generalize from it. Just facts and right answers are not a good foundation for secondary school science. Primary work needs to help 'a first grasp of that dialogue between ideas and evidence that is science's contribution to every person's understanding of the world' (Peter Black and Wynne Harlen, *Times Educational Supplement*, 24 September 1989). In other words, we seek resources and approaches which help children proceed as young scientists – investigating, observing, hypothesizing and applying.

Key Stage 1

The illustrations – pictures, diagrams and photographs – are as important as writing in communicating ideas. At this stage it is particularly important that the pages are inviting – cluttered jumbles of too many things are unhelpful. Thus teachers have to pick and choose from packages of materials on the market. The Ginn Science Key Stage 1 information books convey information by attractive photographs and just a little text and are worth considering along with the large Group Discussion books which can be a focus for reviewing ideas developed in children's science activities. However, other books and resources would need to be included as well to meet National Curriculum requirements.

As a reviewer of materials for the journal *Primary Science Review* I see a great number of new books. I look for attractive illustrations that, whether photographs or drawings, are well integrated with the text, good retrieval devices if appropriate and good ideas for activities. I like the Look At . . . Ourselves books – *Eyes, Hands,* and so on by Ruth Thompson and *Faces and Feet* by Henry Pluckrose – as they encourage discussion; the playfully named Look At . . . Nature series including *Paws and Claws* and *Fingers and Feelers* (Henry Pluckrose) and *Keeping Minibeasts* with delightful close-up colour photographs. (All these are from Franklin Watts.)

One of the most accessible genres for the under-7s (as explained in Chapters 3 and 8) is the chronological organization appropriate in describing life-cycles of creatures. Amongst the finest examples are A & C Black's Stopwatch books which are perceived by children as information books but which communicate by 'telling the story' of how a writer, fly, tomato, butterfly and ladybird develop and change through time (Barrie Watts). These books operate partly on the principle that the very young often like quite a lot of detail about something specific. There are bold headings for the youngest readers and more detailed information for older infant children. Children's own writing in their first book is usually in narrative form about things they have seen and done.

One of the best things about the National Curriculum is its encouragement of cross-curricular work. Of course, good teachers have always exploited the potential for this. Some publishers have produced lively books to support this, for example Take One first reference library. This series offers a range of topics in simple non-narrative text encouraging talking and reflection. Photographs are outstanding. For example, one of the books, *Under the Sea*, which has a science focus includes a photograph of a sea-bird pathetically weighted down by oily wings from a polluted sea. As mentioned in Chapter 5, disturbing images can make us think. It is never too early for children to learn the facts that are not neutral.

For helpful reviews of science books which are too numerous to mention here see *The Signal Selection of Children's Books* edited by Nancy Chambers, The Children's Book Foundation which has exciting lists on topics like Trees and Sheep, and the reviews in *The School Librarian, Primary Science Review,* and *Junior* and *Child Education.*

Key Stage 2

The same qualities detailed above – good, clear illustrations, lively text which encourages doing and reflecting, sound retrieval devices, and so on – apply to our search for suitable books for older primary school children. However, they are able to tolerate more writing in proportion to illustration and to tackle more challenging information and ideas. We must not forget that many children have interests appropriate to their chronological age but are not yet reading confidently enough to understand mainstream books for their age group. Some publishers make it clear in their publicity material which series suit these less forward readers (for example, Franklin Watts, Tel: 071-739-2929, and Wayland, Tel: 0273-722561). The Children's Book Foundation has a very good, and frequently updated, annotated list of science information books for special needs (Tel: 081-870-9055). The Starting Science series, published by Wayland with titles like *Waste, The Weather, Animals* and so on, aims to cater for children with a reading age of 5–7, but the interest age goes up to 9. Franklin Watts' Science Starters by Barbara Taylor have beautiful photographs and an inviting text. Topics include *Energy, Wet and Dry* and *Making Things Move*.

Starting Points by the same publisher and written by Ruth Thompson are visually pleasing with a text that many 7-plus children could manage on their own. There are quizzes and ideas for activities and imaginative treatment of topics like *Water, Fire, Air* and each of the seasons.

I think there is room for playfulness and originality in some of the science books we offer at the younger junior stage. One of my favourites is Vickie Cobb's *Sticky and Slimey* (A & C Black) – a wonderfully involving science book which classifies all kinds of slithery things (nicely arranged in the contents page) and encourages the development of some science concepts at the same time. Another favourite is Aliki's *Dinosaur Bones* about a child's search for fossil evidence.

There is a huge category of books which support our study of the ways in which human activities affect the earth (Attainment Target 5: Science). Books tend to come in series like the Watts/Gloucester World About Us series – *Ozone Layer, Tropical Rainforest, The Greenhouse Effect* and *Acid Rain*. For older juniors who need more depth, Franklin Watts' Save Our Earth series with topics like *Habitat Destruction, Polluting the Sea* and *Toxic Waste* are all well illustrated and thought-provoking. It is well worth scanning the Friends of the Earth Earthworm award short list for good books on conservation.

According to a colleague who is an international expert on primary science and who has published widely for children, students and teachers, there is a lack in some areas of books to challenge and stretch able older juniors. He told me that he often has to direct these young readers to adult books to find information, visual and written, in the right depth.

In spite of the huge numbers of information books, particularly in the science area, by publishers like A & C Black, Hamish Hamilton, Kingfisher, Usborne, Franklin Watts and Wayland, sometimes there just does not seem to be the right book at the right level for a particular purpose. Recently a special needs group of older juniors were researching about the rain forest with my support. What they wanted was very detailed information about particular rainforest plants and creatures. There were lots of excellent rainforest books, but none with the depth of information in accessible text on the sub-topics they were interested in.

Some good features to bear in mind when choosing science books are as follows:

- Visually appealing with involving text appropriate to age, ability and interest of the children.

- Useful retrieval devices.

- Sensible activities involving easily available and inexpensive materials.

- For younger children some books which have a lot of detail about something specific – snails, a particular kind of tree or making a cake – often in story form.

- New technical vocabulary well contextualized.

- For older children books that are accurate, detailed, inviting and capable of explaining difficult concepts clearly using examples and analogy.

- Books which encourage reflection on the ethical issues in science like conservation, space travel and animal experiments.

- Provision of some books which are amusing and playful make us realize what a strange but fascinating world we live in. Science should be exciting!

Mathematics

Key Stages 1 and 2

When we think of non-fiction we do not normally think first of texts for teaching mathematics. Nevertheless, how they are written is important as children using them are at different stages in their reading development. Some teachers use a scheme or framework like Peake, Nuffield or Scottish Mathematics and supplement this with their own materials written with the needs and abilities of particular children in mind. Children's own books can join the collection too.[3]

The National Curriculum guidelines have given rise to many new teaching schemes for mathematics. The thematic approach of some of these incorporates a flexible set of topic-based books for each year of Key Stages 1 and 2. Cross-curricular approaches are now becoming increasingly favoured. For example, the team developing HBJ Mathematics Years 1–6 have such links very much in mind. The theme 'The Park' in the book prepared for Year 2 involves the development of the kind of mapping skills which matches with geography while 'Wet and Dry' in the Year 1 book dovetails well into science work.

The HBJ materials integrate all aspects of the National Curriculum including the non-statutory guidelines, and the collaborative, sociable approach is very much in line with the recommendations in this book. The giant, wordless books with pictures of teddies and other everyday things to encourage discussion at Key Stage 1 are likely to emphasize the playful, enjoyable side to mathematics.

Still with the emphasis on fun, David Kirkby's 'Maths Challenge' (Walker Books) includes both Activity and Games books for Key Stages 1 and 2. A main aim is that parents and children should enjoy learning about shape, space and handling data through games to support work being done in school.

Language in the best material is clear and accurate. While we want children to use their own language to describe mathematical ideas and concepts we also aim to introduce them to the technical terms. Children might use the word 'oval', for example, and we would welcome this in discussion but explain that the word 'ellipse' used in mathematics books means the same (HBJ Teachers' Resource Book, 1990, p. 5).

There are several mathematics dictionaries which help children check the meaning of words like 'mass', 'weight', 'tessellate' and 'estimate'. A good example is the dictionary compiled by Klaebe and published by HBJ.

The better texts include suggestions and questions which help extend children's investigation skills. As in other areas of the curriculum the teacher is a role model researcher, and as one of my colleagues described it 'a kind of living information resource'. I heard one teacher say in response to a question, 'I don't know but I'll look it up for you – and me'.

My mathematics colleagues, when I told them of my work for this book, said that it is particularly important to avoid stereotyping (or omitting) girls and ethnic minorities in mathematics books and resources as children all need to see positive reflections of themselves as young mathematicians.

We therefore seek mathematics materials which:

- are in line with National Curriculum guidelines, attractively presented and, where appropriate, playful;
- support cross-curricular work and relate to children's everyday experience;
- are likely to encourage a collaborative, sociable approach;
- are lucid and accurate, written in simple lively language, but which introduce technical terms with strong contextual support;
- encourage children's investigations;

- show both sexes and children from all social and ethnic groups positively.

Involving parents

Over the past two decades schools have tried in various ways to involve parents in children's learning and particularly in children's early reading.[4] Home-school liaison is likely to be most fruitful where it is genuinely two-way and where 'information about children is shared in a common purpose, of helping children towards literacy' (Beard, 1987, p. 112). The practice of encouraging parents and children to enjoy stories is fairly well established in many schools. It is less usual to find an organized approach to reading non-fiction at home, although many parents do give some help with reading in the context of supporting homework projects. If we accept the principle that parents should be encouraged to think of themselves as having joint responsibility with teachers for helping children find reading rewarding both emotionally and intellectually how can the school help, particularly where non-fiction is concerned?[5]

A very successful initiative in the UK known as 'Family Reading Groups' (FRGs) brings about the joint involvement of parents, teachers and children. This idea was put forward by members of the research committee of the United Kingdom Reading Association (UKRA) in response to the lack of books in some homes and the need for parent-school collaboration over developing children's reading. Some groups are held in parents' homes, others in infant and junior schools, often at the end of the day. The books and resources, which are provided by the school library service, are taken home and parents and children return to discuss their reading in groups of about 10. The promising features of FRGs include: their voluntary nature, the availability of a wide variety of books, informed group discussion, their flexibility and the joint involvement of parents, professionals and pupils (Pumfrey, 1991, p. 225).

Three main aims make this initiative a useful one from the point of view of reading non-fiction. Firstly the emphasis is on enjoyment, secondly positive attitudes to all kinds of genres are encouraged and thirdly discussion encourages reflective reading.

Clearly the family reading group approach has much to recommend it. Further advice can be provided at special talks about the work of the school or in the school prospectus. However obvious these points might seem, it is always useful to have a checklist.[6]

- Joining the public library and encouraging visits.
- Talking about non-fiction books, including:
    (a) those associated with school projects;

    (b) those which support 'out of school' interests;

    (c) those which are enjoyable for browsing.

● Teaching about using dictionaries, encyclopaedias and contents pages to reinforce what is being done at school.

Let us look at each of these in turn. Joining the public library gives children the opportunity to find information books from a source other than school or class libraries. In her interesting study of young successful readers Margaret Clark noted that both boys and girls 'used it (the public library) intensively' and sometimes borrowed non-fiction on science, geography and astronomy from the adult section (Clark, 1976, p. 64). Adults who read non-fiction themselves and visit the library on their own account provide strong role models for children.

Just talking about some factual reading even if the parent does not know a lot about the topic is very helpful and motivating.[7] Providing an interested rather than necessarily a knowledgeable audience for a developing idea allows a child to explain something to someone else and therefore organize it more clearly for him or herself. (Attainment Target 2: Reading: Level 1(d) reinforces this idea of the value of talking about non-fiction.)

Schools can assist by letting parents know at what stage it would be helpful to reinforce learning about how to use a reference book. (Attainment Target 2: Reading: Level 2.6 requires that children be able to use a dictionary.) Margaret Meek in *Learning to Read* (1982), addressed to parents and teachers, suggests parents choose a 'big dictionary, the giant atlas, the real *Britannica*. Look up something together: the speed of light, the distance to the moon, the Battle of Waterloo, not as a homework chore, but in the context of something you have already begun to discuss' (Meek, 1982, p. 128). However, she adds a delightful anecdote admitting to her own 'over-conscientious didactism' which made her children circumspect about asking for explanations. 'Is spring in Australia in March?' they might ask, adding 'Don't explain it, just say yes or no.' Yes, home must not become too like school!

Assessment and the National Curriculum

At the time of writing the reading progress of 5–7-year-olds is formally assessed by talking about and reading from suitable story books. Modified versions of the SATs used in summer 1991 are being prepared for summer 1992. Progress in reading non-fiction can be written on pupils' record cards. It is also part of children's general language development to discuss with parents. In the non-fiction area, the 'knowledge, skills and understanding in reading' part of National Curriculum guidelines in English includes becoming able to:

● Talk in simple terms about information in non-fiction books (AT2: Reading: Level 1(d)).

- Read accurately and understand straightforward signs, labels and notices (AT2: Reading: Level 2(a)).

- Demonstrate knowledge of the alphabet in using word books and simple dictionaries (AT2: Reading: Level 2(b)).

- Read a range of material with some independence, accuracy and understanding (AT2: Reading Level 2(f)).

- Devise a clear set of questions that will enable them to select and use appropriate information sources and reference books from class and school libraries (AT2: Reading: Level 3(f)).

- Find books or magazines in the class or school library by using the classification system, catalogue or database and use appropriate methods of finding information, when pursuing a line of inquiry (AT2: Reading: Level 4(a)).

- Demonstrate, in talking or writing about non-fiction, that they are developing their own views and can support them by reference to some details in the text (AT2: Reading: Level 5(b)).

- Show in discussion that they can recognize whether subject matter in non-literacy and media texts is presented as fact or opinion (AT2: Reading: Level 5(c)).

- Select reference books and other informational materials and use organizational devices to find answers to their own questions and those of others (AT2: Reading: Level 5(d)).

- Show through discussion an awareness of a writer's choice of particular words and phrases and the effects on the reader (AT2: Reading: Level 5(e)).

These abilities as set out provide a basic checklist as children move through Key Stages 1 and 2 at different paces. However, nothing of the excitement we hope the best non-fiction will generate comes through here. I would also like more emphasis on the acquisition of library and study skills in context. In lists like this inevitably abilities which are quite advanced and sophisticated sound easier to acquire than they are. For example, knowing whether subject matter is opinion or fact (Level 5(c)) depends partly on how information books are written (see Chapter 5 p. 51) and the quality of conversation about such matters between teacher and children. Awareness of the impact of a writer's linguistic choices (Level 5(e)) is often in my experience achieved through children's writing of their own books for a particular audience.

Our assessment of children's progress as readers and writers of non-fiction is best made by observing them as they work with some interest and commitment on real tasks. Some of these tasks will be collaborative and I believe talking together and with the teacher helps brings alive the ideas and information in books. Such interaction where the young readers are truly involved leads to the quality of reflection we seek to encourage in this quite challenging kind of reading.

Notes

1. Helpful checklists on library procedures and suggestions for organizing a book week are in David Howe's book on *Primary Libraries* available from County Education Department, 22 Northgate Street, Warwick CV34 4SR; £1.25 per copy.
2. See Jones, L. and Richards, R. (1990) *An Early Start to Mathematics*, Simon and Schuster, p. 52, for a good section on children making books.
3. I have augmented my own first list with extra items from David Howe (1985, p. 2).
4. See Beard, 1987, Chapter 6, for a detailed account of the recent history of parental involvement in schools.
5. See Longman's Head Start for the National Curriculum series, by Terry Cash and Jan Morrow, for books parents and children can enjoy together; for example, *Discoveries* (science for 5–6-year-olds) and *Emma's Busy Day* (technology for 5-year-olds).
6. See Pumfrey, 1991, pp. 224–52 for a helpful account of home-school initiatives in helping reading progress.
7. *The Primary Language Record Handbook* and its explanatory sequel, *Patterns of Learning: the Primary Language Record and the National Curriculum* by Barrs *et al.* (1988) includes advice about the role of parents. For copies write to The Centre for Language in Primary Education, Webber Row, London EC1 8QW.

Further reading

Blyth, Joan (1988) Primary Booksheet, *History 5–9*, Hodder and Stoughton, London.
Beard, Roger (1987) *Developing Reading 3–13*, Hodder and Stoughton, London.
Chambers, Aidan (1991) *The Reading Environment*, The Thimble Press, Glos.
Howe, David (ed.) (1985) *Better School Libraries in Primary Schools*, National Association of Advisers in English.
Meek, Margaret (1982) *Learning to Read*, The Bodley Head, London.
Orbrist, C. and Stuart, A. (1990) The Family Reading Groups movement, in Hunter-Carsch *et al.*, *Primary English in the National Curriculum*, Blackwell Education, Oxford.
Pumfrey, Peter (1991) *Improving Children's Reading in the Junior School: Challenges and Responses*, Cassell Educational, London.
Somerfield, M., Torbe, M. and Ward (1983) *A Framework For Reading*, Heinemann, London.

PART 2

INTO THE CLASSROOM

8
TOPIC WORK: USING AND SHARING INFORMATION AND IDEAS FROM BOOKS

> Knowledge has to be constructed afresh by each individual knower, through an interaction between the evidence (which is obtained through observation, listening, reading, and the use of reference materials of all kinds) and what the learner brings to bear on it.
>
> (Wells, 1987, p. 116)

Whenever we read a book we bring to it our relevant existing knowledge and experience. The depth and quality of this is one factor in determining the level of text we can manage. Another is our motivation: the interest, purpose and commitment we feel towards the topic. Mature readers are able to assimilate new information without the help and companionship of others, although this is a welcome part of some reading contexts, for example the university seminar. Young readers in the primary school need the teacher's support with the more challenging kinds of reading. In Chapter 2 it is argued that the non-narrative organization of many children's information books poses special difficulties. Yet in my work in schools, both as a teacher and as a supervisor of students, I find teacher support, in many otherwise excellent classrooms, patchy and uncoordinated. Often there is something of a mismatch between what teachers think they are achieving and what is actually the case. We now know much more about how to mediate fruitfully between children and informational texts. For example, because this kind of writing tends to be densely packed with material, children need to be encouraged to reflect on the total sense of what they are reading. In other words, they need help in discovering what the most important facts and issues are. This chapter examines the kind of mediation teachers can provide to help with the special challenge of this kind of reading, building particularly on the analysis of Chapters 5 and 6.[1] Firstly promising pre-reading activities are examined and secondly the many ways in which support can be provided when children use books and other secondary sources. Reference will be made throughout to a recent classroom example: the work of 9- to 10-year-olds on the topic 'Squirrels'. The project took place on a half-day each week over the space of a term. A main aim was to help the children improve their ability to learn from non-fiction.

Pre-reading activities

The organization of prior knowledge

In Chapter 1 it was suggested that Piaget's powerful adaptive model of learning could be helpfully applied to learning from books. According to this model all new learning has to be assimilated into an existing framework of knowledge which in turn changes to accommodate the new input. This process takes place whether the new knowledge or experience is first hand, visiting a farm or using mathematical or scientific apparatus, or second hand, from a video film or a book. When we apply this to reading an information book the new ideas encountered there have to be modified to fit with prior knowledge and understanding. How far we can make use of the new ideas depends on how well they can be integrated with what we already understand.

At the beginning of a new project or topic children can be helped considerably by the opportunity to make explicit what is relevant from what they know already. Teachers will find the following example familiar. Ten-year-olds at the beginning of a project on Squirrels shared their existing knowledge. The many anecdotes and comments included the following insights: that in their county, Kent, the grey squirrel predominates; squirrels are usually timid but when encountered in parks they can be tame enough to take food by hand; in urban areas the squirrel is often perceived as a 'pest' as it damages lofts and forages in domestic dustbins; foxes, cats and owls eat baby squirrels, but they are as likely to meet their death on the road in urban areas; squirrels are small, furry, have bushy tails and climb trees; they eat nuts and berries. At the end of the discussion I provided a summing up using these ideas.

This pre-reading discussion can achieve three things. Firstly teachers are able to determine the levels of sophistication of the concepts of the individual children within the group or class as evidenced above. Secondly the kind of language they are able to use to explain their ideas is revealed. Some of the children in the Squirrel work were able to use terms like 'drey', 'habitat' and 'predator', others were using everyday terms like 'home', 'where it lives' and 'enemy'. Thirdly the ideas raised help the teacher glean how much background information is needed before the children use the book and what kind of intermediate experience might be helpful.

Beginning with a specific example

The three major developmentalists, Vygotsky, Piaget and Bruner, differ in many of their views, for example on the roles of social interaction and instruction in learning, but I think they would all broadly accept the principle that children usually learn by moving from the specific to the general.[2] This is evident in the anecdotes and personal experience shared in discussions like that preceding the Squirrel work. Thus, once some attempt has been made to help children organize relevant prior experience, new information probably comes best in the form of an example of the new phenomena. Such examples are familiar to primary school specialists – a visit to a farm, an outing to a museum, a dramatic enactment of a specific incident in history, a science demonstration or, as in the squirrel work, a video film *Squirrel on My Shoulder*.[3] This true story of John Paling's attempt to bring up an orphaned baby squirrel with his cat and her kitten proved an inviting beginning. Indeed the children still mentioned the film after many weeks, sometimes in relation to the information they were observing in the books they were using.

As well as beginning with a specific focus 'the story of a very special grey squirrel', it was also a sympathetic way of confronting the children with book language. David Attenborough's narration takes us through a sequence of events – the finding of a motherless squirrel, the stages of its development, its preparation for release and its return to freedom. But within this broad narrative framework the commentary often breaks off to make generalizations about squirrels. For example, 'the safest nests are cradles of dry grass and twigs hidden in the forks' and 'blind and helpless, they are totally dependent on the mother for protection'. Much of the language was thus close to book language. Sammy's story was accompanied by asides about squirrels in general: their preferred habitat, 'oakwoods are ideal habitats for grey squirrels'; how they eat, 'squirrels tear into the bark'; and how they behave, 'squirrels don't really hibernate for long periods but to conserve energy in winter they sometimes stay in their dreys'. The children were thus introduced in a sympathetic way to the syntax and vocabulary of non-narrative text. Few would have managed to read the script themselves, but listening to the reading, together with the appealing visual element, made some difficult concepts and ideas accessible.

In this example the video film served as a bridge between the children's discussion of their existing knowledge and their work with the information books. Some of the terms they were to meet in the books were introduced. In some cases their assumptions were challenged: for example they had to modify their belief about squirrel hibernation. The video film provided a focus for further discussion and encouraged genuine reflection. Individuals learnt from the questions and observations of others.

Some children noted that the structure of an animal, in this case the squirrel's tail and its teeth and claws, is related to function, how it moves and eats. Often, of course, they did not express it in these terms. Their new understanding of the power of instinct came across in their comments. Although they were raised by the same 'parent', the behaviour of kittens and squirrel are very different. The kittens practise their 'capture kill' technique using Sammy's tail for target practice, while Sammy tries to gnaw the milk and buries food in the sand of the litter tray.

I have spent a little time on this example as I believe it shows the benefit of increasing children's knowledge and understanding on a subject before they use the books. The integration of appealing visual input with book language made this a good bridging experience, but there are other ways of feeding in relevant knowledge: outings, demonstrations and talks from visiting experts to name a few. The important thing is that, through whatever means, the children have been able to gather their own thoughts and ideas to bring to the texts.

Formulating their own questions

Chapters 2 and 3 examine what is currently known about how information books work and the features of the books which make learning from them easy or difficult. Good retrieval devices – contents page, index and glossary – work well together in the better books. We also look for clear headings and subheadings, and illustrations which integrate with the text. Above all, we seek books in which the language is clear and alive and which shows the author has the likely needs of a young learner in mind.

However, even an information book which meets all these criteria is the end result of the author's thinking and organizing of the material. An active reading of the text requires a young reader to confront the text with his or her own purposes and intentions. Of course, simply reading can sometimes create an interest in some new topic and it is not suggested that children can never manage to enjoy a book without our mediation, but when it comes to more systematic content-based work it is useful to make intentions and purposes explicit. Until fairly recently it was not uncommon for teachers to set out what they felt were a useful set of questions to take to the books the children were to use. This was felt to provide a systematic approach to the material or topic, but all of us feel more motivated to answer our own questions rather than those of other people. In the course of my work in schools with students I find many teachers are now encouraging children to formulate their own questions to take to their book research. I find it helpful to give children advance warning. In the Squirrel work, for example, after our preliminary sharing of what the class knew already, I suggested they might like to write down anything they would like to find out in their jotters. They had their notebooks with them during the showing of *Squirrel on My Shoulder*. I took in the jotters to look through

Table 8.1   Children's questions for the Squirrel project

	No. of children asking this or similar questions
General	
1. Where does the squirrel get its name?	15
2. Why is a squirrel's nest called a 'drey'?	1
3. What is a 'habitat'?	1
4. What is a 'rodent'?	1
5. How can you study squirrels?	1
Behaviour	
6. How do squirrels survive in the woodland?	1
7. Do squirrels really hibernate?	20
8. Do squirrels have any interesting habits?	1
9. How do squirrels manage to climb trees so well?	4
10. Do grey squirrels kill red squirrels?	21
11. Can a squirrel make you laugh?	1
12. How do they crack nuts?	2
13. Do squirrels attack people and bite them?	1
Kinds of squirrel	
14. Do some squirrels live underground?	1
15. How many kinds of squirrel are there in the world?	25
16. How do flying squirrels fly?	4
Appearance	
17. What is different about red and grey squirrels' looks?	1
18. How do they use their tail?	2
19. How big is the biggest squirrel and how small is the tiniest?	1
20. What are their teeth like?	2
21. Are males and females the same size?	1
Health, predators, prey, etc.	
22. Which creatures kill squirrels?	22
23. How do we control squirrels? (when population gets too great)	1
24. What creatures are killed by squirrels?	20
25. Have squirrels a good sense of smell and hearing?	1
26. What diseases do squirrels suffer from?	3
27. How long do squirrels live?	1
28. How much does a squirrel weigh?	2
Food	
29. What kinds of nuts do squirrels like best?	15
30. Is it true that squirrels kill baby birds and eat eggs from nests?	3
31. What do squirrels eat?	25
32. Do grey squirrels eat more than red squirrels?	1
Breeding, etc.	
33. What do they build their nests with?	20
34. How many litters do they have each year?	2

35. How many babies do they have? (in each litter)	10
36. Are squirrels good parents?	1
37. When do squirrels mate?	1
Total number of different questions	37
Total number of questions	235

Note: These questions arose in the course of discussion. Each child then compiled his or her own list to take to the books in sessions 3 and 4.

the children's questions. Sometimes children ask questions which need to be modified if they are not to become frustrated in attempting to answer them. Jack had written down 'How many squirrels are there in the whole world?' I explained this would be difficult to find out and was unlikely to be answered in any of the books we had. After some discussion he was happy to look instead for how many different squirrel species there are.

Some of the children's questions were familiar – 'How does a flying squirrel fly?' 'What do squirrels eat?' 'How many babies do squirrels have?' Others were less predictable. Rakhee, who had a splendid list of fifteen questions, included 'Why are red squirrels smaller than grey ones?' 'How much does a squirrel weigh?' 'How do you control squirrels?'[4] 'Where does the squirrel get its name from?'

Table 8.1 sets out the range and relative numbers of each category of question.

The children now had clear aims to take to their first encounter with the books and resources, and after the summary which follows the kind of support we can provide is considered.

Summary

- The existing beliefs and assumptions meant by the term 'prior knowledge' is the framework into which new learning about a topic has to be integrated. It seems likely to be helpful therefore to make this knowledge explicit before confronting secondary sources.

- Children usually cope better with a specific example of the topic under consideration before dealing with the often more generally organized information in books. Outings, talks by experts, demonstrations, drama work, slides and video films are all examples of how this experience can be provided.

- Truly involved reading is more likely if children take their own intentions and purposes to the texts. Formulating their own questions is one way of encouraging active reading.

Using the Books

The many factors involved in choosing non-fiction, and particularly information books and materials, are discussed in Chapters 3, 4 and 5. Here we are mainly concerned with strategies to help children interpret and use the new material. It is not just a matter of acquiring study skills – using the library system efficiently, managing dictionaries, encyclopaedias and thesauruses and finding out by using retrieval devices – but also of learning to reflect on all that is read so that it makes sense in more than a superficial way. This is often partly achieved by embedding the use of books within a rich project which offers reading alongside other activities.

The contribution of three interrelated elements in encouraging the quality of reflective reading we seek is discussed in the rest of this chapter. First the importance and nature of the teacher's role, then the collaborative emphasis of the children's reading and other activities, and finally the 'sense of audience' which adds point and vitality to the work.

The teacher's role

There are five main ways in which teachers can help embed the books and other secondary sources into the total learning situation. First we need a framework of knowledge identifying the core of ideas and concepts which form the content of the topic. Secondly the situations for learning are set up and partly controlled by the teacher's selection and introduction of materials and resources, including information books, for the different ability levels within the class. Thirdly the teacher plays an important part in supporting children's interpretation of the new ideas and information in the text, diagrams and illustrations in the books. Fourthly teachers aim to offer children a choice of imaginative and appropriate tasks which encourage the use of ideas from books in their language activities and art and craft and sometimes dramatic work. Fifthly the teacher provides an interested audience for the children's developing ideas, expressed orally or in writing. Let us see how these five roles were realized in the Squirrel topic.

Providing direction and knowledge

Each day teachers make judgements about what children need to be told fairly directly and what they can, with help, find out for themselves through practical activity or through secondary sources. On the one hand, to expect to transmit chunks of information in a pre-packaged form runs against all we know about the active nature of children's learning discussed in Chapter 1. On the other hand, misinterpretation of progressive approaches and philosophy has sometimes led to teachers providing too little input and too little direction. The National Curriculum guidelines in core and foundation subjects give guidance on the content and ideas to be covered. These guidelines are constantly being developed and refined, partly in the light of feedback from the classroom. Many now consider that as long as we resist allowing the guidelines to be a strait-jacket they can provide a welcome framework and be at least a partial solution to the dilemma. Parts of the Squirrel project helped develop knowledge and understanding of the processes of life including survival and reproduction (National Curriculum Science AT3). My own research before beginning the project helped me to identify a central core of topics and sub-topics to produce a flexible framework of knowledge. This included the placing of the squirrel in the rodent category and more generally with the mammals, knowledge about physical attributes and how structure and function were related, kinds of squirrel and their habitats (particularly the United Kingdom red and grey squirrels), feeding, life-style and conservation issues.

Although I think it is essential for the teacher to do his or her own research before introducing a topic, the children need to feel they have had a share in deciding on the pattern of the work. After bringing the fruits of their research on their own questions to class discussion we drew up a list of some of the areas we wanted to cover. This turned out to be quite close to my own list above: squirrels as part of larger animal categories, kinds of squirrel, habitat, physical attribute, food, life-cycle and conservation issues. We agreed each topic would have a special focus for one or two of the twelve afternoons we worked on the project, but as children work in such different ways we did not stick rigidly to this structure. The children brought their findings to the class meetings which began and ended the sessions. My role was partly to show how each contribution fitted into a broader picture. However, I provided quite a lot of input myself, often indicating where my information had come from. In this way I hoped to provide a helpful model of how we can organize information from books.

I think it is important that children should have an idea of the total task so that they can see that each activity fits into a larger plan. It was made clear at the beginning of this second part of the chapter that all three elements explored interrelate, and the frequent class meetings to share work and discuss progress and the sense of audience built in from the beginning affected both the structure and direction of the work.

Selecting books and other resources

Teachers use their knowledge of different reading levels in the class to guide their choice of a variety of resources to support the work (see Table 8.2 for the range of books used in the Squirrel project). The wildlife wall chart and *Squirrels* by Jessica Holm stretched the reading abilities of the most mature children. Books like Davies' *Discovering Squirrels* were

Table 8.2 Books and resources used in the course of the Squirrel project

Author	Book	Publisher	Series	Contents page	Index	Glossary	Notes etc. at beginning or end	Brief description
Angela Sheehan (1976) (illustrator M. Pledges)	*The Squirrel*	Angus and Robertson	Eyeview Library	–	–	–	X	A simple narrative taking reader through a squirrel's year. Nature notes at end. Drawings. 25pp.
E. & A. Propper (1977) (illustrator P. Oxenham)	*The Squirrel*	Macdonald Educational	Animal World	–	–	–	X	Simple text. Introduces non-narrative text within an overall season sequence. Drawings. 21pp.
C. Butterworth (1988)	*Squirrels*	Macmillan	–	–	–	–	–	Bold print, simple text. Continuous present tense. 32pp.
A. Davies (1986)	*Discovering Squirrels*	Wayland	Discovering Nature	X*	X	X	Suggestions for further reading	Clear format,* very good retrieval devices.* Photographs integrate well with text.* Key words in bold print. Clear text, more demanding than books above: 'Like all rodents squirrels have two pairs of chisel-shaped incisor teeth'. 46pp.

Table 8.2 (*cont*).

Author	Book	Publisher	Series	Contents page	Index	Glossary	Notes etc. at beginning or end	Brief description
L. Bomford (1986)	*Squirrels*	A & C Black	Nature in Close Up	X	X	–	–	Clear inviting text.* 'Did you know the grey squirrel comes from America?' Excellent photographs which are well integrated into text.* Key words in bold print. 25pp.
S. Coldrey	*Grey Squirrels*	André Deutsch	–	–	–	–	Introductory notes for teacher and abler readers	A picture book with a challenging introduction using vocabulary like 'independent', 'native' and 'undoubtedly'. Two lines under each photograph. 32pp.
S. Coldrey (1986)	*The Squirrel in the Trees*	Methuen	Animal Habitats	–	–	X	–	Key words in bold print. Beautiful photographs by Oxford Scientific Films.* Food chain diagram. This text takes the young reader further in dealing with book language than the first six. 'Squirrels that live and shelter in trees are common in many countries.' 32pp.

Table 8.2 (cont).

Author	Book	Publisher	Series	Contents page	Index	Glossary	Notes etc. at beginning or end	Brief description
A. Tittensor (1980)	*The Red Squirrel*	Blanford Press with The Mammal Society	Mammal Society Series	X	–	–	Points about further study at end	Clear but quite challenging text by a naturalist. Goes beyond basic information. Good photographs* and diagrams.* Latin names of species given. 'Red squirrels are most abundant in large and continuous areas of mature coniferous forest, whether these originate from planting or from natural regeneration.' 43pp.
R. Whitlock (1974)	*Squirrels*	Priory Press Ltd.	Young Naturalist Books	X	X*	X	Further reading and places to visit	Inviting but detailed text.* Fine black and white photographs.* Introduction raises interesting questions, e.g. 'Do squirrels really hibernate?' 'Are grey squirrels killing off their smaller red cousins?' 80pp.
J. Holm (1987) (illustrator G. Troughton*)	*Squirrels*	Whittet Books	Companion volumes on *Hedgehogs, Bats, Robins*, etc.	X	X	–	Further* information – books, and useful addresses	A text which manages to be accessible, humorous and scholarly:* 'they wrongly see the grey squirrel as the baddie who drove out the reds by chasing and killing them'. 127pp.

Table 8.2 (cont).

Author	Book	Publisher	Series	Contents page	Index	Glossary	Notes etc. at beginning or end	Brief description
A. Leutscher (1979)	*Animals, Tracks and Signs*	Usborne	Usborne Spotters Guides	X	X	X	Further reading, etc, and guide to making nature notes	A field guide for abler readers.
H. Huass (1961 edition)	*Mammals of the World*	Methuen	–	X	X	–	Foreword	Reference book, 17 chapters with chapter on rodents. 212pp.
J. Taylor (1981)	*Sciurus: The Story of a Grey Squirrel*	Collins	–	Chapters with story-type titles, e.g. 'Sciurus Waking Up'	–	–	Reading list, Foreword	An 'information story' with much authentic detail from a naturalist author. Parts read to class by teacher. 92p.
J. Reynolds	*Rules of the Game*	Article in *Country Life* 4 May 1989	–	–	–	–	–	An article by a zoologist, which needed to be paraphrased by teacher, on the theme – what is the role of the grey squirrel in the decline of the reds? Colour photographs.*
D. Harbour (Design and drawing by D. E. Walton)	*The Grey Squirrel*	World Wildlife Fund Education Dept., with Lloyds Bank	One of a series of Wildlife Wall Charts	–	–	–	–	A green and white wall chart with well-integrated text and illustrations. Small print and quite challenging text. Children liked the diagrams.*

Table 8.2 (*cont*).

Author	Book	Publisher	Series	Contents page	Index	Glossary	Notes etc. at beginning or end	Brief description
John Paling (script writer and photographer)	*Squirrel on My Shoulder*	BBC Wildlife video film	One of a series of wildlife films	–	–	–	–	A BBC video film narrated by David Attenborough. Book language flavour – technical vocabulary, 'gestation', 'arboreal' – but unfolding time sequence aids understanding, giving a narrative framework for non-narrative elements.
P. Heeley Jessica Holm Scientific Editors	*The Case of the Vanishing Squirrel*	Wildlife on BBC1	One of a series of nature films	–	–	–	–	Jessica Holm,[1] zoologist, investigates the cause of the red squirrel's decline. Very little technical language. Fascinating glimpse into a working life observing squirrels – weighing, tagging and checking them for disease. Stresses the painstaking nature of scientific investigation.

* Particularly strong feature.

accessible, partly through headlining and good integration of text and illustration, to most of the children, while Bomford's *Squirrels* was managed by even the few children with special learning needs. The reading out loud which was a feature of the work allowed children to hear parts of texts they would not have been able to read for themselves. Chapter 2 looks at the qualities we look for in information books children can learn from. Not all books worth including will have all the good features and in Chapter 9 the children's assessment of the sources they used is discussed.

Mediating between children and books

It was at one time assumed that once children had acquired the ability to locate books in the library and use the retrieval devices, then with perhaps a worksheet to guide them they could find out for themselves. However, we also need to consider what children do with the information they find. Children working on their own on topics miss out on the very interaction and sharing of ideas that help the assimilation of new material. The talking to peers and teacher needs, I think, to be built into the programme by making a direct invitation to children to share what they have been reading with the class or group. One-to-one help from the teacher is also of great value in taking on unfamiliar information. We cannot assume that diagrams and illustrations communicate information clearly to children. A food chain diagram in Coldrey's *The Squirrel in the Trees* (see Fig. 8.1) puzzled several of the children until it was explained that the arrows pointed to the creature which consumed the food.

The teacher will already have decided what the core key concepts are in the topic and those identified in the Squirrel project are set out earlier. However, the children's comments and questions guide us in how we present the information and indicate which aspects of a topic are of special interest to particular groups and individuals. As I circulated among the children certain areas of special interest were evident. Over the ten-week period of the project these included: the issue of whether or not squirrels hibernate; squirrels as both predators and prey; and the puzzle of the role of the grey squirrel in the red squirrel's decline in Britain. These current preoccupations or 'key concepts' (Langer, 1981) were taken up collaboratively. This talking and sharing which brings alive information and ideas is discussed further in the next section.

Planning appropriate tasks

The most appropriate tasks are those which encourage children to interpret and use new information. In the Squirrel work nearly all the writing was produced for the children's individual information books for the 7-year-olds

Food chain

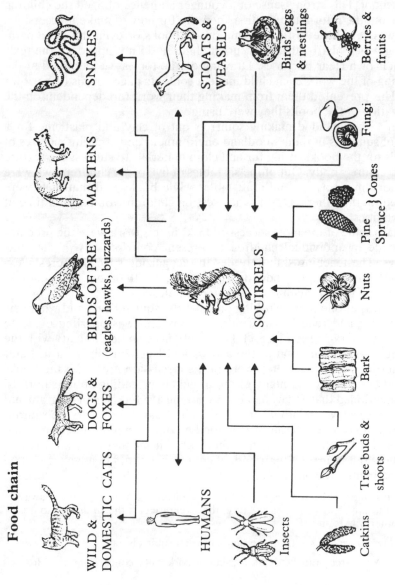

Fig 8.1 The food chain diagram from *The Squirrel in the Trees* (Coldrey, 1986)

in the school. This strong sense of a younger audience obliged the children to write out the information with a keen eye for how to make it accessible. There was very little of the copying out of books or even the close paraphrasing which nearly always occurs if children do not approach the texts with their own clear purposes. Drawing on the topics we identified at the beginning of the work each child made a contents page for his or her own book. This prevented them from making their work too dependent on the organization of the books they were using.

Other tasks included making squirrels out of clay and plasticine for a model of squirrels in their woodland environment and creating pictures of squirrels for the books, using fur and cloth materials to suggest the texture of the creature's body. Out of the six tables of five or six children, two were always organized as art and craft tables while books and materials were arranged on the others. During each session children would spend time at both activities.

Perhaps some of the most successful tasks in this work were the preparations made by individual children to present contributions in the class meetings. The teaching skill here lies in recognizing special interests, extending them and helping individuals share them with others. The best way of explaining what I mean is to give an example.

Stuart was at one point working on what the squirrel eats and what eats squirrels. He had read Susan Coldrey's book and was puzzling over the food chain diagram (see Fig. 8.1). He experienced some difficulty with the meaning of the orientation of the arrows and I helped him with it. Later that afternoon all the children were in the discussion area with the books they had been using and many of them had been reading about squirrels' diet. I mentioned that Stuart had been working at a food chain diagram and asked him to show the others and explain it. Stuart pointed to the squirrel in the middle of the diagram surrounded by other animals and plants and fruit and I asked him to tell the others what it means when an arrow is pointing at the squirrel. Stuart had, of course, been told in advance that he would be invited to contribute.

> *Stuart:* It means the food is eaten by the squirrel and if it is pointing away from the squirrel to another creature, that creature eats the squirrel – so it is the other way round.
>
> *Teacher:* So we can see from the diagram what squirrels eat.
>
> *Stuart:* Yes – tree branches, catkins, shoots, bark, nuts, cones, fungi . . . birds' eggs.
>
> *Teacher:* What about what eats the squirrel?
>
> *Stuart:* Predators are – fox, birds of prey, martens and snakes.

Stuart had been given the opportunity to share one of the main bits of learning he had achieved that afternoon, making it more secure. His researches had also been given a value by the invitation to share them. Everyone's attention had been focused on the diagram. Stuart had gained practice in making his thoughts explicit and the idea that everyone involved can help and share was reinforced. Something like the 'negotiation of meaning' that Gordon Wells (1987) believes is so educative was happening here.

Children were also invited to read out loud to the whole group from books they had been using during the afternoon. These passages were about topics or sub-topics they were preoccupied with and they were always given the chance to prepare before their reading. I always said they were not obliged to read, but no child ever refused. One of the main things I learnt as a teacher was that children enjoy being asked to read to the group as long as they are given notice and it is something they would like to share.

Teacher as audience

The teacher can provide different kinds of audience at different times for the children's oral and written work. Sometimes the role as assessor is uppermost. The 'partner in dialogue'[5] kind of audience is particularly appropriate when children are interpreting new ideas from books. As I circulated amongst the children when they researched their topics and sub-topics they would often tell me what they had been finding out. Sometimes my response would be a genuine question, sometimes a suggestion about where they might find out further information. Ben, for example, became the class expert on the relationship between red and grey squirrels. Often the teacher is the first audience for a child's developing idea and is able to recognize where a child's findings are worth sharing with the whole group.

The writing element in the Squirrel work was all to do with making a book for a younger class. Children tended to ask me whether I thought what they had written was appropriate for their main audience.

The way in which the teacher receives children's developing ideas and findings affects the classroom climate. My aim was to encourage a community of young researchers eager to share new information, using me as a sounding-board before they presented what they had learnt to other audiences.

Collaboration and sharing

One of the main educational achievements of the last few decades is the recognition that learning in the primary years is essentially social. Good teachers have always recognized that children's talk about their activities, and particularly talk about their reading and writing, is central to their learning.

This principle was given official sanction in the Bullock Report (DES, 1975) and explored in many of the Schools Council English Committee's reports. More recently talk has been given status by becoming an essential and assessed part of the English General Certificate of Secondary Education. Talking and listening and their development are Attainment Target 1 in the National Curriculum English statutory guidelines.

It is a main theme of this book that children's talk, both with the teacher and with each other, can help bring alive ideas and information in their reading. This 'making sense' together was a strong feature of the Squirrel case study. Discussion was important at the early stages of the work when the children made their existing knowledge explicit. Their first contact with the information books was in the context of answering their own questions. Once headway had been made with this early research we came together as a class to share the information and ideas.

Rakhee was eager to tell us that she had found out from Coldrey's *The Squirrel in the Trees* that the name comes from a Greek word meaning 'shade' or 'shadowtail' because squirrels often use their tails 'like parasols to shade their bodies from the sun'.

Michael found in Bomford's *Squirrels* that there are 'more than two hundred different kinds of squirrel'. Ben added to this the information that he had found in Davies' *Discovering Squirrels* that the three broadest categories are tree, ground and flying squirrels. He showed us the diagram and talked us through how the flying squirrel moves through the air. 'He has a special bit of skin and this skin stretches from his front legs to his back legs and it opens up a bit like a parachute when he wants to glide through the air'. We learnt from Ben's research that this special skin is called a 'patagium'.

The collaborative centre to the learning added special point and interest to the children's work. They became a community of young readers and writers with a shared purpose. This co-operative aspect was evident when Jack asked why a squirrel's nest was called a 'drey'. Marie suggested 'If you just say "nest" people would think of birds, so you need a special word to show it is a squirrel's home'.

Another important feature of our work was the reading of appropriate passages out loud from the books being used: I would urge teachers to exploit children's eagerness to do this. Here are my reasons.

First, when we attempt something quite difficult, especially if we are a young learner, we need to feel motivated – to find our task rewarding and enjoyable. Recent thinking (for example, Bruner and Haste, 1987) suggests that too many of us have, for too long, favoured individual rather than collaborative learning when all the evidence shows the child to be an essentially social being. By reading out loud from the parts of information books on which they were working the children shared their learning and often got some feedback from the others. I was surprised at how willing even some of the less confident readers were to read from both the books they were using and from their own writing. Children who could not have read some of the more difficult books themselves listened to others reading out loud and were moved forward in their developing understanding of the information book genre.

The children brought their books to the discussions and read out parts which seemed to move our discussion forward. Here is Tara reading to the whole class from Coldrey's *Grey Squirrel* in the context of our discussion about the relationship between red and grey squirrels: 'The grey squirrel is less prone to disease'. Earlier I had asked Tara what she thought this meant and she suggested that 'The grey ones catch it but it don't harm them much, but the red ones die if they catch the disease'. If a context is strong enough children can often be helped to understand quite challenging book language. Making their struggle to grasp the meaning explicit helps children become aware of their own thinking. This growing self-awareness is strongly linked to Donaldson's (1978) notion of disembedded learning or what Bruner terms 'analytic competence' (see Chapter 1). In other words, the special concentration we apply in trying to understand what we read rather than what we do brings within our range concepts and ideas which are context free. I feel sure that this process is best set in motion by collaborative negotiation of meanings.

A sense of 'audience'

The Schools Council Writing Research team working in the 1970s drew attention to the importance of a writer having a sense of 'audience'; this affects the writing as much as its function or purpose. These ideas are fully integrated into National Curriculum Attainment Target 1: Speaking and Listening and Attainment Targets 3–5: Writing. We seek 'a growing ability to construct and convey meaning in which written language matches style to audience and purpose' (English in the National Curriculum, Statutory Document, May 1989).

There are four potential audiences for children's oral and written work: the other children in the group or class; the teacher; individuals outside the immediate classroom context, for example younger children in the school; and parents or an even wider audience. The kinds of audience the teacher can offer has been considered above under 'the teacher's role'. Here we are concerned with two other audiences: first the other children in the class and second the children from the younger end of the school.

Children can learn from each other's efforts to make sense of new bodies of information. The questions children ask and their early attempts to answer them are of great interest to others engaged in a similar task. In the

Squirrel work each session would end with whole class discussion in the book area. It is often suggested that the whole class context is inhibiting (see, for example, Wells, 1987, p. 107) and it is certainly true that we also need small group and one-to-one interaction, but I found the children welcomed the chance to read out loud from books and to share their own writing with the others. During the research children would ask 'can I read this out to the others later on?' Questions were directly addressed by the rest of the group to the child presenting his or her findings.

If we can encourage children to see each other as an interested audience for new ideas and information, the class can begin to become a community of young readers and writers. We might call this a 'research culture' which recognizes that learning is a continuing process.

The children's work was greatly affected by the knowledge that younger children, whom they had consulted informally, would be the readers of their books. The 9-year-olds were impressively aware of motivation factors. I remarked to Tara, 'I'm sure as you write you are thinking about what might make the book interesting for the younger ones?' Tara replied, 'Yes – pictures. You could have a squirrel saying "where's my nut?" Then you could have a flap in the page – lift it up and there could be the nuts and fruits squirrels eat.'

Ben remarked that it was best to have a squirrel 'doing something' in the pictures rather than just sitting on a branch. 'Pictures can tell you a lot about the creatures.'

In the following few lines from Rakhee's book we find a clear description which would help the younger children understand how structure and function relate in the nut-gnawing activity of a squirrel:

> The squirrels' teeth always grow because when they eat the nuts bits of their teeth break off and if the teeth did not grow all the time they would not be able to eat their nuts and berries.
>   Their front teeth are most important because they have to gnaw the nut and split it open. They have two big teeth at the front and two big teeth at the bottom. They gnaw the nut from the end of the teeth.

The climax of the whole project came when each 9-year-old took one or two 7-year-olds to read the books. Gregory read to Wayne and Michael and was extremely skilled in the way he explained his ideas to the younger children. I think it is worth including part of his explanation:

> *Gregory:* That's a drey (pointing to his drawing). Do you know what a drey is? (Pause) It is a kind of nest squirrels have.
>   Now there's two kinds of drey, a winter one and a summer one. The summer drey is out in the branches, cooler, the winter drey is closer to the tree trunk . . . so they don't get cold.
>   Now (turning page) there are two kinds of squirrel here, the red squirrel and the grey squirrel. The red squirrels are disappearing because they cannot get enough food.

(Pointing to his pictures) That is a red squirrel and that is a grey one. Now can you tell me the difference?

Michael: (Looking at Gregory's drawings) Well that one has pointed ears (indicating the drawing of the red squirrel).

Gregory: Yes, that one has pointed ears and that one there has rounded ears (pointing to the grey squirrel). 'The grey squirrel is more vicious than the red squirrel. And red squirrels have more predators'! (reading from his book)
   (Gregory now explains to Michael and Wayne what a predator is.)

Gregory: Well, if I was a squirrel and a lot of animals are after me – right? – they are predators. Like an owl or snake is to a mouse. What do you think the squirrel's predators are?

Wayne: A fox?

Gregory: Yes, and hawks.

Michael: How high do they climb?

Gregory: Well, to the top of an oak tree.

Michael's spontaneous question was one of many and suggests a genuine interest in the topic of conversation.

Conversations of this type could be heard all over the two classrooms and library where the children spread to enjoy the books. It was satisfying for the children to find their efforts were appreciated. It was interesting for me to hear their explanations, because this revealed how far they had gone in their own thinking and learning about the topic.

Summary

- Teachers have an important part to play in helping to embed knowledge from books in a broader framework of learning. Their role includes: providing direction and knowledge, selecting an appropriate range of books and materials, sensitive and skilful mediation between children and books, the setting of interesting tasks and provision of different kinds of audience.

- Non-narrative text is often densely packed with information and children need to be helped to reflect on the overall sense of what is being read.

- Paradoxically the quality of reflection on information and ideas we feel is often achieved by placing alongside other activities which enrich the children's research. This broad-based topic work is a good context in which to include book research.

- It is increasingly being recognized that learning takes place in a social context. Collaboration and sharing have an important role in integrating ideas and information from books. Research becomes less intimidating and more enjoyable.

● A strong sense of an audience – for example, the teacher, the other children, younger children in the school – for both oral and written work enhances a sense of purpose and interest when children are trying to interpret challenging information.

Notes

1. This case study draws on the analysis of Margaret Mallett's unpublished Ph.D. thesis.

2. For an interesting discussion see David Wood (1988), p. 81, 'Learning and generalisation: first thoughts on a thorny issue'.

3. *Squirrel on My Shoulder* produced for BBC Wildlife by John Paling, narrator David Attenborough (1983).

4. When asked Rakhee explained she meant how do you deal with our population of squirrels. This question was answered in detail in Jessica Holm's *Squirrels* (1987).

5. Schools Council Writing Research audience category (1975).

Further reading

DES (1975) *A Language for Life* (The Bullock Report), HMSO, London.

Britton, James N. *et al.* (1975) *The Development of Writing Abilities*, Macmillan, London.

Bruner, J. and Haste, H. (eds.) (1987) Making Sense: *The Child's Construction of the World*, Methuen, London.

DES (1989) *English in the National Curriculum*, Key Stage 1 (Final Orders), HMSO, London.

Fry, Donald (1985) *Children Talk about Books: Seeing Themselves as Readers*, Open University Press, Milton Keynes and Philadelphia. See Chapter 3.

Heek, P. (1982) *Ways of Knowing: Information Books for 7- to 9-Year-Olds*, Thimble Press, Stroud.

Langer, J. (1981) in J. Chapman (ed.) *The Reader and the Text*, Heinemann, London.

Lavender, R. (1983) Children using information books, in *Education 3–13*, vol. 11, no. 1.

Lunzer, E. and Gardner, K. (1979) *The Effective Use of Reading,* Heinemann, London.

Mallett, M. and Newsome, B. (1977) *Talking, Writing and Learning 8–13* Schools Council Working Project 59, Evans/Methuen. Chapter 1. Contexts 4 and 6.

Meek, M. (1977) What is a horse? in *The School Librarian,* vol. 25, no. 1.

Paice, S. (1984) Reading to learn, in *English in Education*, vol. 18, no. 1.

Perera, K. (1986) Some linguistic difficulties in school textbooks, in B. Gilham, *The Language of School Subjects*, Heinemann Educational Books, London.

Southgate, V., Arnold, H. and Johnson, S. (1981) *Extending Beginning Reading*, Heinemann Educational Books, London, for the Schools Council.

Wells, Gordon (1987) *The Meaning Makers: Children Learning Language and Using Language to Learn*, Hodder and Stoughton, Sevenoaks.

9
BECOMING CRITICAL READERS

Children become critical readers as they begin to realize that some books do
the job better than others.

(McKenzie and Warlow, 1977, p. 48)

Researcher: What do you think makes a good information book?
Charlotte (age 10 years): it all depends what you want to use it for . . . for
browsing perhaps or for finding out something in particular.
Tommy (age 8 years): If you already know a lot you need a more detailed
book.

There is no blueprint for the ideal information book, as Charlotte indicates
so competently. This does not mean that there are no general guidelines
which can be applied flexibly and Chapters 3, 4 and 5 identify some of the
features of information books which usually help children use and learn
from them. Sometimes we include a book because it has some excellent
aspects, outstandingly good photographs, perhaps, or clear line drawings,
which compensate for other deficiencies. The purpose for which the book is
to be used helps us decide on the important strengths. Are we seeking a
broad range of fairly basic information or more detailed attention to a sub-
topic? A book can be good for a particular purpose. This was the main
observation of the many young readers I talked to about using books for
research.

The previous chapter concentrated on children's developing knowledge
about a subject. Here the interest centres on children's growing ability,
encouraged throughout the work, to consider and make explicit what they
think are the strengths and weaknesses of the particular books they have
been using.

I find this critical awareness is not always something children just acquire
as they proceed. The teacher needs to plan structured discussions drawing
on the children's work and comments. My observations, notes and tape
recordings led me to certain useful headings (used also in Chapter 5) in
organizing my account of children's developing competence: retrieval devices, illustrations, format and the language of texts. The later part of this

chapter suggests some possible stages in children's increasing control over some of the different kinds of non-fiction and finally considers the contribution of 'expert' writers.[1]

Retrieval devices

Contents page, indexes and glosaries work together to help readers see the scope and level of the book and help locate particular information. Where a book is at an appropriately advanced level a detailed contents page giving chapters with main and subheadings is helpful. Several children praised the contents page in Davies' *Discovering Squirrels* which was organized in this way. For example, in Chapter 2 the main heading is 'Different Kinds of Squirrel'. Subheadings are 'Tree', 'Ground' and 'Flying' squirrels. This more detailed contents page helps children become familiar with the way material is organized in information books and textbooks.

Most of the children knew you read the index like 'a dictionary'. Others needed a practical demonstration in context. Ralph Whitlock's book, *Squirrels*, and Jessica Holm's, with the same title, featured good, detailed indexes to guide the abler young reader. The contents page and index should not be too similar although some overlap is inevitable. While a contents page provides the overall scope, the index directs us to more detailed information on more specific topics and sub-topics. For example, under words beginning with 'C', Holm includes 'cacheing', 'cars and squirrels', 'chipmunk', 'classification', 'claws', 'coccidosis', 'colour', 'competition', 'conservation', 'coppice' and 'courtship'. During one of our discussions we talked about dangers to squirrels and how we might read about this in the books. 'Dangers' is not in Holm's index so together we thought of some other possible index terms and came up with 'cars and squirrels', 'predators' and 'persecution'. Rakhee suggested 'illness' which was not in the list, but we found what we wanted under 'disease'. This collaborative work was helpful in sharing strategies and retrieval techniques but some children needed one-to-one help from the teacher in becoming adept at using the index. Making their own indexes for the books for younger readers gave an opportunity to apply their developing knowledge in a satisfying way.

The concept of a glossary was new to many of them but they came to appreciate this gathering together of technical words in some of the books and many included glossaries when writing their own books for the younger children. We found some glossaries were more helpful than others. Michael commented on Whitlock's full and helpful definition of a rodent: 'a group of animals which have two pairs of long and sharp front teeth especially suited for gnawing'. He then helpfully adds examples of creatures in the category – 'squirrels are rodents. Other rodents are rats and mice' – thus helping the children's concept of what a rodent is to become more secure.

The children became increasingly aware that taking on the new words and therefore the new concepts was part of becoming able to control the new information. This was a constant talking point. Michael pointed out that nearby pictures and the general sense of what is written before and after often helps us make a sensible guess about the word meaning. Some books put technical words in bold print to indicate they were glossary items. I wondered if too many emphasized words might disorganize the reading process for the young readers, but Ben assured me he liked to be warned 'a difficult word is about to come up'. Part of learning about any topic involves coming to understand the meaning of relevant new words. As we saw from Vygotsky's work, discussed in Chapter 1, a brief verbal explanation, whether written in a glossary or expressed out loud, is not likely to communicate the complexity of the more difficult concepts. Pictures, anecdotes, role play and demonstrations all help clothe the words in meaning. The children were encouraged to use these ways of explaining new ideas to each other. For example, in the previous chapter Stuart demonstrated the function of the platagium in the flying squirrel's movement. Discussion can help children understand the purpose and the limitations of the glossary.

Illustrations

In the context of planning their own books as well as appraising the books they were working with, the children talked about the role of illustrations in information books. Rakhee remarked that diagrams, pictures and photographs should be 'near the writing' which refers to and explains them. This was mostly the case in the books we used, for example, Tittensor's distribution map is opposite the paragraph explaining how widespread the red squirrel is over much of Europe and Asia. This matching of appropriate illustrations to the text is what I understand by good integration between the two elements in a book. Useful mention of the illustrations in the writing also helps make the connection clear. The children all preferred colour photographs to any other kind of illustration. Michael said that the colour photographs in *The Squirrel in the Trees* revealed the creature 'in its environment'. He added that particularly in autumn 'the surroundings provide camouflage'. I thought Michael made a good case for using colour photographs, but I did suggest that black and white photographs, drawings and diagrams are sometimes more appropriate.

The simplest books, which retained a broad time structure by taking the squirrel through each season, tend to have drawings rather than photographs. These can be successful, for example, those in Propper's *The Squir-*

rel are attractive and the result of careful observation. Others like the wide-eyed squirrels in Angela Sheehan's book are, I think, in danger of giving a misleading Disneyland view of animals.

The children were eager to draw their own squirrels. Ben pointed out it was best to draw an animal doing something – eating a nut or stripping bark – to match with what had been written. Ralph Whitlock nearly always includes a comment beside an illustration drawing attention to the important feature, for example, 'Note how the bark of the tree has been stripped away'.

What about diagrams? There were distribution maps and drawings showing squirrel body dimensions (Tittensor), wire-mesh handling cones for biologists, a circular diagram showing what squirrels eat during the year and squirrel skeletons (Jessica Holm) and a food chain diagram (Coldrey). Most children need help in interpreting diagrams. The positioning of the arrows in the food chain diagram seemed to confuse some children until it was pointed out that the arrow heads pointed to the creature which ate the food and not the creature or plant that was eaten (see Fig. 8.1). Diagrams can be discussed by a group or by the teacher and one pupil. We cannot assume children know how to interpret and use them. *The Grey Squirrel* World Wildlife wall chart was included near the display table. Ben remarked that while 'the writing was hard' the labelled drawings were very clear and capable of being quickly referred to.

Format

The quality of the general format and organization of the books seemed to play a considerable role in whether the children found them inviting or not. Children do notice whether print is clear, pages uncluttered and pictures attractively positioned. Some quite up-to-date publications (though none of those used in this project) present cluttered pages with hotchpotches of diagrams and photographs arranged so as to cram as much as possible on to one page. Far better to include less and produce a well-integrated and aesthetically pleasing book. Several children commented on the clear and attractive layout of Davies' *Discovering Squirrels*. Headings can help organize the information. Some books have different colour flashes to indicate whether a section provides information or whether it suggests practical activities and projects. The less mature readers liked the balance of illustrations and text in Bomford's *Squirrels* where rather more than half of each page was taken up with excellent colour photographs. These provided a good talking-point about particular aspects of squirrel characteristics or behaviour. Christine Pappas (1984)[2] believes the way the book is organized as a whole, and even the order in which the elements are arranged, affect how far children are able to learn from them. We do not, however, want publishers to make the format a strait-jacket: this inhibits the emergence of a truly individual book.

The language of the texts

What are the features of a 'well-written' text in an information book for primary age children? Teachers tend to choose books for the different levels of ability within their class intuitively. Making explicit some of the judgements behind these intuitions helps children develop their own criteria for appraising resources.

The texts used in this project ranged from Angela Sheehan's informational narrative – 'The Squirrel spends almost the whole day eating the seeds from pine cones' – to the interesting but quite demanding non-narrative writing in Jessica Holm's *Squirrels* – 'Not hampered in the same way by the parapox virus and better able to survive in the small broad-leaved woodlands left after conifers had been felled for wartime use, grey squirrels expanded their numbers enormously'. Even the abler children needed considerable help with this.

Vocabulary, syntax and the sheer length of the sentence contribute to the challenge this presents. Often Jessica Holm has a lighter touch than this but the sentence is not untypical of the writing in many parts of the book. Most of the other texts were between these two in the demands they made upon the young readers. The children were at different stages in becoming readers of information books. What are these stages and how far did the books offered meet the children's abilities and needs?

Stages in becoming a reader of information books

Two children, Jack and Andrew, both statemented on account of special learning needs, were still very much more comfortable with narrative and Angela Sheehan's information story was provided mainly, though not exclusively, with these children in mind.[3] The teacher and I read parts of the narrative to them as, although the genre was familiar to them, some of the vocabulary was difficult. The important point here is that they were not required to cope with generalizations about squirrels, but merely to follow through a year in the life of one particular squirrel. Some of the children mentioned to me that they found the 'More About Squirrels' nature notes at the end of Sheehan's book helpful.

The next stage from Sheehan's information story is, I think, a text like Propper's which provides a very broad time framework – we follow a squirrel family through the seasons but the flow of the narrative breaks sometimes to give information about squirrels in general. For example, we read 'As long as a squirrel's tail is really clean and light, he can use it as a parachute' and 'some animals spend the whole winter sleeping. This is called hibernating. Squirrels do not hibernate'. The non-narrative asides are often conversational: 'If you see bits of broken hazelnut shell on the ground in a wood, look around for squirrels'. This seems to me a sympathetic way of introducing children to the simpler forms of the mode within the general context of a more familiar genre.

Then we come to the form most of us think of when we imagine an information book for children, a fully non-narrative organization of the material but combined with a writing style that still retains some features of the spoken language. Bomford achieves this by making contact with the reader's likely experience in an inviting introduction. 'Perhaps you've fed peanuts to the grey squirrels in a park near your home? If you keep very still, they will come down from the trees where they live. Then you can watch them quite easily.' Children need help in using the headings and subheadings typical of this kind of book and, as mentioned earlier, this way of organizing the book should be evident in the contents page.

Davies' *Discovering Squirrels* is written in clear, simple language but until the last chapter on 'Studying Squirrels' no personal pronouns are used. The generalizations take the reader a step further towards mature non-narrative book language. 'Many squirrels live in forests and spend all their time in the tree tops. Some squirrels can glide quite long distances from tree to tree. Other squirrels dig burrows and live underground in large colonies.' Vocabulary and concepts likely to be new to some readers – 'incisors', 'arboreal', 'patagium' and 'predator' – are in bold print in this and some of the other books.

The writing in *The Squirrel in the Trees* was considered by the children to be more difficult than Davies' text. There is a greater proportion of writing to illustration and the print is much smaller. However, the writer has tried to make a link with likely experience of the reader: 'when you next walk through some trees, look up into the branches – and if you are lucky you may see a squirrel climbing and hopping about in the tree tops'.

Even in a text which is relatively demanding in conceptual and linguistic terms, if some of the language echoes the patterns of speech, the young reader familiarizing himself or herself with non-narrative organization will find it much less intimidating. Even a text written by a distinguished zoologist can relieve the necessary imparting of weighty information by varying the tone. This Jessica Holm does to perfection in *Squirrels*. The quotation from her book near the beginning of this section reveals the challenging content of much of this book. Yet several of the children liked it best. I asked Michael, who was reading the section on 'Dreys', if he found the text difficult. He said he did 'but the questions and the humour and all the drawings help me understand'. He was greatly entertained by the section on 'Do squirrels bite?' and particularly by the head of a very fierce looking grey squirrel saying 'Yes!'.

Appreciating what experts offer

A writer who is an expert on the topic is usually able to share a store of engaging anecdotes gathered in the course of their work with wildlife. Jessica Holm's book is full of lively first-hand experience with squirrels, including this humorous one: 'I have seen a female red squirrel feverishly cacheing hazelnuts and making repeated journeys to and from the canopy to collect them. She followed at a discreet distance by one of her offspring, who promptly dug them all up again and wolfed the lot!' This kind of amusing story is greatly appreciated by children and provides some light relief from the weightier parts of such texts. Holm's writing shows that book language can be scholarly without being dull. She probably knows more about squirrels than anyone else and her syntax and vocabulary reflect the complexity of the information, yet the abler 9-year-olds made quite a good attempt at reading the book with some help from the teacher. One stylistic device which makes a link with spoken language is, as Michael pointed out, the peppering of her work with questions such as 'when are squirrels active?', 'how far do squirrels travel?', 'do squirrels steal birds' eggs?', 'can squirrels swim?' and 'are squirrels sociable?' She also helps by anticipating what a young reader might not know and providing an explanation. 'Each time a new crop of youngsters, which biologists call a "cohort" (like a year set at school), comes along, the population swells'.

Two other books we used, which like Holm's were in the more challenging category, were also written by experts: *The Red Squirrel* by Andrew Tittensor, published in association with the Mammal Society, and *Squirrels* by the naturalist Ralph Whitlock.

What is most noticeable about these is their individuality. Tittensor's text is accessible only to mature readers in the upper primary school. The following extract shows that much of Tittensor's writing is in the textbook style: 'Red squirrels are most abundant in large and continuous areas of mature coniferous forest, whether these originate by planting or from natural regeneration'. Vocabulary and syntax are much more difficult here than in *The Squirrel in the Trees* and this text is really for primary school readers who see themselves as young naturalists. Occasionally the reader is addressed in a more personal tone: 'You can learn a lot from studying signs, so do not be downhearted if you cannot actually see the squirrels'. Primary teachers often remark to me that there are relatively few books to extend the mature primary school reader. This one does and even the most advanced readers in this class used the book mainly for its illustrations, tackling only parts of the text.

Equally scholarly but rather more accessible is Ralph Whitlock's beautifully integrated text. The children needed more coaxing to try this book as they so much preferred the colour photographs in many of the other books to these black and white pictures. Those that tried the written text coped well and learnt much. Whitlock's writing is mature book language with few echoes of spoken language. However, his account is never dull and shows an information book can be as individual and absorbing as a story. The following description of how squirrels move in trees shows the vitality of Whitlock's writing:

> Squirrels are extremely agile in trees. We may see one sitting high in a tree in a park and think it will have to come down and run along the ground to the next tree. But no! It gathers itself for a mighty leap across a gap twenty feet or more wide and lands, a little lower down, on a branch of the next tree.

Reading out loud to the group seemed a particularly promising strategy in helping convey information not only about the topic in hand but also about the information book genre. The rhythm and patterning of these texts is not familiar to primary age children and hearing the teacher reading helps them get to know how information is organized at sentence level. I found children very willing to read out loud to the group. It is kind to give a warning as children can then check how to pronounce new words rather than be left to struggle or be helped in front of the others. Actually using terms like 'subheading', 'section' and 'glossary' when discussing the book helps greatly.

We think of the language of stories and poetry as being worthy of comment. Children can also be encouraged to admire a lucid explanation or perhaps an apt metaphor or other comparison. I asked Maria if the section on habitat and dreys in Coldrey's book had helped her. What new ideas had she uncovered?

> *Maria:* That the drey is quite easy to see. And they line their nests with moss.

> *Teacher:* Yes. We already knew the nests were ball shaped. I like the way it says they were 'wedged' in the tree fork. Nice way of putting it, isn't it?

Becoming an expert on a topic allows us to be playful in communicating knowledge. I thought it worth sharing with the group, at the point where we were discussing how function relates to structure in a successful species, this delightful picture of agile squirrels moving about in their environment in Holm's book:

> Squirrels' feet and claws are so efficient at climbing that they find no difficulty in scaling brick walls and tall garden fences. One of the funniest sights is youngsters playing and learning about their wonderful feet. Favourite exercises include suspending yourself upside down, and hanging from one leg before dropping in on an unsuspecting sibling, or racing round and round a tree-trunk rather like the legendary tiger that turned into butter.

It is by sharing such lively writing that children come to understand that some books just give the information while others invite us to be fascinated, intrigued and sometimes entertained at the same time.

Summary

- Discussion and demonstration of how to use retrieval devices can helpfully be built into everyday work. The ability to evaluate this aspect of an information book is part of becoming a critical reader.

- An information book is 'good' if it serves the reader's particular purposes well.

- Children often need help in interpreting diagrams. They can be helped to judge the worth of the illustrations in books for their particular purpose.

- The format of a book is important in attracting young readers. Clear organization, headings and subheadings and aesthetically pleasing and useful illustrations are desirable. However, children often like quirky, individual books and publishers should not be encouraged to reduce all information books to a predictable formula.

- Mature information book language is less familiar to children than other kinds of text. Reading out loud from books helps children to appreciate good examples of the genre.

- Non-fiction organized on a less general principle than the typical information book may meet the needs of children moving from story to fully non-narrative text.

- Early information books are more accessible if some of the language echoes conversational patterns.

This book was almost complete when the report of the 'Three Wise Men' on the quality of children's learning in primary schools appeared. Among other things they pointed out what has been known for a long time: that work organized round a 'topic', sometimes referred to as 'thematic' or 'project–based' can, if not carefully planned and monitored, 'lead to fragmentary teaching and learning'. These problems are not, however, confined to topic work; subject–specific, timetabled lessons can be equally unsatisfactory if not conscientiously and imaginatively prepared. Often difficulties arise in either approach, when children are left to cope with challenging secondary sources without adequate direction and support.

One of the strengths of the National Curriculum is that both project-based work, with its special potential for cross curriculum problem solving, and more subject–specific lessons are encouraged. I hope the present book makes a contribution to our understanding of how both kinds of work can be well planned, directed and evaluated, and particularly to how children can be helped to use and reflect on the information in books which can enrich their learning.

Notes

1. This chapter draws on my analysis in 'Children using and sharing information books in the context of primary school project work', in *British Educational Research Journal,* Spring 1992.

2. Pappas, Christine (1986) Exploring the global structure of children's 'information books'. Paper presented at the Annual Meeting of the National Reading Conference, Austin, Texas, 2–6 December. Page 7. The 'elements' are the obligatory features of an information book that give it the status of a genre. First the topic (e.g. 'Squirrels') is introduced, followed by attributes (e.g. creatures' size, physical structure and mobility), and then characteristic events (e.g. hibernation, birth, death, etc.) are described. Pappas' point is that children develop an expectation about the order of these elements.

3. There are different views about whether an information narrative might lead to genre confusion or not. My experience leads me to believe it can be a helpful transitional genre between story and information book forms.

Further reading

Heeks, P. (1982) *Ways of Knowing: Information Books for 7–9-Year-Olds,* The Thimble Press, Stroud.

Lavender, R. (1983) Children using information books, in *Education 3–13*, vol. 11, no. 1.

Neate, B. (1985) Children's information books, in *Gnosis,* 13 September.

Paice, S. (1984) Reading to learn, in *English in Education,* vol. 18, no. 1.

Wade, E. (ed.) (1990) *Reading for Real,* Open University Press, Milton Keynes and Philadelphia. Chapter 8.

10
CLASSROOM CONTEXTS FOR READING NON-FICTION

The National Curriculum faces teachers with the task of providing books that keep personal interests alive and flourishing, so that each subject invites enquiry and discovery, rather than involving only the transmission of knowledge and facts.

(John Dixon, 1990, personal correspondence)

I aimed through discussion to discover what the children themselves wanted to find out, so that the books became tools to assist their investigations rather than just used for information retrieval exercises set by me.

(Gemma Amphlett, student teacher working on a science topic, June 1991)

Teachers have developed some very effective and detailed ways of giving stories a context in the classroom. Fictional texts with first-class illustrations tended to be at the centre of reading programmes for the younger children in British primary schools. This is in keeping with the great tradition of the 1960s, to place children and their 'personal development' at the centre of the educational process.

The National Curriculum assumes a different starting point for the 1990s, subject learning: science, history, geography and so on. The question facing teachers is, can reading to explore the 'world' opened up by such subjects be welded into existing practices and traditions?

One encouraging observation is that cross-curricular topic work, one of the strengths of primary practice in the last few decades, is compatible with the National Curriculum framework. It is evident also to anyone visiting and teaching in primary schools regularly, as I do, that geography, history and science often provide the content for the talking, listening, reading and writing activities set out in the English curriculum guidelines. Thus the flexibility and unity of the good primary school programme can be maintained. The following glimpses into actual classrooms where things are going well seems the most helpful way of indicating how some of the principles proposed throughout the book can be realized in practice. It is not claimed that this collection of examples is comprehensive. Some subjects and activities place non-fiction books in a more central role than others. Thus there is concentration on science, history and geography rather than on mathematics where teachers themselves provide many of the written materials. What the examples have in common is that situations where the active nature of acquiring knowledge is emphasized are encouraged. Teacher input in the choice and organization of materials and in the direction of the learning activities is fully recognized. However, in keeping with the central theme of the book, in each example the children themselves have a good understanding of the purposes the books are serving.

Some of the problems of learning from books are raised and some of the strategies which can help are described and evaluated. A main assumption is that becoming a reader in each of the curriculum areas is achieved through encountering books as part of the everyday work in science, geography, history and so on. The examples reflect the requirements of the National Curriculum at the time of writing. Inevitably changes will be made as programmes of work are evaluated. However, the ways in which we can successfully embed learning from books into the other complementary learning activities will remain a central concern whatever modifications are made. These examples aim to share the strategies some teachers have used.

The Earth in Space: Science with 7-year-olds
(AT16: Levels 1–4)
Background to the work

G., a student in her third year of a BA(Ed.) degree course, was asked by the class teacher to carry out the following National Curriculum programme over her four-week teaching practice, summer term 1991. The 32 first-year juniors attended a small suburban Roman Catholic School. Most of the children enjoyed reading and received encouragement at home and school.

Science AT 16
(Since this work was carried out, the organization of the attainment target has been revised)
Level 2

- be able to explain why night occurs
- know that day length changes throughout the year
- know that we live on a large, spherical, self-contained planet called earth
- know that the Earth, Moon and Sun are separate bodies

Level 3

- ability to measure time with a sundial
- knowledge that the inclination of the sun in the sky changes in the year

Level 4

- know that the solar system is made up of the Sun and planets and

- have an idea of its scale

- understand that the Sun is a star

Aims

G. planned to provide an interesting introduction to the topic. The challenging ideas and concepts involved in a study of space, the planets and stars would be revisited at later points during the children's school years, so G.'s main aim was to awaken interest and to help the children to achieve some understanding of the relative size and movement of the planets.

Another important aim was to make cross-curricular links to enrich the work: with English work through discussion, reading both poetry and information books and writing (indeed the topic gave a worthwhile content for the English Attainment Targets); with art and CDT by making two- and three-dimensional representations of stars and planets; with mathematics by learning to recognize and name spheres and their nets (AT10 Shape and Space, Level 2), work on time, sundials and 12-hour clocks and by measuring the relative sizes of the planets and their distance from the Earth (the children were helped to make a 'voyage to the Moon' game with dice); with geography in looking at continents and oceans and night and day on opposite sides of the earth; with drama through role play to demonstrate the movement of the planets and the turning of the Earth on its own axis. Aesthetic appreciation of the sheer beauty of planets and stars was encouraged by the art and English activities.

Our particular interest in the work is of course the way in which non-fiction was to be used to develop and expand the knowledge children achieved through observation and activity. Here aims included:

- helping children to learn to use retrieval devices in context;

- encouraging discussion, observation and activity before reading so that the books were more likely to be tools to aid their own investigations;

- reading out loud from information books at appropriate points in the work to help familiarize the children with the game.

The progression of activities

The many activities were carefully planned within the framework stipulated by the National Curriculum programme, but G. sought an atmosphere likely to sustain the wonder and excitement of a first structured look at space. The whole topic was approached on three fronts:

- focus on night-time (English emphasis);

- focus on the Sun and daylight (shadow sticks, sundials, our need for the Sun);

- focus on the Earth and Moon in space (stars, planets and the solar system).

Week 1
Focus on night-time

What children feel about phenomena like the Sun, Moon and planets as well as their prior ideas is the basis on which learning is best based. Work began with a focus on night-time. Children shared thoughts, feelings and experiences in group discussion and G. read Roger McGough's poem 'Bully Night'. The children brought in their own favourite night-time or night sky poems and some of them began to write their own poems and personal accounts. Discussion extended to people who work at night and nocturnal creatures, leading to personal written accounts of night-time.

Focus on the Sun and daylight

In this first week teacher and children planned how they would make shadow sticks and sundials.

Focus on the Sun and Moon in space

The children shared their existing knowledge about the Sun and Earth and their relative movements. Most of them had the impression that the Sun seems to move across the sky. The teacher explained that in fact the Sun is stationary and it is the Earth that moves around the sun in a pathway we call its orbit. It takes a year to move completely round the Sun. Some of the children who were already interested in space knew that the Earth also moves on its own axis. A complete revolution takes one day, that is twenty-four hours. It is daytime when our part of the Earth faces the Sun and night-time when it faces away. Drama seemed an appropriate way of crystallizing the contents. G. comments: 'We had a demonstration of the movements of the Earth to ensure that those who might not already have a grasp of the concepts could see what we were talking about.'

In their first session they were shown a poster of Earth taken from 180,000 km into space. This led to prolonged discussion and considerable interest.

G. read out loud to the children from Robin Scagell's *How to be an Astronomer*. The children loved the illustrations but the text had to be paraphrased.

Bringing in secondary sources

At the end of the first week G. explained that as well as the activities, observations and discussion they were planning they would need to develop their knowledge through books. Attention was drawn to a classroom display of information books on space. Several children said they had space books at home and that they would bring them in to school. G. comments in her notes that 'Tommy H. was particularly well informed about the subject and could hardly contain himself from bursting out with information about it!'

The children took turns to look at the books on the display and to read about some of the things they had talked about. Some of the books were too difficult and the student felt she had in some cases overestimated what 7–8-year-olds could manage. However, she remarks that response was often 'as much aesthetic as born of scientific curiosity'. G. read the section on the Sun (pp. 14–17) in M. Chown's *Stars and Planets*. She paraphrased where necessary and talked about the striking pictures constantly making links with children's experience.

At the end of this first week G. introduced a collaborative writing task, writing with the children's help the main things they had understood so far about the Earth and Sun. The children made notes on this using the shared writing for their project folders.

Week 2

The children made their shadow sticks and began looking through the books to find out about the Sun. They came together to talk about their findings: what the Sun is made of, its size relative to the Earth and its distance from the Earth.

The children were able to talk from their everyday experience about how we need the light and heat of the sun, how it moves or seems to move across our sky, change of inclination in summer and winter, change of time of sunset and sunrise.

Work started on models of the planets and the Sun. Together teacher and children worked out a reasonably realistic scale. Saturn, Jupiter and the Sun were too large to be modelled in three dimensions so were represented in 2D card or paper. Asteroids and comets were made in 3D with papier mâché, card, newspaper, plastic junk materials – all were used to create models of planets, space stations and rockets. Children negotiated how they would make their models in groups of three. It was decided the small models would be made of scrunched up paper (Mercury, Pluto and Mars), medium models of balloons blow up to the right size (Earth, Venus, Neptune and Uranus), and large models in 2D, painted paper (Saturn, Jupiter and Sun). As the groups worked on the models G. asked them what they had found out from the books. One boy said that if we tried to make a model of the Sun, if the other stars and planets were the right size in relation to it, it would be as big as the classroom! In the end only a segment of the Sun was shown as on the scale worked out it was 10 metres in diameter. Louise commented that looking at the books had made her realize that stars are 'not really star shaped'. 'They are round, but the light makes them glitter into star shapes.'

Work on the solar system, and particularly how far each planet is from the sun, began in this second week. The children took turns to use the books to find the distances between the Sun and planets and with G.'s help worked out a scale. G. had her own notes on distances for children unable to find the information themselves. The information found in the books had a direct relationship with the children's activities – making their models and carrying out role play both in the classroom and later on the school field to show the spacing and movement of the planets. G. writes in her lesson notes that she intended to demonstrate

> the scale of the universe through art work to show relative sizes of the planets and a practical demonstration outside to show the relative distances between them. This will involve two differing scales which will not be fully comprehensible to the whole class. However, I feel it will be valuable to give an impression of the great size of the universe and an experience which will be valuable as a starting block to future, more sophisticated, learning in the same area.

G. had sorted through all the information books from her college, the school library and those brought in from public libraries to find those which had the information needed on distances and which could be read by most of the children. Small groups took turns to use the books while the other children worked on less teacher dependent activities such as folder decoration and art work.

An interesting feature of the work was the collaborative writing teacher and children did using the blackboard, children being invited to formulate sentences. Thus what had been read was integrated with what they did in the writing to accompany the wall displays and 'washing line' solar system representation.

The basic concepts in the National Curriculum guidelines set out earlier were written by teacher and children on the board, with teacher acting as scribe, and then expanded by the children in their project folders. Some children aged only 7 or 8 find informational writing difficult and I felt the collaborative approach and demonstration of note-taking was a useful strategy employed by this student. It also encouraged good integration of book knowledge and practical observations and experience.

Week 3

The children were helped to construct a sundial and understand its practical use. They recorded movements of the Sun across the sky and recorded the making of the sundial. To recap on information about the Sun the teacher read out of K. Perry's *The Sun* (1985) and showed the pictures.

The other planets being made for the displays were discussed and children chose a particular planet to research in the information books. Again the reading was focused by discussion about what was of most importance to know about the planets: size, distance from Sun and Earth, what they were made of, temperature.

G. writes that at the end of this third week

> We had a summing up session and those who had not been involved in making the 2D planets were interested and amazed at the relative differences in size between the giant planets of Jupiter, Saturn and the Earth. This work is advancing them into AT16: Level 4. I would say that probably all of them are now working at Level 4: they understand that the Sun is a star, know what 'solar system' means and that it is made up of the Sun and planets. They now have a better idea of its scale, with reference to the difference in the size of the planets but few, if any, have a real concept of the distances between planets either relatively or in real terms. They know from the book I showed them that it would take a space rocket ten years to go from the Earth to the sun, if that were possible, and therefore have the notion that it is an extremely long way. It is impossible for most of them to grasp the concept of millions of miles, because it is so vast a number that one of them suggested it was the same as infinity, and because some of them do not understand place value anyway. Today's work and discussion with the children shows me that they have developed their understanding of the topic of the Earth in space in the short time I have been working with them.

Week 4

All the activities needed finishing off. G. comments that the papier mâché work took much more time than she expected. The 2D large shapes took a lot of painting but were an important visual aid. Children worked in pairs to write descriptions of each planet for the wall display.

There was some new input on the Moon. G. read from the books about why the Moon shines, why it changes in the sky, how long it takes to orbit the Earth (Myring and Snowden, *Finding Out about Sun, Moon and Planets*, 1982, pp. 6–9).

G. told the children that before we had the scientific facts, the origins of the Earth, Sun, stars and Moon seemed very mysterious to women and men living years ago. Two myths were read, one English and one Eskimo, about why the Moon looks as it does, how the 'man' got into the Moon (Hadley, *Legends of the Sun and Moon*, 1983). G. comments,

> I pointed out that people all over the Earth had stories like these, such as 'Woman in the Moon' from North American Indian culture. The children listened attentively to the stories, which I half read and half told, and they were young enough for a couple to ask me whether it was actually true!

The children marked the position of shadows on their sundials as the Sun was shining one day in this last week. G. showed them a picture of a Saxon sundial. 'This would probably have little meaning for them except, as I explained it, as an example of how people who lived in England over a thousand years ago (i.e. a very long time ago) told the time using the Sun before they had clocks and watches.'

This week the children were shown pictures of the Moon's surfaces from books. One illustration which particularly captured their interest was a photograph of an American astronaut actually standing on the Moon. G. notes that while the girls and boys were both active in making the models of planets, and if anything the girls were more inclined to do the writing, it was mainly the boys who asked questions about the Moon.

When I asked G. what she felt the contribution of books and secondary sources had been she said she felt all but the simplest information books were too difficult for most of the children to read independently. The diagrams needed a lot of explanation. While the children enjoyed browsing through the books, when it came to more systematic work she felt it helped to give a focus to their research, for example to search for an answer to a specific question they or someone else had raised using the books' retrieval devices or to work in detail at a particular star or planet.[1]

Several of the children were interested in reading books and came up to show them to me. Mandy brought a book on the Sun and G. showed her appreciation by reading part of it to the class. Using the books directly for research nearly always results in copying unless we can help the children write their accounts from brief notes. G. thought copying the odd bit of information from a book may '. . . be of value in assisting their assimilation of not only the factual knowledge but also the style of language and spellings which will stand them in good stead for the future.'

G. mentions, 'The main problem is obtaining sufficient books which are suitable for younger children. While most of the books are relevant and suitable for browsing through, many of them are quite densely packed with information expressed in such a way that the language causes problems even to these articulate youngsters.'

Other books used apart from those mentioned in the text

Davis, Don P. and Hughes, D. (1989) *The Moon*, Planetary Exploration: Books about the Solar System, BLA Publishing Ltd. A good up-to-date book with stunning illustrations (for example, p. 43 shows the Sun with 9 planets, sizes depicted to scale). Text for older juniors. Teachers would need to read it out loud as G. did to younger children. They browsed through the pictures on their own.

Davis, Don P. and Hughes, D. (1989) *Jupiter*, in same series as above. The text, part of which we read out loud, is often almost poetic, for example on p. 6 we read 'Jupiter is a giant planet wrapped in clouds that reflect sunlight. . . . The pattern of colours produces graceful swirls across the disc, and in the planet's southern hemisphere, a giant whirling spot peers out like an angry red eye.'

Moore, Patrick (1972) *Stars and Space*, A. & C. Black Ltd. A little scholarly for this age group but they liked the illustrations.

Fenwick, Jill (1980) *The Moon*, Macdonald Starter. Some of the children loved tracing the spacemen.

Maché, D. (1978) *Mars*, Franklin Watts. Good computer pictures but the children said, 'The moon is not blue!'

Petty, Kate (1985) *Comets*, Franklin Watts. Clearly written text.

Macdonald Starter (1971) *The Universe*. G. remarked that children need to be told the significance of different print styles, for example that under illustrations, to explain them.

The Mysterious Universe: Earth Our Planet (1978) Christenson Press. Several of the children enjoyed looking through this question and answer book.

Lafferty, Peter (1989) *Astronomy*, Science in Action series, Cherry Tree Books. Some of the children managed quite well on their own with this well set out book. Good retrieval devices and clear headings. Interestingly written, for example 'Some nebulae glow because, inside them, stars are being born.'

Focus on geography

Children: 7–8-year-olds.
School: RC primary – small suburban school.
Teacher: 3rd year BA(Ed.) student, summer 1991.
Week 3 of the Earth in Space project described above.

Map work: continents and oceans

The children knew that their study of the Earth and planets was going to include a close look at the land masses and stretches of water on planet Earth. Paul brought in a globe and helped the teacher recap through demonstration the mechanism of the Earth turning bringing about day and night. Together children and teacher looked at the British Isles on the globe and then turned it to find that Australia was on the opposite side to the UK, hence when it is night there it is day here and vice versa. G. comments,

The children are familiar with the name of Australia if only because of the *Neighbours* programme. However, I was quite surprised at how few of the class had any idea what a continent is. Those who knew some of the names could not necessarily identify the relevant land mass on the globe. It is easy as an adult to forget how abstract a coloured blob on a globe or map is and how difficult to relate to where we actually live. It also becomes easier to understand as children become able to understand larger numbers and larger distances.

It was clear that a lot of talking and demonstrating was needed to increase the children's understanding of the subject matter before map work could begin. Discussion was made personal by looking at places children had or would be visiting. For example, since David was going to America at the end of the week we included a look at this continent. The children needed a lot of help to transfer their reading of the globe to their reading of maps. The *Philips Junior Atlas* was used to help children identify and label the continents and major oceans. A map worksheet provided a labelling task.

G. noted that she was 'caught by surprise when half the class began work with their map worksheet upside down.' In line with AT2 Geography (knowledge and understanding of places): Level 3, the children coloured an outline of a map of the world to show the sea and land and used the atlases to label the continents and oceans.

This science work also included a geographical focus when the sundials were constructed in Week 3. The use of a compass was explained in the context of an actual task in which the children had interest invested.

In the fourth week it was sunny enough to carry out some 'shadow' work in the playground and G. tied this in with compass directions to link with the sundial work.

The children were now familiar with the four main compass points, many could use eight, and they were clear that the Sun rises in the east and sets in the west. G. comments,

> Many were able to explain how we can use the Sun to tell the time, but when I asked them what the problems were with using a sundial they mentioned the problems with cloud and rain but none of them realized that the shadows would be different in summer and winter. However, this is quite an advanced concept requiring a considerably more sophisticated understanding than that required by AT16: Level 3, which only requires the children to know 'that the inclination of the Sun in the sky changes in the year'. The majority of the children's understanding of this was secure by the fourth week. There was doubt, however, as to whether the differences between winter and summer were caused by the Sun changing its movements in some way such as moving more slowly. I do not find this surprising or a problem as I distinctly remember the first time I understood the seasonal changes, and I was by then in the secondary school.

History: the Wordsworths and Dove Cottage

This case study differs from all the other children's work I quote in several respects. Firstly, much of the activity took place out of the classroom in the context of a school visit. Secondly, while I either taught or at least observed the work of the children in other examples, in this case I base my reflections on children's writing and drawing, on materials provided by the Education Department of The Wordsworth Trust and on the comments teachers were kind enough to send me. Thirdly, the secondary sources were booklets, worksheets, museum objects, and the journals of Dorothy Wordsworth rather than information books. My involvement with all this began with a summer holiday visit to Dove Cottage and Museum. Above the shop was a display of the work of children who had made school visits. I discovered that the educational team offered children from 5 to 18, from Key Stage 1 to Advanced Level, an appropriate programme including an exploration of social, historical, literacy and environmental themes to bring alive the life and times of the Wordsworths.[2]

Let us look at the materials and experiences provided with special reference to a visit made by 10-year-olds from a Colchester School.[3]

Preparation for the visit

The children whose experience we follow were staying at Ashley Bank Centre to carry out a broad and varied programme of work which included map reading, nature study, sketching, science and mathematics as well as history. It is a splendid exmaple of the rich cross-curricular work which I think is the best way of interpreting and carrying out the National Curriculum in primary schools. However, here my special concern is with the history focus in the work Mrs B. prepared for the visit to Dove Cottage and the museum by reading selected Wordsworth poems together with extracts from Dorothy Wordsworth's journals. The pre-visit school pack contains information about the walk, the artefacts in the museum and a copy of Nancy Martin's booklet, *William and Dorothy Wordsworth at Dove Cottage*. Some abler older juniors would be able to read this interesting, illustrated material on their own but Mrs B. reads it out loud so that all the children can begin reflecting on what they are going to experience.

The walk

This starts and finishes at Dove Cottage and the education staff adapt it for any age group. The walk is based on the eighteenth-century picturesque convention of having special stopping points from which the landscape can be viewed. The guides read extracts from Dorothy's journals and William's poems. Dorothy Wordsworth's journals are worth reading as a source of information about one particular sort of life in the early 1800s. She often writes like a naturalist bringing alive the countryside and creatures that

lived in Grasmere. The journals also give fascinating insight into Wordsworth's poetry, particularly the experience that inspired it, and children
preparing for visits to Dove Cottage often hear extracts from it. A favourite anecdote from the journal is the entry for 3 October 1800, as it sheds
light on the writing of Wordsworth's poem 'Resolution and Independence',
called 'The Leech-Gatherer' before its publication in 1807.

> When William and I returned from accompanying Jones we met an old man
> almost bent double, he had on a coat thrown over his shoulders above his
> waistcoat and coat. Under this he carried a bundle and had an apron on and a
> nightcap. His face was interesting. He had dark eyes and a long nose.

There follow further details about the man's origins and family, then
Dorothy explains his work had been gathering leeches to sell for medical
purposes.

> His trade was to gather leeches, but now leeches are scarce and he had no
> strength for it. He lived by begging and was making his way to Carlisle where
> he should buy a few godly books to sell. He said leeches were very scarce
> partly owing to this dry season, but many years they have been scarce – he
> supposed owing to their being much sought after, that they did breed fast, and
> were of slow growth. Leeches were formerly two and sixpence a hundred;
> they are now thirty shillings!
> (Dorothy Wordsworth, *The Grasmere Journal*, illustrated 1987
> edition, Michael Joseph, London)

Children find this fascinating, and in the course of a nature walk the
places where leeches were gathered are pointed out.

> He told, that to these waters he had come
> To gather leeches, being old and poor:
> Employment hazardous and wearisome!
> And he had many hardships to endure
> From pond to pond he roamed, from moor to moor:
> ('Resolution and Independence', 'The Leech-Gatherer', lines
> 99–103)

In the Dove Cottage booklet it is explained: 'The man had made a living by
collecting leeches from ponds which he would sell to doctors for use in
bleeding patients!'

Thus children are offered a very rich experience through both poetry and
biographical writing brought to life by being read out loud in the very
places which gave rise to both kinds of writing; questions, discussions and
collaboration were encouraged.

Visit to Dove Cottage

School parties are taken on a guided tour round the cottage. Here is part of
Richard's response to the experience.

Dove Cottage
It was Monday morning, everybody was excited, we were going on a trip to Grasmere to see Dove Cottage. Dove Cottage is where William Wordsworth lived with his wife and two children, his wife was called Mary. A guide showed us round the house and told us how it used to be. She said that it used to be an inn, and that the walls were painted with pigs' blood so that the walls didn't get stained by tobacco smoke. She said most house floors were just beaten earth, but Dove Cottage was stone, because if someone spilt ale it would turn into mud. William Wordsworth bought the inn and turned it into a house. He bought the house because it was close to the hills, and he loved to walk through the hills and write poems. William Wordsworth was Poet Laureate.

Wendy also responded in writing to the experience:

Who lived in Dove Cottage?
Dove Cottage was William Wordsworth's first house. It was an inn for a while and then it got changed to a house and William and his sister Dorothy moved in on the Christmas Eve of 1799. A couple of years later William married a lady called Mary Simpson. She then moved into Dove Cottage with William. During their marriage they had five children. Three of them were born in Dove Cottage. When the first three children were born Mary's sister Sarah moved in with them to help look after the children. After a while the house started to get a bit cramped with everyone in it so the Wordsworths family moved out and into a cottage called Alban Bank. This was where the other two children were born.

   Mary and William had a favourite daughter and she was called Dora.

   I enjoyed Dove Cottage very much and I think that it was because we were looking at things that had actually belonged to William Wordsworth and were antiques. They were so precious that you were not allowed to touch most things and we weren't allowed to sit down on any of the chairs. The stairs were also a bit rickety.

   After we had seen downstairs we went upstairs and saw William's study. William never wrote himself: he always dictated to Mary or Dorothy as he complained it gave him hand and backache.

This account seems to me to be a successful integration of what had been read from Nancy Martin's booklet before the visit and what had been heard in the guided tour and what had been touched and seen. Terms like 'for a while' and 'a couple of years', 'a bit cramped' and 'stairs were also a bit rickety' are clearly not copied out of written materials and suggest this young writer is in full control of her material. She enjoyed it all because they looked at the actual possessions of the Wordsworths.

   Neil picks out an interesting detail in his writing: 'Wordsworth's cottage was quite interesting, especially the burn mark that the coal bucket had made.'

   Helen uses the information in a fictionalized account which nevertheless draws very successfully on all the information she had acquired.

I rushed into the family room and looked out of the window. The sun had come up showing up the whiteness of Dove Cottage. Lilac flowers climbed the wall: upstairs I could hear father talking to guests so I went outside. I walked around the house peeping into open windows and looking. The sparrows had built their nests under Aunt Dorothy's window. I could hear them talking and quarrelling just like human beings.

The first drop of rain came and got heavier and heavier. I raced indoors. Mother was sewing and Pepper was sitting washing his whiskers. Peeping into the wooden basket I saw a lost visiting card at the bottom.

'Mother, mother, look at this, a visiting card,' I cried.

'Who from?' asked mother.

'Walter Scott,' I replied, reading the faded writing. Mother took the card and left.

This is only about a quarter of a very well sustained account by a young writer who has made a creative attempt to bring alive a little bit of the past.

The museum

In line with the National Curriculum guidelines on the value of 'hands on' opportunities to handle and reflect on objects from the past, children can now handle, discuss, draw and write about selected objects from nineteenth-century domestic life in the education room at Dove Cottage.

The children are encouraged to explore and ask questions about the objects and to have a guess at what they think they might have been used for. One boy jotted down the following hypotheses after cogitating on some rake-like objects: 'I think these are garden rakes and tools, or they could be used to scrape the coals out of the fire.' Thus thinking like an historian is encouraged from the earliest stages.

The visit to the museum is partially structured by The Wordsworth Collection of Discovery Sheets which children can use either individually or in pairs. These are not the 'one-word answer' type of worksheet but specially designed aids to provoke written response about Wordsworth and about 'wider aspects of writing, language and life in the past'. Pupils are guided towards a variety of types of writing including original manuscripts which show the drafting process, notebooks, letters and diaries. The discovery sheets constantly encourage the linking of past and present. For example, the children are asked to look at a picture of Wordsworth's schoolroom at Hawkshead and to 'write down some of the ways in which it is different from our own classroom'.

They are also asked to read one of Dorothy Wordsworth's letters to Coleridge and to consider how it differs from a letter they might write today.

Let us return to Richard's account to see what he made of the museum visit:

After the guide had shown us around the house we went into the Wordsworth Trust Museum. It was interesting and we found that William was born in

1770, and died in 1850 at the grand old age of 80 years. It gave us his life story on earphones, he liked ice-skating on Grasmere.

Nothing passive about this – Richard writes briefly but with his own voice about his visit.

Making their own information books

One satisfying outcome of the Ashley Bank, Grasmere visit for the Colchester 10-year-olds was the making of large, hardbacked, individual and shared books, beautifully presented with hessian binding, cloth collages and pictures with a protective cellophane covering. Enormous care had gone into each of the four sent to me: Wendy's with beautiful marbled mounts and inviting headlining; C. and S.'s splendid combined book with a twenty-item contents page; Neil's well-illustrated book with touches of humour about the social side of the trip; Lisa's with an exquisite cloth collage of the kinds of flower common in Grasmere and with a separate contents page for each chapter.

These fine books show that this kind of writing can be extremely satisfying. It is evident that the children had learnt not only about retrieval devices and setting the information down clearly and accurately, but about how information books work, how, for example, the order of sub-topics matters and that headlining can be a device for taking the reader through the text. Use of maps, labelled diagrams, photographs, quizzes and illustrations all indicate control over the information book genre and an awareness of what might be of interest to the readers.

On their return they read out their work at assembly to the rest of the school, parents and other visitors and finally presented a display of all the work.

Summary

- This example shows how history can be brought alive by a range of experiences, including collaborative discussion, 'hands on' experience like exploring the museum artefacts, actually seeing the things mentioned in the poetry and journals during the walk round Grasmere, secondary experiences like listening to the guide's talk and reading pamphlets, booklets and museum materials.

- Constant help was given through the museum's materials in making links between past and present.

- The 10-year-olds whose writing was included were managing to integrate all this and to find their own voices in their informational and fictionalized accounts.

- The special presentation and display brought all the experiences and efforts to a climax and made it possible to share all this with an audience.

- Books, however good, are not a sufficient resource to support primary history work. A range of first- and second-hand experience is often needed to make the past accessible and significant.

Shorter glimpses

Identifying birds: 6-year-olds in a Croydon infant school

The teacher had helped the children to set up a bird table in the quadrangle just outside their classroom with bird seed and water. Inside was a table with books about birds and children's own writing and drawings. The window above the table was partially covered with paper with a viewing space to allow the children to watch the birds without frightening them away. Some of the children had bird-spotting diaries with dated sightings of particular birds. While I was there I noticed that identifying the birds from the books was often collaborative. While Sarah hunted through, Sam shouted reminders, 'Don't forget it has a pinky chest and grey bits'. When the picture of a chaffinch was reached the little group of children who had seen it all shouted 'Yes, that's it' and proceeded to record the details in their bird-spotting diaries. Using the books here had a purpose the children could understand. The teacher told me that they often browsed through the books as well as using them when a bird actually alighted on the table. All sorts of exciting work arose from this enterprise including graphs to show which birds visited the table most frequently and lively art work.

Books used
Ladybird Book of Garden Birds.
Watts, Barrie (1989) *Bird's Nest,* Stopwatch Books, A. & C. Black, London.
Usborne's Bird Spotting Book, Usborne, London.
Gree, Alain (1990) *Birds,* Questions about Nature series, Franklin Watts.

From fiction to fact: 8–9-year-olds

This class, in a junior school in Croydon, enjoyed the teacher's reading of *Mrs Frisby and the Rats of Nimh* by Robert O'Brien (Victor Gollancz, 1972, London). Mrs Frisby, a field mouse, seeks the help of rats in moving her home from the dangers of the farmer's tractor and becomes involved in turn in helping them. The children were very interested in Nicodemus' account of how some of the rats were caught and locked in cages in a laboratory.

> That cage was my home for a long time. It was not uncomfortable; it had a floor of some kind of plastic, medium soft and warm to the touch; with wire

walls and ceiling, it was airy enough. Yet just the fact that it was a cage made it horrible. I, who had always run where I wanted, could go three hops forward, three hops back again, and that was all. But worse was the dreadful feeling – I know we all had it – that we were completely at the mercy of someone we knew not at all, for some purpose we could not guess. What were their plans for us?

What was in store soon becomes clear: captivity, injections, experiments.

Many of the children were usually rather reserved, but they asked a lot of questions about keeping animals in laboratories. Was it right to experiment on animals? Why was it done? Was it all right for medical purposes, less so for cosmetics?

The teacher brought in Miles Barton's *Why Do People Harm Animals?* (Aladdin Books, 1988) to help structure the discussion. A photograph of a monkey hideously made up and dressed dominates the front cover. The impact of this picture was considerable and the teacher felt it summed up for the children the most unacceptable side of animal experimentation. Animals are made to live extremely unnatural and miserable existences often for relatively trivial purposes like yet another shampoo or perfume. However, the good thing about Miles Barton's book is that it takes on the complexity of the issues and makes it clear that there is more than one point of view. The teacher read it out loud and also the children took turns to borrow it. In a way that the children could understand it explains that some people think all animal experiments are wrong on principle; others think as animals are less intelligent than us having only a present, not a past and future as well as humans have, that we should feel free to do whatever seems necessary; a middle way is to distinguish between experiments for cosmetics and experiments to help find cures for human diseases. It was partly coming to appreciate the way different arguments could be supported that was so educative. This seemed to me an example of the provision of just the right book at the right psychological moment. It also confirms the power of the best fiction to start off speculation and interest that go beyond the enjoyment of the book.

Rainforest creatures: special needs group, 10–11-year-olds

South East London Primary School.

Danny, Dean, Lisa and Chris had not yet achieved the ability to write down their ideas and thoughts without a great deal of support. My task was to work with them for an hour each week and to help them with informational reading and writing.

They all agreed they were interested in animals, and, as the class teacher was working with the whole class in the area of conservation, we finally decided to make our special topic 'rainforest creatures'.

We gathered together wall charts and books. I read *Where the Forest Meets the Sea* as a beginning and the children liked the unusual pictures which were photogrpahs of collages made of natural objects like sand, leaves, nuts and tree barks. A young boy is taken by his father to the Australian rainforest where they spend the day exploring and enjoying the beauty of the surroundings. The final picture shows in faint outline superimposed on a picture of forest what could replace all the loveliness of nature if the forest was to be cut away to make way for technological progress. This was a useful background to our study and seemed to communicate to the children, in a way that a more conventional information book might not have, the threat the rainforests face. It was a focus for lively discussion.

There are large numbers of books and materials about the rainforests, or more generally about conservation with a section on this topic. The children enjoyed talking about the pictures in books like *Earth Watch* (P. Horton *et al.*, 1990) but found the text far too difficult. With help they managed to read some of the writing in the information boxes, for example 'As many as eight out of ten of all known insects live in the rainforest. 41,000 kinds of insects were found in a study of the Peruvian rainforest including 12,000 different kinds of beetles.' This led to our search for pictures and further information about rainforest insects like the rhinoceros beetle, the praying mantis, the thorn shield bug, ants and ant spiders, hercules beetles and long-horned grasshoppers. I have to say that the children preferred to draw and label the insects rather than attempting any extended writing.

One of the most accessible of the books we used was M. Bright's *Tropical Rainforests* (World About Us series, Franklin Watts). The print is very clear and the pictures showing the animals living in the canopy and understory clear and attractive.

A main problem was finding books which went into more detail about particular animals as the children wanted to write about their chosen creatures: tigers, snakes, toucans and parrots. It meant searching through a lot of books to find the required information, and sometimes motivation sagged. The headteacher asked if the children would produce some writing and pictures to make a presentation to a group of younger children. This gave the group a renewed sense of purpose. They produced beautiful drawings on labelled charts, some poems, and with a great deal of help from me a few sentences in their own nicely illustrated books about the rainforest and their chosen creature.

Danny and Lisa asked if they could read 'Where the forest meets the sea' at the beginning of their presentation. They practised it and discussed how they would introduce each double-spread illustration.

The presentation went well and I think the children benefited from small group discussion and special help in finding their way round contents pages and indexes. However, progress was slow and as teachers know, even by age 10 a small minority of children have not managed to achieve enough success in reading and writing abilities to confront the more book-based work of the secondary school with confidence. I am not going to suggest there is an easy answer to this. Collaborative work with an adult in small groups seems to be one way forward. Unfortunately schools cannot often afford this kind of extra human resource.

Notes

1. G. agrees that Ian Redpath's *The Giant Book of Space* would, if it had been available, have been a helpful and inspiring resource for this age group.

2. The Wordsworth Trust won the Sandford Award for Heritage Education in 1990. The Heritage Education Trust citation includes the following praise: 'The organization of educational groups is an object lesson for small properties. A place to make the spirits soar.'

3. I asked Nancy Martin how the experience was made valuable and appropriate for the very youngest children. She said that many 5- and 6-year-olds were brought to the cottage in the context of work on 'old houses'. They very much enjoyed seeing and handling the things the Wordsworths used, jugs, garden implements, items of clothing and so on. Many of the children were helped to write their own version of the happenings in Wordsworth's poem 'Lucy Grey'.

11
YOUNG 'EXPERTS' TALK ABOUT THEIR READING

When some of the children asked Mrs E. about fossils she told them what she knew . . . but then she said they should talk to Michael and me as we were the class experts, especially on dinosaur remains and we know the books that explain things best.

(Kieron, age 8 years)

There is no doubt in all our minds that one of the most important tasks facing the teacher . . . is to increase the amount and range of their voluntary reading.

(The Bullock Report, DES, 1975, p. 126)

If we want children to look upon books as a necessary and rewarding source of knowledge then we need plenty of non-fiction books in our classrooms, for two particular purposes. One is to support areas of learning which we, as teachers, are anxious for the children to study, such as the local environment or the Norman Conquest. The other is to allow them to pursue their own particular interests and enthusiasms.

(McKenzie and Warlow, 1977, p. 45)

This final chapter celebrates the sheer enthusiasm of some young readers who have found great satisfaction in reading non-fiction on subjects of special interest to them. Some general observations which suggest how we might encourage all children to delight in voluntary reading are made.

Sex differences

When I was researching in school with this chapter in mind one thing pressed itself on my attention: for some reason teachers in general tended to suggest boys rather than girls when asked who was an eager reader of non-fiction on a particular topic. There is some evidence that boys as young as age 5 seek out reading associated with their other interests while girls often prefer to extend their reading of stories (Clark, 1976, p. 11). The Extending Beginning Reading project also found boys chose more information books than girls (Southgate *et al.*, 1981, p. 223).

A teacher working at the older end of a primary school suggested to me that girls and boys may model their reading preferences partly on what they see their parent of the same sex read. Girls tend to notice their mothers and older sisters reading novels and watching fiction on television. The boys, on the other hand, often see their fathers reading newspapers and non-fiction like car manuals and sports magazines. This may be connected with the fairly consistent finding that boys are very generally more forthcoming about their interests and hobbies than girls and more likely to perceive themselves as 'experts'. A very interesting case study is set out in detail in Donald Fry's *Children Talk About Books* (1985), Chapter 2: Clayton at age 7 is very involved with his father's job in agriculture. He looks at his father's journal, *Farmer's Weekly*, accompanies him to shows and helps him with combine harvesting and other farm tasks. In his home are books on trains, horses, wild flowers and all aspects of farming and agriculture.

Whenever the opportunity to write a book at school arose Clayton's choice would be something like tractors or farm animals. On one occasion he produced an information leaflet on 'Bugs' which he took home for his father. While welcoming Clayton's interest and expertise his teacher's reports make it clear they wanted him to enjoy fiction as well as informational material. Here is a clear case of a boy modelling his reading interest on his father's occupation.

Of course, we must not make the mistake of adding to the stereotyping of reading interests by over-stating the case. Many men read and enjoy fiction and many women read newspapers and a variety of non-fiction. The teacher making the original observation went on to say that in her experience girls made sense of non-fiction at least as well as boys when they used books for a particular purpose like a school project. It occurred to her that this year in her class, three girls had produced outstanding project books on pollution, and had researched in a thorough and mature way, seeking out a range of resources including pamphlets, charts and publicity material as well as books.[1]

Another teacher who was aware of this issue told me she tried to notice special strengths in all the children and to encourage both girls and boys to share interests and knowledge in group and class discussion. Stereotyped assumptions about who is likely to be interested in dinosaurs, space or wild flowers are best avoided.

It was good to find that in this classroom the 7-year-olds unanimously agreed that Sarah was the computer expert. Using a computer manual as a rough guide she managed to rewrite the instructions in a simplified form for the other children.

In another classroom 5-year-old Gemma sought out books in the classroom on spiders and minibeasts. While I was waiting to talk to the headteacher after school and she was waiting for her older sister to take her home she talked to me about spiders and insisted on showing me every picture in Lionel Bender's large book *Spiders*. She very much wanted to talk about the pictures and asked for help in understanding some of them. 'Where is its head?' 'Has it got eyes?' 'Why is that picture so big?' The pictures of rare spiders, often exotically coloured and many times magnified, looked very different from the little brown garden spiders she and her friend had found outside the classroom. Her concept of what to include in the 'spider' category had thus been broadened by what she saw in the book. This is the kind of involvement we need to encourage in children of both sexes from the earliest stages.

Less able readers

Just as we should not think inflexibly about which topics each sex might find interesting, we should not assume only the most able readers are likely to become experts. 'It is a restatement of a fact often noted by junior teachers that reluctant readers can often be won over by being introduced to books at an appropriate level concerned with their individual hobbies, pets or other interests' (Southgate *et al.*, 1981, p. 222). There is a perfect example of a keen interest providing the motivation for two boys who found reading hard to try again in *Reading Matters* (McKenzie and Warlow, 1977). Two 9-year-old friends found a toad under a log and in order to set up a terranium and to care for the creature they consulted the *Clue Book of Freshwater Animals* (Clue Books, Oxford University Press, 1964). Judy Hargreaves comments that one of the boys basically learnt to read using Judy Hawes' *What I like about Toads*. The boys found that their toad could leap 47 centimetres. But the books they consulted, sometimes getting abler readers to help them, said different things about how far a toad could leap and whether frogs or toads leapt further. The teacher felt the boys became able to classify, corroborate, analyse and interpret by relating their first-hand study of the creature to the information they felt motivated to find in books (McKenzie and Warlow, 1977, p. 47).

Favourite topics

Over some years of working and teaching in primary schools I have come across many young experts. Enthusiasms encountered most often include:

- phenomena made by human beings – vehicles like cars, boats, trains, aeroplanes and trams and objects like guns, windmills, space technology and machines;

- the huge category of course, of natural history – wild flowers, trees, minibeasts, birds (particularly owls and birds of prey like hawks) and pet animals like rabbits, guinea pigs, hamsters, mice, rats, fish, cats, dogs and horses;

- geographical enthusiasms like volcanoes and earthquakes;
- music and modern dance;
- history (often centring on a period like The Romans or The Tudors);
- making collections, for example of stamps or stickers;
- sport and games like chess.

Some of these interests and hobbies are by their nature more likely to involve first-hand experience than secondary sources. If your hobby is playing chess or dancing, reading about it would at best be secondary. Sometimes an interest lends itself instead of reading to writing your own book. Other hobbies like collecting stamps and pictures are gathered together in an album and any writing tends to be basic labelling. Children make all kinds of books at school and the sense of achievement and ownership that accompanies this is extremely satisfying. However, the young expert is just as likely to make a book at home. Eight-year-old Richard made 'A Book of Chess' which had a contents page detailing the twelve sections on the different pieces, on symbols, castling and co-ordinates. Diagrams as well as writing explained the rules.

Summary

- There is some evidence that boys are more likely to choose non-fiction in preference to stories than girls and to be perceived as 'experts' by teachers.

- It is a good thing for teachers to know this so that both kinds of reading can be encouraged in both sexes.

- Some of the topics which seem to interest children during the primary years involve more reading of non-fiction than others. Commitment to a hobby or enthusiasm can lead to increased motivation to read.

Naturally the more detailed examples that follow centre on children's reading to develop an interest. Provision of exciting books and materials at school can inspire enthusiasms and teachers can help children extend their voluntary reading. But one thing I have learnt as a parent and a teacher is that you cannot be enthusiastic for someone else! My own children promptly dropped embryonic interests if I made the mistake of being over-eager on their behalf. The whole point about being a young expert is that you are self-motivating.

First I offer a glimpse of 5-year-old Samantha's reading interest. I find the youngest children often change their favourite topic frequently as they become excited and interested in what they experience first hand and what they read. I include Samantha's because her understanding of how an information book works was so impressive and interesting. By the junior school stage interests have sometimes stabilized and I include Michael and Kieron's reading interests because of the great degree of commitment they bring to their researches into fossil evidence. 1991 is the year of the dinosaur as so much new evidence seems to be emerging, but Michael and Kieron have been interested for a long time. In the final case study I consider an example of an interest awakening as a result of something offered in school which for Charlotte, Andrew and Stephen became a more permanent focus for their reading.

Samantha: Dinosaurs

Samantha, who is 5 and in the reception class of a small suburban Roman Catholic primary school, enjoys reading both stories and non-fiction. She told me she has a lot of books about animals at home and at the moment her special reading interest is in dinosaurs. In her school tray was a huge, beautifully illustrated book entitled *Dinosaurs* by Ron Taylor (Picture Facts series, Grisewood and Dempsey, 1981).[2]

Samantha was eager to show me the illustrations and was able to read out loud the bold headlines at the top of each double spread. She read the headline 'Spikes and shields' to me and then pointed to the distinctive head shapes of the dinosaurs in this group. When she came to the headline 'Jurassic jaws' she had a strategy for reading out the word 'Jurassic' but did not of course understand the meaning. But 'jaws' was easily within her grasp and she pointed to the fierce looking dinosaur head on this double spread remarking, 'If I put my hand in his mouth he would bite me and I would be in tears . . . sharp, sharp teeth and look at that one, there is a skeleton of that one. His teeth are the same.' Thus she seemed aware of how the illustrations in an information book are organized: how they relate not only to the text but to each other. Further evidence of her understanding was apparent when she showed me on another page a series of cartoon-like pictures showing how a dinosaur body would gradually decay and change until it became a fossil. She explained to me that 'First he has his skin, then he has only got his bones.'

Her favourite page showed a young dinosaur emerging from her egg (p. 15). 'It is lovely and pink,' she said 'and they come out of eggs like chicks. The shell breaks and out they get.' Again her understanding of how to interpret pictures an diagrams was impressive.

It was the beautiful, large illustations which had invited this young reader into the book. She remarked that 'the pictures look real.' Samantha was able to concentrate until we had turned every page and she insisted on attempting to read out loud every headline. She expected what she read to be shown and extended in the accompanying pictures. Not all of the ideas in the book, which was probably intended for older children than Samantha, were accessible to her. She asked me why one of the major headings was 'The second age of the dinosaurs', and using the diagrams of the layers of the earth I tried to explain that we get a clue from where a fossil is found, how deep it lies in the earth, about whether it was one of the very earliest creatures or amongst those that lived later. Such great stretches of time are difficult for all of us to comprehend but Samantha listened attentively.

Finally we came to the end of the book and the headline 'What happened?' Samantha said, 'I think it got colder and colder and their food could not grow and they got very hungry and then they died.' Samantha had other dinosaur books at home and it may be that someone suggested this to her. Even so I think she expressed a hypothesis about why dinosaurs died out very clearly for a child of this age.

Michael and Keiron: fossils and extinct creatures

Michael, age 9, and Kieron, age 8, were in the second year of their junior school when I made my series of visits to their classroom to visit one of my students carrying out his first teaching practice. Mrs E., the class teacher, mentioned that Michael had expressed an intention to become a palaeontologist when he grew up. His considerable knowledge about how fossil remains are interpreted came to light when the whole class were learning about fossils and bones in science. Kieron, also an enthusiast, brought in his ammonite, one of his nine fossils at home, for the science interest table and explained that he shared Michael's interests and this had led to them being friends out of school. They swapped books and tried to encourage joint family outings to the Science Museum. Kieron told me that while he enjoyed reading about fossils he did not claim to match Michael in degree of dedication and knowledge, although he was catching up. Of course, you find a number of children in nearly every classroom who claim an interest in fossils and dinosaurs, but Michael's interest seems to me out of the ordinary in its maturity and intensity. Both children talked to me for lengthy periods and brought books from home in carrier bags as well as directing me to the relevant section in the school library which they knew intimately (see Table 11.1). I learnt a great deal about both fossils and about the children's books available on the topic. In all about fifty different books were discussed and evaluated and quite complicated matters were explored, for example the latest theories on why dinosaurs became extinct, the precise dating of other extinct species and the different ways in which experts categorize the different creatures. It is possible only to give a flavour of all this here. Although many of the conversations involved both children, and the collaborative element clearly made their research more enjoyable, I focus on each young reader in turn.

Table 11.1   Talking about fossils with Kieron (8) and Michael (9) summer term 1991; both boys have brought in favourite books from home to show me

Key

M: Michael
K: Kieron
R: Researcher

Speaker	Utterance	Notes
K	This one on prehistoric animals is copyright	*Prehistoric Animals* by Peter Zallinger.
R	Meaning?	
K	You've no right to copy the pictures or writing!	
R	You can write for permission to quote.	
K	This book is more for children like Michael and me who already know something about the topic. The colours of the creatures are good . . . the camouflage of the edaphosaurus is clear there. And you can see the texture of the skin of the struthomian.	
M	This picture dictionary has a good contents page and index and also helps with pronouncing dinosaurs' names. And it shows you how to make things – a trilobite, how to make a time dial, how to identify fossils.	*Children's Picture Dictionary* by Anne McCord, Usborne, 1977.
R	Do you think some books have too much on a page sometimes?	
M	Yes. But it depends what they include. If it is all related you can have a lot. This book is good because it puts special bits in boxes with borders round them – that helps. And headlines to guide us – 'The first reptile', 'Land animals of 200 million years ago'.	Mature Understanding of how the format of a book can help the reader. A grown-up reviewer could hardly do better!

K   I like the quiz and the dinosaur timetable on page 14. And look, this picture shows you the heads and jaws of plant-eating and meat-eating dinosaurs to compare.

M   The sort of things I want to know are whether tyrannosaurus was a predator or scavenger, and which theory about how they died is right – climate change, meteorite or predators, and how long it took for them to die out.

       Kieron bought a new book which looks a little bit at the dinosaur period and then shows you what might have happened after the dinosaurs died out, which creatures dominated then.

> An example of a reader confronting books with his own purposes in mind.
>
> Dinosaur fact file, *Life after the Dinosaurs*, by Mary O'Neill, Hamlyn, 1988.

K   It's more original to look at the time just after the reign of the dinosaurs. On page 8 it says it seems to have been a sudden ending – a mystery – it says it might have been a dramatic climate change or a meteor crash. There is about half writing, half illustration – just right.

R   It is kind of you to bring in your fossil books from home to show me.

K   These are not all of them! I could not carry all 20 of them.

M   I've got over 20. Some are the same as Kieron's, but if we have a different one we swop them. We made friends when we found we both liked fossils and dinosaurs.

> Clearly collaborating with a friend over reading is very motivating.

K   I think Michael knows a little bit more than me about some things. We try to get our parents to take us both to the Natural History Museum to see the fossils and models. Last time there was a wonderful display of evolution. You walked from room to room to see how creatures evolved. We spent hours in there.

R   How did Mrs E. find out you both had an interest in fossils?

M   We were doing rocks and bones in science and she said we knew more than she did about fossils and things. She said we were experts!

Michael

Michael thinks his interest in fossils began at about the age of 3 when he was taken to an exhibition of bones and animal skeletons at the Natural History Museum. The first book he remembers is the *Ladybird Book of Dinosaurs,* followed swiftly by Anne McCord's *Dictionary of Dinosaurs,* Michael Benton's *A–Z Guide of Dinosaurs,* Steve Parker's *Dinosaurs and How They Lived* and David Lambeth's *The Age of Dinosaurs.*

He gains great enjoyment from reading and writing about his interest, and although he is less extrovert than Kieron he is very willing to share his knowledge and enthusiasm with anyone willing to listen. At the time of writing he is greatly looking forward to giving a talk to his cub pack on fossil evidence.

His reading has led to an ability to make generalizations about his topic – the result of internalizing information over several years. He can apply what he has read appropriately too. Kieron had just remarked that when you find an animal's fossilized jaw bone you can tell by the bluntness or sharpness of the teeth whether a creature is a vegetarian, meat-eater or omnivore. Michael adds, 'Yes, but you can also find out about the diet from the dinosaur coprolites – the droppings that might still be preserved, specially in swamps.'

Michael constantly speculates and hypothesizes: when he, Kieron and myself were considering ways of dinosaurs protecting themselves, he suggested

> the small ones could probably run away quite quickly. Some were more intelligent than others, I think. The tall ones might position themselves so they could see into the distance and check whether danger was coming. But no one is really sure which meat-eating dinosaurs were predators and which ones were just scavengers.

Michael understands that non-fiction can be placed in categories too. He remarks that the information stories which can invite new enthusiasts into the topic tend not to have contents pages and indexes but that there may be notes at the end 'so that parents and teachers can answer the children's questions.' Dinosaurs and other prehistoric creatures lived in a very different world from our own; Michael recommends books like the *Ladybird Book of Dinosaurs* and Kieron's *Dinosaur Pop-up Book* as these show young children 'the kind of environment the creatures lived in.' Books which help children pronounce the difficult names, like McCord's *Dictionary of Dinosaurs,* meet with his approval and books which encourage 'doing and making things – making a trilobite or a time dial, your own time line and checklist for identifying fossils.'

He has mature ideas on what makes an information book clear and inviting. A lot of pictures and information on one double page is all right as long as it is all 'related'. Clearly he is not in favour of the kind of miscellaneous jumbles the less appealing books inflict on us! It helps if special bits of information are in boxes with borders round them. Headlines like 'The first reptile', or 'Land animals of 200 million years ago' can guide us in using the book. He approves of *Althea's Dinosaurs* (Dinosaur Publications, 1987) as 'it says the author was advised by the palaeontology department at the Natural History Museum.'

In developing his interest further, Michael says he is always on the look out for books with the latest theories and the kind of detailed information he feels ready for: books which assess the very latest material or theories of how dinosaurs died. 'Was it climate change, a meteorite, predators or a mixture of all these?' He also sought books which would help him answer his questions about the period before and after dinosaur domination and was delighted when Kieron offered to lend him Mary O'Neill's *Life after the Dinosaurs* (Dinosaur Fact File, Hamlyn, 1989). He considers the guide and books on fossils written by the Science Museum specialists are likely to be the most up-to-date source of information.

Another thing I noticed about Michael was his mature peception of himself as a reader. Not only had he come to understand relatively simple things like how to pronounce the lesser known dinosaur names, but he realized that even fossil evidence could only offer partial answers. He was in Bruner's sense coming to think like a scientist.

Kieron

Kieron tends to defer to Michael's greater knowledge about fossils ('I think Michael knows more than I do about some things') but I found his enthusiasm just as convincing. His approach was more playful than Michael's: in a book he had made he wrote a little piece about 'the author' and part of it read thus: 'Kieron Miles is aged 9 and has been interested in dinosaurs for a very, very long time (but not as far back as when the dinosaurs lived!)'. His illustrations usually showed a creature doing something, for example, a plesiosaurus catching a fish or a tyrannosaurus grabbing a victim. He thinks he was interested in the topic as far back as he can remember, perhaps at age 3. When he was younger he remembers gaining great enjoyment out of drawing dinosaurs and fossils and playing with dinosaur toys and games.

What struck me most about Kieron was his appreciation of the social side of learning. Dipping into his carrier bag of books to share with me he drew out Barry Cox's *Prehistoric Life* (The Children's Illustrated Library 8–12, Macmillan, 1978) explaining, 'I got this for my birthday – people know I'm interested in bones and that kind of thing'.

A lot of his comments on the book were directed towards Michael as well as myself. Still looking at *Prehistoric Life* he said of a picture of a sloth, 'Look at this one Michael, it shows a skeleton – what we would find – then the next picture shows where the flesh would be and the third picture adds the fur.'

I think that while anyone would admire Michael's mature attitude to his research, if I were another child, Kieron's approach might invite me into the topic more enjoyably. After all, dinosaurs can encourage an imaginative response. Story books came out of the carrier bag as well as information books:

> I've just brought this story book, *Nessie goes to Mars* by Francis Mosley (Grafton Books). I've got the others in this series. It is about fantasy creatures – look at those space spiders! But the Loch Ness monster might not be fantasy, it might be a plesiosaurus – people claiming to have seen it say it sort of slides out of the water so it might be an amphibian. I would love to go to the Museum at Loch Ness. And look here is my *Dinosaur Pop-up Book* (Grandreaders Ltd, 1986). I used to cover up the names of the dinosaurs and guess what they were.

One of the next books to emerge was *Time Machine 2* by David Bischoff: *Search for Dinosaurs* (Bantam Books, 1984). 'I like this one. You can travel back 65 million years and find what it would have been like – you can choose different bits of the story.'

Kieron is able to evaluate the books he reads. He praises *All About Dinosaurs* by Rupert Oliver and Bernard Long (Hodder and Stoughton, 1983). He notes that the illustrator uses the strategy of including familiar things like an animal (hen) or a building (house) to suggest the relative sizes of different dinosaurs.

He has read enough books to find discrepancies in information. 'It says' (in the Ladybird *Dinosaurs*) 'the diplodocus was the largest, but books say different things. Some say the supersaurus is bigger, some say the ultrasaurus. I think the dimetrodon was probably the biggest.' He has his own thoughts on how appropriate the meaning of 'dinosaur', mentioned in 'nearly every book', is – 'terrible lizard'. 'But in fact the tiny dinosaurs were not terrible or frightening at all.'

He had read widely enough to understand there are different ways of classifying dinosaurs and had some ideas of his own. 'You can group them into plant- and meat-eaters or ways of protecting themselves. Some used speed, others armour. Some were probably very ferocious and aggressive to put off a predator.'

I asked for his view on a book I was reviewing, *Tyrannosaurus* by Robert Matthews (Firefly Books Ltd, 1990). Kieron commented 'it is large print and quite easy writing. It is a good idea to choose one dinosaur and study it. Yes – for little ones it is good.' He recommended *Dinodots* by Dougal Dixon (Simon and Schuster, 1980) for 'children just beginning to get interested'. He drew out his copy of one of his first books, *Dinosaur Days* by Joyce Milton, and laughed as he showed us the pencil drawings and little bits of writing he had done 'when I was little'. The beginning sentence has always stayed in his memory and clearly made a considerable impact on him: 'Millions of years ago the world belonged to the dinosaurs.' Kieron thought the story form, 'Saltopus lived near a river. Snap! went the croco-diles', would make it a good first book. Kieron read the *Ladybird Book of Dinosaurs* (C. Douglas, 1974) to his younger brother as it starts with a wonderful picture of how the world might have looked long ago. 'I read this to my brother. He was just learning to read – "amphibians" was one of his first words. I explained that "ph" is sometimes said as "f". He liked it as the pictures were quite big and there was not too much writing.'

Michael and Kieron were happy to be a sort of human resource for anyone in the class wishing for advice on bones, fossils and dinosaurs.

Charlotte, Stephen and Andrew: Bats

The next three young 'experts' became enthusiasts as a result of an oppor-tunity in school and we need a little background information first. A class of thirty 10–11-year-olds in a South East London primary school were following a class project on conservation issues. Different groups followed their chosen topics within this and five children chose to study bats as an endangered species. I joined the class on Friday afternoons for a term to help support their reading of non-fiction: the class teacher and headteacher felt that the children's informational reading and writing needed support. Two of the children, Keelley and Kerry, were co-operative and interested while in school but did not carry on their interest further, while Charlotte, Stephen and Andrew became voluntary readers and are therefore the subject of this final case study.[3]

The work included many activities: looking at slides and video film, listening to tape recordings of different species of bat echo-locating, writing and reading poems, writing and reading stories about folklore, reading from a range of non-fiction and writing up the fruits of their research.

The imaginative and informational aspects were mutually enriching. For example, the poetry about bats the children wrote seemed to be effective partly because they integrated their increasingly detailed knowledge about the creatures.

Charlotte

Charlotte was an able child whose abilities to communicate very well in conversation were not yet matched by her written accounts. When I told the group about the association for people interested in bats which had a magazine called *The Young Bat Worker* she wrote down the address and told me the next time we met that she had paid for membership out of her pocket money and awaited the first issue.

Charlotte spent a lot of time at the table I had set up with books and material about bats. She had chosen to make a special study of the Natterer's bat species and said she wanted to use some of the slides and pictures to give a talk to the whole class. The other children liked this idea and the thought of their presentation at the end of their research gave a special sense of purpose.

Charlotte had the most sociable approach to her enthusiasm, often pointing out to the other children parts of books relating to their species of bat, and offering to read out loud items of general interest.

She showed the group the photograph of the hairless bat which is 'ugly and without fur' from *Bat* in the Young Naturalist series (Edward and Clive Turner, p. 68). Charlotte praised this book on account of the unusual and interesting anecdotes. Under 'Unusual pets' Charlotte read, 'Lady Cullen wrote: I had a partly tamed bat when I was a girl. I never handled it but it lived in my room and fluttered down from the ceiling when I called it.' She also found the contents page and very detailed index (75 items) helped her find what she wanted quickly. Illustrations were 'very simple and clear, for example the drawings on page 8 of three kinds of wing – bat's, bird's and pterodactyl's to show the bat's wing is most like a human's hand.' She did say that in a book including all bat species there was relatively little on her chosen bat.

Charlotte felt she had improved her writing during this project. The note-taking strategy we tried as a group – making notes on a sub-topic from several sources and then binding them together in a synthesis – was effective in her case. There was no one book on the Natterer's bat and Charlotte worked hard to find the relevant pages in general books like Phil Richardson's *Bats* and James Robertson's *The Complete Bat*.

Here is just a short example of the sort of writing Charlotte was managing towards the end of our project:

> Baby bats are normally born in June, but the mating is done in the autumn before and the baby does his or her growing inside the mother bat during the spring. Most bats only have one baby but Natterer's bat often has twins. As soon as the baby is born the mother catches it in her tail so he/she does not fall. The baby is at first blind and unable to fly and has special little hooks so it can hang on to the mother's teats when it is feeding.
>
> When the baby is still too young to fly the mother puts the baby in a crevice in the cave wall while she searches for food so she can produce milk for the baby. When she comes back she can tell quickly which is her baby by its sound!

This still does not do justice to Charlotte's ability to give very detailed and coherent oral accounts, but it does suggest that she is beginning to find her own 'voice' in her writing.

Stephen

Stephen was described to me as a lively, athletic boy who was not yet a voluntary reader of either stories or non-fiction. He did read when school work demanded it and managed well with instructions on mathematical and science materials and with reading encyclopaedia items. The teacher noted he liked reading highly illustrated information books on topics like animals and sport. He told me he had always wanted to learn more about bats and his oral contribution to the bat group was considerable. The many visual materials I had provided – video film, slides and recordings of bat sounds – appealed to him more than books with a lot of writing. In fact at first, as you might expect from this thumb-nail sketch, his main intererst in books centred on the illustrations, the photography and diagrams.

The challenge was to encourage Stephen to see writing in books as a way of developing and making more enjoyable his enthusiasm.

I suggested to him that when he took part in the presentation he might be asked questions and he needed to write down some of the things an 'expert' on bats might be expected to know. I put it to him that this would give a structure to his research. This is his first piece of writing:

> I saw a white or greyish coloured bat once on holiday. So far as I know at present, bats are like mice with wings. This is what I would like to find out:
> 1. Why do bats come out at night and not very much during the day?
> 2. Why do some bats have tails and some don't?
> 3. What are a bat's teeth like and how many do they have?
> 4. How high and fast can bats fly?
> 5. Can any kind of bat go under water?
> 6. More about the chosen bat the mouse-eared bat which is getting rare.

Stephen agreed with me that to find the answers to these questions involved looking at written accounts as well as pictures. The group had decided that as well as giving a presentation to the whole class on how to contribute to the conservation of bats, as part of the general work on conservation, they would tell a small group of interested first-year children about their chosen species of bat and answer questions.

This gave Stephen a sense of purpose to take to the written materials and, like the others, he brought back snippets of particularly interesting information to the group discussion which began and ended all our 10 sessions.

I do believe that, while one of our ultimate aims is to encourage independent reading, most children need some input and direction from the teacher. My contribution, as well as providing materials and audience for developing ideas, was to give short talks about, for example, how we classify bats into microchiroptera (small echo-locating bats) and the larger sized bats termed megachiroptera. We also agreed as a group that there were some central aspects of our study. For example, in studying any creature we need to know about its life-cycle, food, habitat and so on. In this particular study we were also interested particularly in threats to bats. As the children's chosen bats were all in the microbat group we needed to understand the quite complicated activity known as echo-location. Here Stephen took a central role, drawing us his own diagrams adapted from those in the books and reading out loud from section 6 in *The Bat in the Cave.*

I became aware of the extent to which Stephen had integrated all that we had been reading and talking about on the occasion of the presentation to the younger children. Using books and slides he and the other children gave interesting and lucid answers to the younger children's questions on bat sizes, breeding and habits. The headteacher on seeing the video was impressed by Stephen's ability to read relevant bits from books to support his answers. When the summer 1991 issue of *The Young Bat Worker* magazine focused on the mouse-eared bat, the species under great threat that Stephen had studied, one of his drawings with a poem he had written were included to his great satisfaction.

Andrew

Andrew had recently arrived from Hong Kong and was learning English as his second language. His interest in the bat project helped him refine his spoken and written English. The small group context made it possible for him to ask for word and phrase meanings and feel confident we would take the time and trouble to help him. He chose the long-eared bat as his specialism and the pictures, slides and video films invited him into the topic. Once fascinated he was eager to attempt the books and pamphlets. He needed a lot of help and support, but I admired his willingness to read out loud to the group from his own writing and from books. Specializing in one bat meant each child was addressed as the 'expert' whenever their bat came up in video film or in the books and materials.

Andrew's interest led to him taking home some of the books and pamphlets like *The Young Bat Worker.* One of the back copies of the latter concentrated on the long-eared bat and Andrew talked the group through the series of drawing showing this bat folding its ears to go to sleep! Andrew found the language in this magazine 'easier than most of the books'. The questions – 'How would you manage to sleep if your ears were nearly as long as your body?' – and the interesting ideas simply expressed helped him understand. Andrew produced quite a lot of writing from notes he made as he scanned the books for sections on 'his' bat. Here is one of his earlier pieces:

> The long-eared bat, he look like a mouse with very long ears. And he has a small head with a big nose. He live in trees and buildings and eat moths and insects. This bat is a microbat and all microbats echo-locate. Female bat has only one or sometimes two babies. Some bats is in danger, but my bat is not. All the microbats in England are asleep in winter.

It did not seem sensible to fuss over a few faulty verb/noun agreements as I felt nothing should discourage Andrew from his sense of satisfaction in writing in his second language. This is clearly his own organization from several sources which is to his credit. Just occasionally he produced a sentence or phrase very obviously copied neat from a book, for example 'They can snatch meals by landing on the ground to secure their prey before becoming airborne and making good its escape'. Teachers rightly discourage wholesale copying from books, but I wonder if in the case of a young second-language learner like Andrew writing out the words and phrases might contribute to learning the new language.

Andrew enjoyed the collaboration with the other children. Often they would point out passages in books dealing with the long-eared bat which they had noticed when skimming through to find references to their own species. He told me that 'this friendly group helps me with my English!' He preferred some of the pamphlets to the books, and particularly *The Young Bat Worker* magazines which had large print, many pictures and a playful approach to bats, while including much valuable information. In our evaluation of materials discussion towards the end of the work Andrew also praised the large information poster, Save Our Bats, published by the Fauna and Flora Preservation Society. There was a large beautiful photograph of the brown long-eared bat showing the distinctive large ears in great detail, every small vein visible. The writing on the posters was challenging and we read it as a group explaining the terminology. Andrew felt able throughout the project to ask what 'chemical', 'nocturnal', 'hibernate', 'roost' and 'adapted' meant. The other children enjoyed explaining these.

What do we learn from success?

What then do these young readers tell us about successful reading of non-fiction?

- Reading to develop an existing interest or reading which creates a new enthusiasm becomes an essentially enjoyable activity. Children are thus often motivated to read beyond their usual level. Interest greatly increases attention span and the good powers of concentration prized in the secondary school years.

- Very young children like Samantha are forming their attitude towards different reading materials and it is important that early non-fiction is inviting. Good illustrations that integrate well with the text and clear headlines are particularly important. Opportunities to share their delight by talking to adults and to other children help encourage a liking for topic books which should have some transfer to other situations.

- Young children learn not only about the topic – dinosaurs, space, mini-beasts or whatever – but also about how an information book works.

- A paradox is that while we think of some interests and hobbies as being activities pursued alone, such interests can be fed and nourished by sharing them with others. Not only do Michael and Kieron enjoy collaborating with each other, they also delight in sharing what they know. This applies also to the bat group. The comments and questions of others help them organize their own thinking and encourage the speculation and hypothesizing characteristic of a keen reader.

- Once children become voluntary readers of non-fiction they tackle the books with a clear purpose. This makes them truly critical readers not only in their increasing understanding of how non-fiction is organized but in judging the strengths and weaknesses of particular texts.

- Teachers can help by sometimes stepping aside and allowing the other children to ask the child experts in an area the questions. This encourages a growing intellectual maturity.

- Our aim is to encourage all children to find in non-fiction a source of pleasure in the furthering of an existing interest or as an awakener of a new interest.

Notes

1. I wrote to Paul Appleby, producer of BBC's *The Really Wild Road Show*, to ask if boys and girls were equally represented as young 'experts'. He answered as follows: 'the sex difference you mention is less prevalent in natural history, partly because girls have a great love of animals, and also because it involves patience and organization, which I think are definitely female traits in the pre-teens! Although I myself have a degree, and earn a living through biology, I am less expert in many areas than the kids I have worked with.' (Letter dated September 1991).

2. The technique of including different sizes of print at different reading levels in Ron Taylor's *Dinosaurs* means readers of different ages can appreciate the book.

3. A more detailed account of the bat project can be found in M. Mallett (1991) Learning from information books in the primary school: some promising strategies, in *Primary Education*, journal of the Education Department of the Chinese University of Hong Kong.

Further reading

Bissex, Glenda (1980) *Gyns at Work*, Harvard University Press, Cambridge, Mass.
Clark, Margaret (1976) *Young Fluent Readers*, Heinemann, London.
Fry, Donald (1985) *Children Talk About Books: Seeing Themselves as Readers*, Open University Press, Milton Keynes and Philadelphia (Chapter 2, Clayton).
McKenzie, Moira and Warlow, Aidan (1977) *Reading Matters*, Hodder and Stoughton, London, pp. 45–56.
Southgate, V., Arnold, H. and Johnson, S. (1981) *Extending Beginning Reading*, Heinemann Educational Books, London, for the Schools Council.

APPENDIX I
CATEGORIES OF CHILDREN'S NON-FICTION: A SUMMARY

NARRATIVE		
Information stories	Biography, Autobiography	Procedural
Main feature is adherence to a time sequence: a creature's life cycle or a person's activities over a period of time. While the form is close to story, the kind of content permissible is much more restricted than the term 'story' might suggest – authors are expected to stick to what is known factually about the phenomena written about.	Accounts of people's lives organized chronologically. The narrative breaks sometimes to evaluate events. We also include here letters, diaries, children's own books and newspaper accounts. Similar to the adult genre, differing mainly in the complexity of the accounts and the language.	Instruction books, manuals, recipes and notices all belong here as do the booklets children themselves make about the routine care of the class pet or how to use the computer.
Jan Taylor (1978) *Sciurus: The Story of a Grey Squirrel* Collins. Barrie Watts (1989) *Tomato* A P C Black David Macauley (1978) *Castles* Collins.	Olivia Bennett (1988) *Annie Besant* Hamish Hamilton. Ruth Thompson (1990) *Washday* Turn of the Century Series, A & C Black.	Barrie Watts (1991) *Grasshoppers and Crickets, Keeping Minibeasts* Franklin Watts. Roma Gans (1984) *Rock Collecting* A & C Black *Usborne's First Cook Book* (1987) A Wilkes and S. Cartright.

Appendix I (*cont*).

NARRATIVE

Information stories	Biography, Autobiography	Procedural
Avoid 'Disney like' illustrations – good photographs or line drawings, probably best. Choose writers sensitive to the rhythms of language. Not only for the very young – this form can be an appealing way into a topic. Sometimes this can be a transitional genre which includes asides giving general information.	Bland accounts best avoided. Most famous people's achievements are assessed differently by different groups (of course not only well known lives are of interest). Controversy is exciting! Newspaper accounts can be used to aid a discussion on bias in writing and the difference between fact and opinion. Choose writers who communicate their own interest successfully in clear vivid language.	Explanations about how to carry out experiments in books work cards, work sheets and charts need of course to be capable of being easily understood by the young readers for whom they are intended.

Reference	Picture books	Exposition (Information books)
The principle of organization may be alphabetical (dictionaries) or topic based (thesauruses and some encyclopaedias for the very young.) Dictionaries and encylopaedias are simpler, sometimes illustrated versions of the adult genres, but the judgements about what to include and leave out are just as important. Atlases and map books belong here. Look out for computer encylopaedias.	The earliest type within this category are books where the organizing principle is a concept like shape, colour, numbers or the letters of the alphabet. This genre can be for any age – for example the remarkable drawings by the child artist, Stephen Wiltshire in books like *Cities*, Dent & Sons, are enjoyed by a wide age range.	Illustrated books on one topic arranged chronologically. Following elements usually present: topic presentation, a description of the attributes of the phenomena and characteristic events, in case of an animal – feeding, breeding and movement. Most new books have contents pages, indexes and glossaries. Often published in series.

Appendix I (*cont*).

	NARRATIVE	
Reference	Picture books	Exposition (Information books)
Collins School Dictionary John Paton *The Kingfisher Children's Encyclopaedia.* Brian Delf (1991) *The Picture Atlas of the World* Dorling Kindersley	John Burningham. *Colours, Opposites, 123, ABC* etc. Walker Books. Charles Keeping *Railway Passage*, Oxford University Press.	Riley, P.D. (1990) *Electricity and Magnetism* Dryad Press. Coldrey, S (1986) *The Squirrel in the Trees* Belitha Press Ltd.
An alphabetical organization of encyclopaedias is often preferred. Children need help in becoming familiar with the format of all the kinds of reference material mentioned.	Pictures and text need to integrate even if they aim to surprise as well as complement. Best examples are the distinctive work of gifted authors & are aesthetically pleasing whether photographs or drawings are used.	Usually best not to have too wide a focus – 'Ants' rather than 'Insects' for younger readers. Clear and appropriate retrieval devices are important and well integrated attractive illustrations. Avoid jumbles of photographs and drawings. Seek good organization of the topic with helpful headings and sub headings and language that is clear and alive. Favour a questioning approach that encourages reflection and recognizes controversy. Seek up-to-date and socially aware books.

APPENDIX II
CHILDREN'S BOOK PRIZES FOR
NON-FICTION

EARTHWORM CHILDREN'S BOOK AWARD

A short list in age categories is drawn up of books on environmental issues published during the preceding year. Tel: Friends of the Earth, 071-490 4734.

1990: John Elkington and Julia Hail, *The Young Greens' Consumer Guide* (illustrations by T. Ross), Gollancz.

TES INFORMATION BOOK AWARD

The junior prize awarded by *The Times Educational Supplement* is for an outstanding work of non-fiction for children up to the age of 9.

1990: Judy Hindley, *The Tree* (illustrations by A. Wisenfeld), Aurum Books.

THE SCIENCE BOOK PRIZE

Under 8s prize awarded by the Science Museum for a book which contributes to our understanding of science.

1990: Ian Redpath *The Giant Book of Space*, Hamlyn.

APPENDIX III
USEFUL ADDRESSES AND JOURNALS REVIEWING CHILDREN'S NON-FICTION

Books for your children, P.O. Box 507, Birmingham B15 3AL.

Bookseller's Association, 12, Dyott Street, London WC1A. Provides information about booksellers specializing in children's books.

Centre for Language in Primary Education, Webber Row, London EC1 8QW. Myra Barrs *et al.* have written *The Primary Language Record Handbook* and its explanatory sequel *Patterns of Learning: The Primary Language Record and the National Curriculum. Tried and Tested* is a review journal of the centre and includes reviews of non-fiction.

Child Education and *Junior Education*, Scholastic Publications, Marlborough House, Holly Walk, Leamington Spa, Warwickshire CV32.

Children's Book Foundation, Book Trust House, 45 East Hill, London SW18 2Q2. Offers advice and information on all aspects of children's reading and books.

Dragon's Teeth, published by The National Committee on Racism in Children's Books, Notting Hill Methodist Church, 7 Denbigh Road, London W11 2SJ.

The Geographical Association, 343 Fulwood Road, Sheffield S10 2DP. Advises on resources to support National Curriculum work.

Growing Point, Margery Fisher (ed.), Old Ashton Manor, Northampton. Fiction and non-fiction reviewed.

The Historical Association, 59a Kennington Park Road, London SE11 4JH. Includes information about primary school resources and about implementing the National Curriculum.

Letterbox Library Children's Book Cooperative, 8 Bradbuy Street, London N16 8JN. Reviews non-sexist multicultural fiction and non-fiction for children.

National Association for the Teaching of English (NATE), 49 Broomsgrove Road, Sheffield S10 2NA. The associated journal *English in Education* often includes articles by practising teachers on children's reading development.

National Book League, Book House, 45 East Hill, London SW18 2Q2. Selected book lists available. Provides an information service.

Primary Science Review. The Journal of the Association for Science Education, College Lane, Hatfield, Herts AL10 9AA.

Rotherham Libraries, Museums and Art Department, Principal Librarian, Youth and Schools Sections, Maltby Library HQ, High Street, Maltby, Rotherham S66 8LA. Collection of 3,000 recently published children's books.

The School Bookshop Association, 6 Brightfield Road, Lee, London SE12 8QF. Publishes *Books for Keeps* which includes non-fiction reviews.

The School Library Association, Publishes *The School Librarian* which reviews non-fiction. Linden Library, Barrington Close, Linden, Swindon SW3 6HF.

Signal, Nancy Chambers (ed.), The Thimble Press, Lockwood, Station Road, Stroud, Gloucestershire GL5 5EQ. Many guides and booklets and reviews of children's books available.

Special Educational Resources Information Service (SERIS), 11 Anson Road, Rusholme, Manchester M14 9BX.

The Times Educational Supplement, Prior House, St John's Lane, London EC1M 4BX. Reviews children's fiction and non-fiction.

United Kingdom Reading Association (UKRA), Administrative Office, c/o Edge Hill College, St Helen's Road, Ormskirk, Lancashire L39 4QP.

The Wandsworth Collection of Early Children's Books, West Hill Library, 36 West Hill, Wandsworth, London SW18 1RZ (4,000 children's books from 1673 to 1940).

APPENDIX IV
CHILDREN'S BOOKS MENTIONED IN THE TEXT – WITH SOME ANNOTATION

Key:

Co	Contents page	G	Glossary
Ch	Chapters	HL	Headlining
Di	Diagrams	In	Index
Dr	Drawings	Ph	Photographs
1	Key Stage 1 (5–7)	Fr	Further reading
2	Key Stage 2 (7–11)		
3	Key Stage 3 11+		

Adams, R. (compiler) (1982) *Wierd and Wonderful Wildlife,* Secker and Warburg. (Co. Dr. Ph. HL. 2.) Some stunning photographs, e.g. p. 107 shows a flying fox bat.

Ahlberg, Alan and Janet (1982) *The Baby's Catalogue,* Kestrel/Penguin Harmondsworth. Much more from a picture dictionary: we follow through Janet Ahlberg's illustrations. 24 hours in the lives of five families and their babies. Includes jokes and games.

Allen, G. and Denslow, J. (1964) *Clare Book of Freshwater Animals*, Clare Books, Oxford Unviersity Press, Oxford.

Aliki Brandenburg, *Dinosaur Bones*, First Sight series, A. & C. Black, London. (Dr. G. In. 1.) Original book following a child's attempt to find out about fossils.

Anno Mitsumasa (1982) *Anno's Journey, Anno's Britain, Anno's Italy, Anno's Medieval World*, Bodley Head. (Dr. 2/3.) In these original and playful books, we get a delightful idiosyncratic mixture of legend, custom, topology and history that make up a country's character.

Ardley, Neil (1990) *Sound Waves to Music*, Hands-on-Science series, Gloucester Press, London. Good retrieval devices and imaginative activities suggested. (Co. Di. Dr. G. HL. In. Ph. 2.)

Baker, J. (1987) *Where the Forest Meets the Sea*, Walker Books, London. Illustrations are photographs of collages made from natural materials.

Barton, Miles (1988) *Why Do People Harm Animals?* Let's Talk About series, Aladdin Books, Gloucester Press, London. (G. HL. In. Ph. 2.)

Bender, Lionel (1986) *Spiders*, First Sight series, A. & C. Black. (Co. In. Ph.) Very fine illustrations.

Bennett, O. (1988) *Annie Besant*, In Her Own Time series, Hamish Hamilton, London. (Co. Ch. Fr. HL. In. Ph. 2/3.) Series celebrates the contribution to society of famous women. The complexity of Besant's life is well communicated.

Benton, M. *Prehistoric Animals: An A–Z Guide*, Kingfisher. (Dr. In. 2/3.) Specialist dictionary for 10+.

Berry, R. (1982) *Mechanical Giants*, Hamish Hamilton, London, (HL. Dr. I.).

Bischoff, D. (1984) *Time Machine 2: Search for Dinosaurs*, Bantam Books.

Bisel, S. (1990) *The Secrets of Vesuvius*, Hodder & Stoughton, Sevenoaks.

Bomford, L. (1986) *Squirrels*, Nature in Close Up series, A. & C. Black. (Co. G. In. Ph. 2.) Inviting text and beautiful photographs. Key words in bold print.

Bright, M. (1990) *Koalas*, Wildlife series, Franklin Watts. (Co. Ch. Di. Dr. Fr. G. HL. In. Ph. Dr. 2.) Excellent layout, photographs and illustrations. In sufficient depth for older juniors. Good treatment of complicated conservation issues.

Browne, A. (1986) *Piggybook,* Julia MacRae, London.

Bruna, Dick (1967) *b is for bear: an abc*, Methuen, London.

Brunsell, A. (1989) *Let's Talk About Bullying*, Gloucester Press, London. (G. HL. In. Ph.)

Burningham, J. *ABC Opposites Book*, Jonathan Cape.

Burningham, J. (1982) *Would You Rather . . .* Jonathan Cape.

Butterworth, C. (1988) *Squirrels*, Macmillan. (Dr. 1.) Bold print and simple text in continuous present tense.

Chambers First Picture Dictionary, edited by Betty Root. For the very young. Contextualizes terms in sentences.

Childcraft, World Book – Childcraft International, World Book House, 77 Mount Ephraim, Tunbridge Wells, Kent TN4 8AZ. A very lively set of 19 books, including atlas and dictionary, appropriately playful and project based. £239.

Children's Britannica, Encyclopaedia Britannica International Ltd., Carew House, Station Approach, Wallington, Surrey SM6 ODA. 7–14 years. £249. Edited from London. Lively language, 19 volumes plus an index volume.

Children's Encyclopaedia, Heinemann Children's Reference, Halley Court, Jordan Hill, Oxford OX2 8EJ. Up to date and easy to use. 9–13 years. £75.

Chown, Marcus (1987) *Stars and planets*, My First Library series, Macdonald Educational. (Co. Di. Dr. G. HL. In. Ph.) Clear format and lively pictures. Good retrieval devices.

Cobb, Vicki (1983) *Sticky and slimey*, A. & C. Black, London. (Co. Dr. HL. In.) A playful book about how to categorize different slimey substances.

Coldrey, Susan (1982) *Grey Squirrels*, André Deutsch. (Ph. 2.) An attractive picture book with minimal text but with teachers' notes which could also be read by able readers.

Coldrey, Susan (1986) *The Squirrel in the Trees*, Animal Habitats series, Methuen. (Di. G. In. HL. Ph. 2.) Mature non-narrative book language. Excellent photography.

Cole, Joanna (illustrator Kenneth Lilly) (1985) *Night Time Animals*, Walker Books, London. (HL. Ph. 1.)

Collins Children's Atlas, compiled by Michael Cooper, revised edition 1989. A 96-page atlas with each of the three sections indexed. A good section on the world and its formation precedes the clear physical maps.

Crews, D. (1979) *Harbour*, (other titles: *Trains, Freight Trains*) Bodley Head, London (DR. I.).

Cumming, D. (1989) *India*, Countries of the World Series, Wayland, Hove. Other titles include, *Pakistan, Japan* and *Greece*. (Co. In. Ph. HL.)

Dahl, R. (1974) *The Magic Finger*, Puffin books edition, Penguin Harmondsworth.

Davies, A. (1986) *Discovering Squirrels*, Discovering Nature series, Wayland. (Co. Fr. G. In. Ph. 1/2.) Good retrieval devices and clear text and attractive photographs that integrate well with the text.

Dixon, D. (1980) *Dinodots*, Simon & Schuster, Hemel Hempstead.

Dixon, Dougal (1990) *The Children's Giant Book of Dinosaurs*, Octopus, London. Delightfully huge – this classifies dinosaurs into 'ferocious', 'largest' and 'flyers and swimmers'. Good for sharing in a group.

Dorling Kindersley Children's Illustrated Encyclopaedia, £25. 8+. Excellent illustrations, fact-finder list at end.

Dorling Kindersley Picture Atlas of the World, illustrated by B. Delf. A large, beautifully produced atlas with copious information on each continent.

Douglas, C. (1974) *Ladybird Book of Dinosaurs*, (Dr. HL.)

Douglas, Mary (1991) (illustrator G. Humphreys) *The Kings and Queens of Britain*, Sainsbury, Collins. (Co. Ch. Dr. HL. In. 2.) Best-selling history book – well set out and inviting.

Elkington, J. and Hail, J. (1990) *Young Green Consumer's Guide,* Harrap, London. Nicely organized text. Good 'other books to read'.

Forest, W. (1989) *Rosa Luxemburg*, In Her Own Time Series, Hamish Hamilton, London.

Gale, J. (1987) *Common and Endangered Mammals of the UK*, Dryad Press, London. (In. Ph. 2.)

Garland, Sarah (1982) *Going to Play School; Going Shopping; Having a Picnic; Doing the Washing*, Bodley Head Picture Books for 3–7s. 44 words of text – pictures of the activities invite children's comment.

Geistdoerfer, Patrick (1991) *Whales, Dolphins and Seals,* Moonlight Publishing. (Co. In. Ph. 2.) Short-listed for the 1991 Earthworm award, it explores with many illustrations the problems these sea creatures face.

Ginn Science (1991) Key Stage 1 Information Books and Group Discussion Book. Level 1. Attractive photographs. Worth considering as part of resources for 5–7 year olds.

Glease, Hannah (1991) *Bees*, Cherrytree Books. Beautiful paintings illustrate this compact book, full of fascinating information about the life-cycle and characteristics of bees. 7–11.

Graham, I. (1988) *Space Shuttles*, How it Works Series, Gloucester Press (Co. In. Ph. Dr.).

Hadley, E. and T. (1983) *Legends of the Sun and Moon*, Cambridge University Press.

Halstead, B. (1982) *A Brontosaurus: The Life Story Unearthed*, Collins, London. Illustrations by Jenny Halstead.

Hamlyn's Children World Atlas, (1991) text M. Day and K. Woodward, editors N. Barber and N. Harris, illustrations J. Massy. (Co. Di. HL. In. Ph.)

Hamlyn First Picture Dictionary, edited by R. Fergusson. For younger children – words are set in sentences.

Hanson, G. and Fogerstorm, G. (1979) *Our New Baby*, Macdonald education.

Harrap English Illustrated Dictionary, edited by L. N. Dorley. For middle and upper primary age range.

Hasan, K. and Warner, R. (1989) *Rumana's New Clothes*, Hamish Hamilton, London, English and Bengali text.

Hasan, K. and Warner, R. (1989) *Manzur Goes to the Airport,* Hamish Hamilton, London. English and Bengali text.

Hawes, J. (1970) *What I Like About Toads*, A & C Black, London.

Hoban, R. (1964) *A Baby Sister for Frances*, Harper & Row, London.

Hindley, Judy (1990) (illustrated by Alison Wisenfeld) *The Tree*, Aurum Books. Winner of TES information book award, original and superbly illustrated. Excellent even though without page numbers! (For a good list of information books about trees, contact Children's Book Foundation, 081-870 9055.)

Holm, Jessica (1987) (illustrator Guy Troughton) *Squirrels*, Whittet Books (companion volumes on *Bats, Robins, Hedgehogs*, etc.). (Co. Di. Dr. HL. In. Ph. 2/3.) A rare text for older children which manages to be accessible, humourous and scholarly.

Horton, P. *et al* (1990) *Earth Watch*, BBC Factfinders, London.

Huass, H. (1961 edition) *Mammals of the World*, Methuen. (Dr. In. 2/3.) Reference book. 17 chapters, 'Rodent' chapter consulted by Squirrel project children (Chapter 8 of this book).

I Was There series, titles include *Vikings, Ancient Egyptians*, The Bodley Head. Not everyone likes this admittedly quite original approach to history, but some 7–11-year-olds might be entertained by photographs of actors dressed up in period costume.

Kabeer, N. (1988) *Ann in Bangladesh*, A & C Black, London.

Keeping, Charles, *Railway Passage*, Oxford University Press.

King, Clive (1970) *Stig of the Dump*, Penguin.

Kingfisher Book of Words, edited by George Beal. This is really a first thesaurus suitable from about age 6 upwards. The cartoon illustrations (e.g. of crocodile tears!) are great fun and the quotations, proverbs and idioms encourage an interest in language.

Kingfisher Children's Encyclopaedia. 7–11. Has large print, simple language and is alphabetically arranged. Particularly good for the younger juniors.

Kingfisher Children's World Atlas. Good clear illustrations, photographs ana fact boxes.

Kingfisher Illustrated Dictionary (edited by John Grisewood) (1990 edition) Grisewood and Dempsey. Has abbreviations of grammatical functions of words explained at beginning and help over pronunciation (stressed syllable is in darker print).

King-Smith, D. (1985) *The Sheep-pig*, Puffin Books edition, Penguin Books, Harmondsworth.

Lafferty, P. (1988) *Wind to Flight*, Hands-on Science Series, Gloucester Press. (Co. In. HL. Ph. Di.)

Lambeth, D. (1987) Age of Dinosaurs, Kingfisher Explorer Books, (Co. In. HL.).

Leutscher, A. (1979) *Animals, Tracks and Signs*, Usborne Spotters Guides. (Co. G. In. 2/3.) A field guide for abler readers in the primary school.

Llewellyn, Claire (1991) *Under the Sea.* Take One series, Simon and Schuster. For Key Stage 1. Excellent photography with a simple thematically arranged text – links with AT1 English, AT2 English Levels 1–3, Science AT1 Levels 1–3, AT2 Levels 1–3, AT3 Level 3, AT5 Levels 1 and 3.

Lloyd, Errol (1978) *Nina at Carnival*, The Bodley Head, London.

Look It Up, Heinemann Children's Reference (Hally Court) Jordan Hill, Oxford OX2 8LJ. For 6–9. Up to date. £96.

Macauley, David (paperback edition 1988) *Cathedral: The Story of its Construction*, Collins. An engaging narration about the building of a particular typical cathedral. Superb drawings.

Macauley, David with Neil Ardley (1988) *The Way Things Work*. Dorling Kindersley, London. (Co. Ch. Di. Dr. Fr. G. HL. In. Ph.) An excellent tome on all kinds of machines and technology – appeals to all ages.

Martin, Nancy (1990) *William and Dorothy Wordsworth at Dove Cottage*, The Wordsworth Trust, Dove Cottage, Grasmere, Cumbria.

Mathias, B. and Thompson, R. (1988) *My Body A–Z*, Franklin Watts, London. Includes signed English and Finger Spelling Alphabet for non-hearing readers.

Matthews, R., *A Dictionary of Dinosaurs*, Scholastic. A simple but lively dictionary for 8+ age range.

Matthews, R. (1990) *Tyrannosaurus*, Firefly Books.

McCord, A. (1977) *Dinosaurs*, Prehistoric Lives Series, Usborne Publishing, London.

Miller, J.C. (1984) The Birth of Piglets, Dent.

Milton, B. (1982) *Oil Rig Worker*, Beans Series, A & C Black, London, (Ph. 1/2).

Milton, J. (1980) *Dinosaur Days*,

Moonlight First Encyclopaedia, 13 volumes planned. £9.99 each. For 6+. Index to each volume describes as well as lists. Explore and play sections with games, places to visit, quizzes, intriguing facts and glossary as well as information, make these ideal first books of knowledge.

Morris, A. (1989) *Delhi Visit*, A. & C. Black, London. (HL. Ph.), tells the story of preparing for and enjoying a visit to the family's country of origin.

Morris, A. (1989) *Uzma's Photograph Album*, A. & C. Black, London, (HL. Ph.). Uzma shows her photographs to her schoolfriends.

Mosley, Frances (1986) *Nessie Goes to Mars*, Grafton Books, Harper Collins, London.

Murphy, Brian (1991) *Experiment with Water; Light; Air; Sound and Movement*, Two Can. Junior school age range. Excellent science books with 'hands-on' approach. Lively and motivating.

Myring, L. and Snowden, S. (1982) *Finding Out About Sun, Moon and Planets*, Usborne Explainers. (Co. Di. Dr. In. 2.) Children enjoy the exciting drawings in this book.

New Book of Knowledge, House of Grolier Ltd., Grolier House, 1 Watford Road, Radlett, Hertfordshire WD7 8L1. 7 upwards. £299.

Octopus Parent and Child Programme First Dictionary, edited by Deborah Manley. Spellings of inflectional variations – past tenses, spellings of plurals, etc.

Oliver, R. and Long, B. (1983) *All About Dinosaurs*, Hodder & Stoughton, Sevenoaks.

Oxford Children's Encyclopaedia, Oxford University Press, Walkers Street, Oxford OX2 6DP. 8–13 years. £100. Clear text and retrieval devices.

Oxford Children's Thesaurus (1987) compiled by Alan Spooner, Oxford University Press. Uses the same basic vocabulary as the *Oxford Children's Dictionary* (3rd edition).

Oxford Illustrated Junior Dictionary, compiled by R. Sansome and D. Reid, Oxford University Press. Very well laid out with terms in red and explanations in black. Broad definition and usage only.

Oxford Junior Dictionary (1991 edition) compiled by R. Sansome for 7–9-year-olds. The 500 entries include new words from science and modern life and lists of the names of planets, continents, places, etc.

Parish, Peggy (1984) (illustrator A. Lobel) *Dinosaur Time*, World's Work, I Can Read books. Good clear illustrations and an interesting text based on evidence from fossils. Traces the food and habitat of 11 dinosaurs – should intrigue children.

Parker, S. (1988) *Dinosaurs and How They Lived*, Dorling Kindersley, (Co. HL. In.).

Patchett, Lynne (1991) *My Shell* Simple Science series, A. & C. Black.

Pears Encyclopaedia (1991 edition) edited by Edward Blishen, Pelham. Gives facts and brief explanation, handy for projects in the junior years, includes some interesting lists of, for example, historic Acts of Parliament and a diary of world events.

Peppe, R. (1974) *The Alphabet Book*, Kestrel Books, Penguin Books, Harmondsworth.

Perry, K. (1985) *The Sun*, Aladdin Books, Franklin Watts, London.

Perry, K. and Kopper, L. (1988) *Staying Overnight*, First Time Series. Franklin Watts, London.

Philips Children's Atlas, compiled by David and Jill Wright (2nd edition). Clear maps, good contents page, useful fact boxes.

Philips Modern School Atlas (new 1991 Edition). Each page is colour indexed for quick reference and there are statistical charts on health, populations, etc. Astronomical geography included. 11+.

Pitt, V. (1977) *Bats,* Franklin Watts, London.

Potter, B. (1902) *The Tale of Squirrel Nutkin*, Frederick Warne, London.

Pluckrose, Henry (1988) Look at . . . Nature series, Franklin Watts. Witty titles include *Fur and Feathers; Homes; Holes and Hives* and *Tongues and Tastes* (HL. In. Ph. 1.) Good photographs, lucid text and suggested activities.

Pragoff, F. (1989) *Opposites*, Gollancz, London.

Pressling, R. (1990) *My Jumper*, Simple Science series, photographs by Fiona Pragoff, A. & C. Black. (HL. Ph. 1.) (Contact Children's Book Foundation 081-870 9055 for a good list of books on the theme of sheep and wool.)

Propper, E. and A. (1977) (illustrator P. Oxenham) *The Squirrel*, Macdonald Educational Animal World series. (Dr. 1/2.) Overall time sequence with non-narrative asides.

Purkis, Sally (general editor) (1991) *A Sense of History*, A Longman Publication for History at Key Stages 1 and 2. A comprehensive set of materials including topic books, posters and cassettes.

Pye, David (1968) (illustrations by Colin Thredgold) *Bats*, The Bodley Head. (Co. HL. In. Ph. 2.)

Redmond, I. (1990) The Elephant Book, Walker Books, London. Illustrated with superb photographs and in aid of the Elefriend's campaign. (Co. Ph. HL. Fr. 2/3.)

Redpath, I. (1990) *The Giant Book of Space*, Hamlyn.

Regan, M. (1982) *French Family*, Beans Series, A. & C. Black, London, (Ph. 2).

Richard Scarry's Picture Dictionary, Collins. For the very young – 5+. Beautifully and amusingly illustrated.

Richardson, Phil (1985) (illustrated by Guy Troughton). *Bats* Whittet Books, London. (Co. HL. Dr. Di. Ph. In. Fr. 2.) A good example of an excellent series for older juniors.

Riley, Helen (1989) *The Bat in the Cave*, Animal Habitats series, Belitha Press, London. Photographs by Oxford Scientific Films. (Co. Dr. Di. HL. G. In. Ph. 2.) Outstanding photographs.

Robertson, James (1990) *The Complete Bat,* (drawings by Alistair Robertson) Chatto and Windus, London. (Co. Dr. Di. G. In. Ph. 2/3.) Excellent resource book for older junior age group.

Roffey, Maureen (1982) *Home Sweet Home*, The Bodley Head. 3–6 Simple question and answer game. Questions like 'Does a cat live in a kennel?' The half-page flaps, holes and so on greatly add to the fun.

Rosen, M. (1982) *Everybody Here,* Bodley Head, London.

Royston, Angela and King, Colin (1991) *Car*, Frances Lincoln. A very useful book for anyone from about 5 years upwards featuring excellent diagrams of the structure of a car with flaps and tags that can be manouevred to demonstrate how a car can be serviced and mended.

Russell, N. (1990) *The Stream: From a Raindrop to the Sea*, Methuen Children's Books, London.

Scagell, R. (1980) (illustrated by David Mallot and Ron Hayard) *How to be an Astronomer*, Whizz Kids series, Macdonald Educational. (Co. Di. Dr. G. HL. In. 2.) Appealing illustrations but quite difficult text.

Sendak, M. (1967) *Where the Wild Things Are*, The Bodley Head, London.

Sheehan, A. (1976) (illustrator M. Pledges) *The Squirrel*, Eyeview Library, Angus and Robertson. (Dr. 1/2.) Nature notes at the end of a narrative (information story).

Smith, Anne (1989) *Aborigines,* People of the World series, Wayland, Hove. (Ch. Co. Gl. In. Ph. HL), includes a glossary of Aboriginal words in the pitjantjatjara language. Other titles include *Plains Indians* and *Inuit.*

Stones, Rosemary (1989) *Where do Babies Come From?* Dinosaur.

Taylor, B. (1990) *Waste and Recycling*, A. & C. Black, London.

Take One: A Very First Reference Series (1991) Simon and Schuster, Young Books now incorporating Macdonald Educational. (HL. In. Ph. 1.) This cross-curricular approach on topics like *Night and Day, Under the Sea, Boats* and so on, is welcome. The examples I have looked at have clear text encouraging reflection and excellent photographs.

Tames, Richard (1990) *Marie Curie; Helen Keller; Amelia Earhart; Florence Nightingale; Anne Franks; Mother Teresa; Guglielmo Marconi*, Life Time series, Watts. Fact files alongside narratives, many photographs and pictures.

Taylor, Barbara (1991) *Waste and Recycling*, A. & C. Black, London. How do we get rid of rubbish and recycle it? Short-listed for the 1991 Earthworm award.

Taylor, B. (1990) *Weight and Balance,* Science Starter Series, Franklin Watts, London. (Co. In. G. HL. Ph. 2.)

Taylor, J. (1981) *Sciurus: The Story of a Grey Squirrel*, Collins. A mature information story with chapters, drawings and reading list.

Taylor, R. (1981) *Dinosaurs,* Picture Facts series, Grisewood and Dempsey.

Thompson, R. (1978) *Understanding Farm Animals*, Usborne Publishing, London. (Co. In. HL. Dr. 2.)

Thompson, R. (1987) *Making a Book*, Franklin Watts, London.

Thompson, R. (1990) *Washday*, Turn of the Century series, A. & C. Black, London.

Thompson, Ruth (1991) *Eyes; Hair; Hands;* Look at . . . Ourselves series, Franklin Watts. An imaginative and beautifully illustrated series for 5+ which links with AT3 Science – Health Education.

Thompson, Ruth and Emery, Nancy (1989) *When I was Young*, Early Twentieth Century series, Watts. (Co. In. Ph. 2/3.) Reminiscences of an old lady who was young at the beginning of the twentieth century. Excellent photographs of contemporary scenes and objects.

Thompson, Neil and Jones, Charlie (1989) *World War II*, Early Twentieth Century series, Watts. (Co. In. Ph. 2/3.) An old soldier recaptures the texture of the war years.

Thompson, Wendy (1991) *Schubert; Beethoven; Haydn; Mozart,* Composer's World series. Very attractively produced paperbacks, with imaginative illustrations (contemporary paintings and engravings). 7–11 age range.

Tigwell, T. (1982) *Sakina in India*, Beans Series, A. & C. Black, London. (Ph. 1/2.)

Tittensor, A. (1980) *The Red Squirrel*, Mammal Society series, Blanford Press with the Mammal Society. (Co. Di. Fr. Ph. 2/3.) Clear but quite difficult text by a naturalist.

Turner, Dorothy (1990) *Victorian Factory Workers*, Beginning History series, Wayland. (HL. In. Ph. 2.) About the suffering of child factory workers. For a bookfax on Victorian England, apply to Children's Book Foundation (081-870 9055).

Turner, E. and Turner, C. (1974) *Bats*, prepared by Northants Bat Group, Priory Press Ltd, Sussex, Young Naturalist Books.

Tsow, Ming (1982) *A Day with Ling*, Hamish Hamilton, London.

Watts, Barrie (1991) *Butterflies and Moths*, Keeping Minibeasts series, Franklin Watts. (Co. Dr. HL. In. Ph. 2.) The emphasis is on action, but help is given in how to provide humane treatment. Good retrieval devices and 'interesting facts' page.

Watts, Barrie (1991) *Tomato*, Stopwatch Books, A. & C. Black, London. (HL. Ph. 1.) Transitional between chronological and non-chronological. Begins with general observations about appearance and food, then describes the life-cycle. Beautifully illustrated and clear language (other titles include *Apple Tree, Birds Nest, Bumblebee, Conker and House Mouse*).

Whitlock, Ralph (1974) *Squirrels*, Young Naturalist Books, Prior Press. (Co. G. HL. In. Ph. 2/3.) An inviting, quite detailed text. Good black and white photographs.

Whitlock, R. (1975) *Spiders*, Young Naturalist Books, Priory Press, London. (Co. G. HL. In. Ph. 2.)

Wildsmith, B. (1962) *ABC*, Oxford University Press, Oxford.

Wood, T. (1989) *Doctor* and *Postwoman*, Franklin Watts, London.

World Book Encyclopaedia, World Book – Childcraft International, World Book House, 77 Mount Ephraim, Tunbridge Wells, Kent TN4 8AZ. 8–adult Text graded. A good value intermediate set. £499.

APPENDIX V
NON-BOOK RESOURCES

Information Finder, a CD-ROM using the text of the *World Book Encyclopaedia*, World Book – Childcraft International, £390. Aims to provide the accuracy, up-to-dateness, etc. of the *World Book* in electronic form (older juniors, middle school and secondary).

Bat Groups of Great Britain, 10 Bedford Cottages, Gt. Brington, Northampton NN7 4JE. Leaflets and booklets which provided some of the resources for the bat project (Chapter 10).

Focus on Bats (1984). Slide pack about bats and their conservation, prepared by the Fauna and Flora Society. International Centre for Conservation Education (narration by Bob Stebbing), Zoological Society of London, Regents Park, London NW1 4RY. (Excellent teacher's Bat Pack also available.)

The Young Bat Worker, A termly magazine for the young bat enthusiast. Funded by Bat Groups of Great Britain. Shirley Thompson (ed.), 5 Manor Road, Tankerton, Whitstable, Kent.

Bats, prepared by Northants Bat Group. Published by Priory Press, Sussex, England. Compiler of materials – C. Turner.

Harbour, D. and Walton, D. E. *The Grey Squirrel*, World Wildlife. Chart from World Wildlife Fund Education Department, with Lloyds Bank. Small print and quite challenging text. Children usually enjoy the beautiful diagrams.

Squirrel on My Shoulder, BBC Wildlife Project 1988. John Paling, producer and photographer. Narrator David Attenborough. Quite difficult language used but delightful visual narrative helps make it accessible.

The Case of the Vanishing Squirrel (1988). Nature film video, Wildlife on BBC1. Scientific editors Jessica Holm and P. Heeley. A fascinating glimpse into how scientists observe squirrels, weighing, tagging and checking them for disease.

Junior Education Projects: Space. Poster of a photograph taken 180,000 km into space.

Reynolds, J. (1989) Rules of the Game, in *Country LIfe*, May. Beautiful colour photographs and a report of the latest insights into relationships between grey and red squirrels. For teacher to read to children.

BIBLIOGRAPHY

Adams, P. (1969) *Language in Thinking*, Penguin, Harmondsworth.

Andrews, R. (ed.) (1989) *Narrative and Argument,* Open University Press, Milton Keynes.

Baker, C. D. and Freebody, P. (1989) *Children's First School Books*, Basil Blackwell, Oxford.

Barnes, D. (1976) *From Communication to Curriculum,* Penguin, Harmondsworth.

Barnes, D. (1988) Knowledge as action, in M. Lightfoot and N. Martin (eds.) *The Word For Teaching is Learning: Essays for James Britton*, Heinemann Educational Books, London.

Barrs, M. (1987) Mapping the world, in *English in Education,* Vol. 21, no. 3.

Barrs, M., Ellis, E., Hester, H. and Thomas, A. (1988) *The Primary Language Record.* Inner London Education Authority; available from The Centre for Language in Primary Education, Webber Row, London EC1 8QW.

Bartlett, F.C. (1932) *Remembering*, Cambridge University Press.

Beard, R. (1984) *Children Writing in the Primary School*, Hodder and Stoughton, London.

Beard, R. (1987) *Developing Reading 3–13*, Hodder and Stoughton, London.

Bissex, G. (1980) *Gyns at Work: A Child Learns to Write and Read*, Harvard University Press, Cambridge, Mass.

Blanchard, J.S., Mason, G. L. and David, D. (1987) *Computer Applications in Reading* (3rd edn), International Reading Association, Newark, DE.

Blyth, J. (1988) Primary Booksheet, *History 5–9,* Hodder and Stoughton, London.

Brice-Heath, S. (1983) *Ways With Words: Language, Life and Work in Communities and Classrooms*, Cambridge University Press.

Britton, J. N. (1970) *Language and Learning*, Allen Lane, London.

Britton, J. N., Burgess, T., Martin, N., Macleod, A. and Rosen, H. (1975) *The Development of Writing Abilities,* Macmillan, London.

Britton, J. N. (1987) Vygotsky's contribution to pedagogical theory in *English in Education* Vol. 21, no. 3, Autumn.

Bruner, J. S., Oiver, R. R. and Greenfield, P. M. (1960) *Studies in Cognitive Growth*, Wiley, New York, London, Sydney.

Bruner, J. S. (1966) *Towards a Theory of Instruction*, The Belknap Press, Cambridge, Mass., and London.

Bruner, J. (1975) The ontogenesis of speech acts, *Journal of Child Language*, Vol. 2, pp. 1–19.

Bruner, J. S. (1986) *Actual Minds, Possible Worlds*, Harvard University Press, Cambridge, Mass.

Bruner, J. S. and Haste, H. (eds.) (1987) *Making Sense: the Child's Construction of the World*, Methuen, London.

Buckingham, D. (ed.) (1990) *Watching Media Learning: Making Sense of Media Education*, Falmer Press.

Butler, D. (1988) *Babies Need Books*, (2nd edn), Penguin, Harmondsworth.

Cass, Joan (1967) *Literature and the Young Child*, Longman, London.

Catling, S. (1991) Mapping out their future, in *Junior Education*, September, pp. 26–9.

Chall, J. (1983) *Stages of Reading Development*, McGraw-Hill, New York.

Chambers, A. (1991) *The Reading Environment*, The Thimble Press, Glos.

Chander, Daniel (1985) *Computers and Literacy*, Open University Press, Milton Keynes.

Chapman, L. J. (1983) *Reading Development and Cohesion*, Heinemann Educational, London.

Chapman, L. J. (1987) *Reading 5–11*, Open University Press, Milton Keynes.

Clark, M. M. (1976) *Young Fluent Readers,* Heinemann, London.

Cook-Gumpertz, J. (1986) *The Social Construction of Literacy*, Cambridge University Press.

Crystal, D. (1987) *The Cambridge Encyclopaedia of Language*, Cambridge University Press.

DES (1975) *A Language for Life* (The Bullock Report), HMSO, London.

DES (1988a) *English for Ages 5–11*, Proposals for the Secretaries of State (The Cox Report), NCC/HMSO, London.

DES (1988b) *Report of the Committee of Inquiry into the Teaching of English Language* (The Kingman Report), HMSO, London.

DES (1990) *English in the National Curriculum*, HMSO, London.

DES (1991) *History in the National Curriculum*, HMSO, London.

Dixon, B. (1976) *Catching them Young*, Pluto Books.

Donaldson, Margaret (1978) *Children's Minds*, Fontana, Glasgow.

Donaldson, Margaret (1989) *Sense and Sensibility: Some Thoughts on The Teaching of Literacy*. Occasional Paper no. 3, University of Reading, School of Education.

Doughty, P. S., Pearce, J. J. and Thornton, G. M. (1972) *Exploring Language*, Edward Arnold, London.

Fisher, Margery (1972) *Matters of Fact*, Brockhampton Press.

Fisher, M. (1981) Growing point, *Mapping the World*, Vol. 20, no. 3, p. 3942.

Feynman, Richard, as told to Ralph Leighton (1986) *Surely You're Joking Mr Feynman*, Unwin/Hyman (based on the BBC Horizon film *The Pleasure of Finding Out*).

Fox, C. (1989) Of shoes and ships, in *The Times Educational Supplement*, 13 October.

Fry, D. (1985) *Children Talk about Books: Seeing Themselves as Readers*, Open University Press, Milton Keynes and Philadelphia.

Gilliland, J. (1972) *Readability*, University of London Press.

Goelman, H., Oberg, A. and Smith, F. (eds.) (1984) *Awakening to Literacy*. The University of Victoria Symposium on Children's Responses to a Literate Environment: Literacy Before Schooling, Heinemann, London.

Gordon, Cecelia (1983) Teaching the young to use indexes, in *The Indexer,* Vol. 13 (3), pp. 181–2.

Graves, D. (1983) *Writing: Teachers and Children at Work*, Heinemann, London.

Hall, Nigel (1987) *The Emergence of Literacy*, Hodder and Stoughton, London.

Halliday, M. A. K. (1975) *Learning how to Mean: Explorations in the Development of Language*, Edward Arnold, London.
Halliday, M. A. K. (1978) *Language as Social Semiotic*, Edward Arnold, London.
Halliday, M. A. K. and Hasan, R. (1976) *Cohesion in English*, Longman, London.
Halliday, M. A. K. and Hasan, R. (1980) *Text and Context*, Sophia Linguistica VI, Tokyo, Sophia University.
Hardy, B. (1977) Towards a poetics of fiction: an approach through narrative, in M. Meek, A. Warlow and G. Barton (eds.) *op. cit.*, pp. 12–23.
Harrison, C. (1980) *Readability in the Classroom*, Cambridge University Press, Cambridge.
Hasan, R. (1984) The nursery tale as genre, in *Nottingham Circular*, Vol. 13, pp. 71–102.
Hasan, R. (1985) Situation and the definition of genres, in A. D. Grimshaw *Perspectives on Discourse: Multi-disciplinary Study of a Naturally Occurring Conversation*, Ablex, Norwood, NJ.
Heeks, P. (1981) *Choosing and Using Books in the First School*, Macmillan, London and Basingstoke.
Heeks, P. (1982) *Ways of Knowing: Information Books for 7–9-year-olds*, Thimble Press, Gloucester.
Hilgard, E. R. (ed.) (1964) *Theories of Learning and Instruction*, University of Chicago Press, Chicago, Ill.
Howe, D. (ed.) (1985) *Better School Libraries in Primary Schools*, National Association of Advisers in English.
Hunter-Carsch, M., Beverton, S. and Dennis, D. (eds.) (1990) *Primary English in the National Curriculum*, Blackwell, Oxford.
Information Skills in Education (January 1990), The British Library Research and Development Department's Publication on 'Research in Progress'.
Jones, R. M. (1972) *Fantasy and Feeling in Education*, Penguin Books, Harmondsworth.
Kerslake, D. *et al.* (1990) *HBJ Mathematics*, Harcourt Brace Jovanovich, London, Orlando, Sydney, Toronto. Teachers' resource book.
Klein, G. (1985) *Reading into Racism*, Routledge & Kegan Paul, London and Boston.
Klein, G. (1986) *The School Library for Multi-Cultural Awareness*, Trentham Books.
Kress, G. (1982) *Learning to Write*, Routledge & Kegan Paul, London.
Langer, J. (1981) In J. Chapman (ed.) *The Reader and the Text*, Heinemann, London.
Langer, J. (1985) Children's sense of genre, in *Journal of Written Communication*, Vol. 12, no. 2, pp. 157–87.
Lavender, R. (1983) Children using information books, in *Education 3–13*, vol. 11, no. 1.
Lightfoot, M. and Martin, N. (1988) *The Word for Teaching is Learning: Essays for James Britton*, Heinemann Educational Books, London.
Littlefair, A. (1991) *Reading All Types of Writing*, Open University Press, Milton Keynes and Philadelphia.
Lock, A. and Fisher, E. (eds.) (1984) *Language Development*, Croom Helm, London, in association with the Open University.
Lunzer, E. and Gardner, K. (1979) *The Effective Use of Reading*, Heinemann, London.

Lunzer, E. and Gardner, K. (1984) *Learning from the Written Word*, Oliver and Boyd, Edinburgh.

MacNamara, David (1990) The National Curriculum: an agenda for resources, in *B.Ed. Res. Journal*, Vol. 16, no. 3.

Macnamara, J. (1972) Cognitive basis of language learning in infants, *Psychological Review*, Vol. 79, pp. 1–13.

Mallett, M. (1991) Learning from information books in the primary school: some promising strategies, in *Primary Education*, Journal of the Education Department of the Chinese University of Hong Kong, Vol. 2, no. 1.

Mallett, M. (in preparation) Non-fiction in the primary years: a study of some factors associated with success in helping children reflect on ideas and information in their reading. Unpublished Ph.D. thesis. London University.

Mallett, M. (1992a) How long does a pig live? in *English in Education*, Vol. 26, no. 1.

Mallett, M. (1992b) Using and sharing ideas from books in the context of a primary school project, in *The British Educational Research Journal*, Spring.

Mallett, M. and Newsome, B. (1977) *Talking, Writing and Learning 8–13*, Evans/Methuen for the Schools Council.

Martin, N., Williams, P., Wilding, J., Hemmings, S. and Medaway, P. (1976) *Understanding Children Talking*, Penguin, Harmondsworth.

McKenzie, M. and Warlow, A. (1977) *Reading Matters*, Hodder and Stoughton, London.

Meek, M. (1977) What is a horse? in *The School Librarian*, Vol. 25, no. 1.

Meek, M. (1982) *Learning to Read*, The Bodley Head, London.

Meek, M. (1991) *On Being Literate*, The Bodley Head, London.

Meek, M. Warlow, A. and Barton, G. (1977) *The Cool Web: The Pattern of Childhood Reading*, The Bodley Head, London.

Meyer, B. J. F. (1981) *Prose Analysis Procedures: Purpose and Problems*, Dept. of Educational Psychology, Arizona State University.

Mills, D. (ed.) (1989) *Geographical Work in the Primary and Middle Schools*, (2nd edn) Geographical Association, Sheffield.

Minns, H. (1990) *Read to Me, Now*, Virago, London.

Moffett, J. (1968) *Teaching the Universe of Discourse*, Houghton Mifflin, Boston, Mass.

Moorman, M. (1971) *Journals of Dorothy Wordsworth Second Edition*, Oxford University Press, Oxford.

Moss, Elaine (1985) *Picture Books for Young People 9–13* (2nd edn) a Signal bookguide, Thimble Press, Gloucester.

Mortimore, P., Summons, P., Stoll, L., Lewis, D. and Ecob, R. (1988) *School Matters – The Junior Years*, Open Books, Wells.

Neate, B. (1985) Children's information books, in *Gnosis*, 13 September.

Neate, B. (in press) *Children's Informative Reading*. Hodder & Stoughton, London and Sevenoaks.

Olson, D. R. (1984) Oral and written language and the cognitive processes of children, in A. Lock and E. Fisher (eds.) *Language Development*, Croom Helm, London, in association with the Open University.

Olson, D. R. (1988) On the language and authority of textbooks, in Suzanne de Castell and A. and C. Luke *Language, Authority and Criticism*, Falmer Press.

Olson, D. R., Torrance, N. and Hildyard, A. (eds.) (1985) *Literacy, Language and Learning: The Nature and Consequences of Reading and Writing*, Cambridge University Press.

Ong, W. H. (1982) *Orality and Literacy*, Methuen, London.
Orbrist, C. and Stuart, A. (1990) The Family Reading Groups Movement, in M. Hunter-Carsch *et al.* (eds.) *Primary English in the National Curriculum*. Blackwell, Oxford.
Osborn, J. *et al.* (1985) *Reading Education: Foundation for a Literate America*, D. C. Heath and Co. Lexington, Mass.
Paice, S. (1984) Reading to learn, in *English in Education*, vol. 18, no. 1.
Pappas, C. C. (1986) Exploring the global structure of children's 'information books'. Paper presented at the Annual Meeting of the National Reading Conference, Austin, Texas, 2–6 December.
Perera, K. (1984) *Children's Reading and Writing: Analysing Classroom Language*, Basil Blackwell in association with André Deutsch, Oxford.
Perera, K. (1987) *Understanding Language*, NATE, Sheffield.
Perera, K. (1986) Some linguistic difficulties in school textbooks, in B. Gillham *The Language of School Subjects,* Heinemann Educational Books, London.
Piaget, J. (1926) *The Language and Thought of the Child*, Routledge & Kegan Paul, London.
Piaget, J. (1967) *Six Psychological Studies*, London University Press.
Piaget, J. (1967) Language and thought from the genetic point of view, in P. Adams, (1969) op. cit.
Piaget, J. and Inhelder, B. (1969) *The Psychology of the Child,* Routledge & Kegan Paul, London.
Pumfrey, P. (1991) *Improving Children's Reading in the Junior School: Challenges and Responses*, Cassell Educational, London.
Raper, R. (1990) Indexes really are necessary, in *The School Librarian*, Vol. 38, no. 3.
Ricks, C. and Michaels, L. (eds.) (1990) *The State of the Language,* Faber, London.
Root, B. (ed.) (1986) *Resources for Reading: Does Quality Count?* Macmillan/ United Kingdom Reading Association, Basingstoke.
Rosen, C. and Rosen, H. (1973) *The Language of Primary School Children*, Penguin Books, Harmondsworth.
School Libraries: Foundation of the Curriculum, Library Information Series, HMSO, London.
Sheldon, S. (1986) Representing Comprehension, in B. Root (ed.) op. cit.
Smith, F. (1988) *Understanding Reading: A Psycholinguistic Analysis of Reading and Learning to Read* (4th edn), Lawrence Erlbaum, Hillsdale, NJ.
Smith, F. (1984) *Reading Like a Writer*, University of Reading: Centre for the Teaching of Reading, in conjunction with Abel Press, Victoria, BC.
Somerfield, M., Torbe, M. and Ward (1983) *A Framework for Reading*, Heinemann, London.
Southgate, V., Arnold, H. and Johnson, S. (1981) *Extending Beginning Reading*, Heinemann Educational Books, London, for the Schools Council.
Spiro, R. J. *et al.* (eds.) (1980) *Theoretical Issues in Reading Comprehension*, Lawrence Erlbaum, Hillsdale, NJ.
Stauffer, R. G. (1969) *Teaching Reading as a Thinking Process,* Harper & Row, New York.
Stones, R. (1983) *Pour out the Cocoa Janet: Sexism in Children's Books*, Longman's Resource Unit for Schools Council.
Temple, C. A., Nathan, R. G., Burris, N. A. and Temple, F. (1988) *The Beginnings of Writing* (2nd edn.) Allyn & Beacon, Boston, Mass.

Tizard, B. and Hughes, M. (1984) *Young Children Learning: Talking and Thinking at Home and at School*, Fontana, London.

Tucker, N. and Timms, S. H. (1991) *The Buyer's Guide to Encyclopaedias*, from Simply Creative, 246 London Road, Charlton Kings, Cheltenham, Glos. GL52 6HS.

Von Schweinitz, E. (1989) Facing the facts, in *Books for Keeps*, March.

Vygotsky, L. S. (1962) *Thought and Language*, MIT Press, Cambridge, Mass.

Vygotsky, L. S. (1978) *Mind in Society: The Development of Higher Psychological Processes*, Harvard University Press, Cambridge, Mass.

Vygotsky, L. S. (1986) (revised and edited by A. Kozusin) *Thought and Language*, MIT Press, Cambridge, Mass.

Wade, E. (ed.) (1990) *Reading for Real*, Open University Press, Milton Keynes and Philadelphia.

Wadsworth, B. (1981 edition) *Piaget's Theory of Cognitive and Affective Development,* Longman, London.

Wells, G. (ed.) (1981) *Learning Through Interaction: The Study of Language Development*, Cambridge University Press.

Wells, G. (1985) *Language, Learning and Education*, NFER/Nelson, Windsor.

Wells, G. (1987) *The Meaning Makers: Children Learning Language and Using Language to Learn*, Hodder and Stoughton, Sevenoaks.

Whitehead, M. R. (1990) *Language and Literacy in the Early Years: An Approach for Education Students*, Paul Chapman Publishing, London.

Wilson, E. (1983) *The Thoughtful Reader in the Primary School*, Hodder and Stoughton, Sevenoaks.

Wilson, J. (1982) Information books, in *Signal*, The Thimble Press, Stroud.

Wilson, J. (1989) Information books, in Nancy Chambers (ed.) *The Signal Collection of Children's Books*, pp. 68–88.

Wood, D. (1988) *How Children Think and Learn*, Blackwell, Oxford.

Wray, D. and Medwell, J. (1989) Using desk-top publishing to develop literacy, in *Reading*, Vol. 23, no. 2, July, pp. 62–8.

AUTHOR INDEX

SUBJECT INDEX